graphis annual 78|79

78|79 graphis annual

The International Annual of Advertising and
Editorial Graphics

Das internationale Jahrbuch der Werbe-
graphik und der redaktionellen Graphik

Le répertoire international de l'art graphique
publicitaire et rédactionnel

Edited by / Herausgegeben von / Réalisé par:

Walter Herdeg

Walter Herdeg, The Graphis Press, Zurich

Distributed in the United States by

Hastings House

Publishers

10 East 40th Street, New York, N.Y. 10016

PUBLICATION No. 153   [ISBN 0-8038-2695-8]

Contents   Inhalt   Sommaire

Abbreviations   Abkürzungen   Abréviations

Argentina	ARG	Aethiopien	ETH	Afrique du Sud	SAF
Australia	AUS	Argentinien	ARG	Allemagne occidentale	GER
Austria	AUT	Australien	AUS	Allemagne orientale	GDR
Belgium	BEL	Belgien	BEL	Argentine	ARG
Brazil	BRA	Brasilien	BRA	Australie	AUS
Canada	CAN	Deutschland (Ost)	GDR	Autriche	AUT
Cuba	CUB	Deutschland (West)	GER	Belgique	BEL
Czechoslovakia	CSR	Finnland	FIN	Brésil	BRA
Ethiopia	ETH	Frankreich	FRA	Canada	CAN
Finland	FIN	Grossbritannien	GBR	Cuba	CUE
France	FRA	Hongkong	HKG	Emirats Arabes unis	UAE
Germany (East)	GDR	Italien	ITA	Espagne	SPA
Germany (West)	GER	Japan	JPN	Etats-Unis	USA
Great Britain	GBR	Jugoslawien	YUG	Ethiopie	ETH
Hong Kong	NKG	Kanada	CAN	Finlande	FIN
Hungary	HUN	Kuba	CUB	France	FRA
Italy	ITA	Niederlande	NLD	Grande-Bretagne	GBR
Japan	JPN	Norwegen	NOR	Hongkong	HKG
Netherlands	NLD	Oesterreich	AUT	Hongrie	HUN
Norway	NOR	Polen	POL	Italie	ITA
Poland	POL	Schweden	SWE	Japon	JPN
South Africa	SAF	Schweiz	SWI	Norvège	NOR
Spain	SPA	Spanien	SPA	Pays-Bas	NLD
Sweden	SWE	Südafrika	SAF	Pologne	POL
Switzerland	SWI	Tschechoslowakei	CSR	Suède	SWE
United Arab Emirates	UAE	Ungarn	HUN	Suisse	SWI
USA	USA	USA	USA	Tchécoslovaquie	CSR
Yugoslavia	YUG	Vereinigte Arab. Emirate	UAE	Yougoslavie	YUG

In his introduction to this volume Jerry Steimle
talks of the high standards of modern international
graphic design. As a mirror of these standards,
our annual has certainly been one of the feedback
mechanisms that have encouraged optimization.
Our own feedback, however, consists of the good
work sent in year by year by our contributors. We are
grateful to them for their support and very much
aware of its value: it helps us to raise our sights
and in the long run it benefits the graphic design
profession.

In seiner Einführung zu diesem Buch spricht Jerry
Steimle über den hohen Standard internationaler
Graphik. Als Spiegel dieses Standards hat unser
Jahrbuch sicherlich auch der Vervollkommnung Vorschub geleistet. Uns selbst jedoch wird Vorschub
geleistet durch die guten Arbeiten, die uns Jahr für
Jahr eingesandt werden. Wir sind den Einsendern
für ihre Unterstützung dankbar, und wir sind uns
sehr wohl ihrer Bedeutung bewusst: sie helfen uns,
unsere Ziele höher zu setzen, und auf lange Sicht
fördern sie das Grafik-Design.

Dans l'introduction au présent volume, Jerry Steimle
évoque le niveau de qualité élevé de l'art graphique
international de nos jours. Reflet fidèle de ce niveau,
notre annuaire a certainement contribué, par un
phénomène de rétroaction, à promouvoir l'optimali-
sation du design. Notre feed-back à nous implique
la réception de travaux d'excellente qualité, année
par année. Merci à nos correspondants qui, élargis-
sant ainsi notre champ de vision, rendent à long
terme un service réel à la profession tout entière.

PAUL DAVIS, our cover artist, needs no introduction
here. His work has appeared in the pages of almost
every major American magazine as well as on book
jackets, record covers and posters all over the world.
He was one of the "Five Designers" featured in
the Last Venice Biennale, he has recently had a
retrospective exhibition at the Centre Georges
Pompidou, and Dutton have published a large paperback of "Paul Davis Posters and Paintings".

PAUL DAVIS, der Gestalter unseres Umschlags,
braucht kaum vorgestellt zu werden. Seine Arbeiten
sind in fast allen amerikanischen Zeitschriften zu
sehen, so wie auch auf Buchumschlägen, Schallplattenhüllen und Plakaten aus aller Welt. An der
letzten Biennale in Venedig war er einer der dort aus-
gestellten «fünf Graphiker», das Centre Pompidou
widmete ihm eine Retrospektive, während im
Dutton-Verlag ein Buch über «Paul Davis' Plakate
und Malerei» erschienen ist.

PAUL DAVIS, l'auteur de notre couverture, n'a plus
besoin d'être présenté à nos lecteurs. On trouve ses
œuvres dans tous les grands magazines américains et
sur les jaquettes, pochettes et affiches du monde en-
tier. Il a fait partie des «Cinq designers» mis en vedette
lors de la dernière Biennale de Venise, a eu sa rétro-
spective au Centre Georges Pompidou, et l'éditeur
Dutton lui a consacré une importante monographie
sous le titre de «Paul Davis Posters and Paintings».

Jerry Steimle

Introduction

JERRY STEIMLE is a California-based freelance writer on media advertising and related design-oriented subjects. His career began with the N.W. Ayer & Son agency in San Francisco. He has written articles on designers and the design scene in Copenhagen, Hong Kong, London, Milan, Paris and Turin as well as in the United States.

It has been said often that the first complete, global co-operation of mankind may come when a common enemy, the long-awaited extra-terrestrial visitor, appears from outer space. Science fiction come to life.

A contemporary view holds that multinational enterprises, proliferating on a grand scale on the wings of the jet airplane and the immediacy of earth-satellite communications, are intertwining our interests with such complexity that it will be difficult to separate one nation's interests from another's.

One small item in evidence: the Soviet Union's emergence as an enterpriser on foreign soil. For example, partnership with local investors in ownership of a fish processing plant in the state of Washington in the United States.

Ideology becomes less and less a barrier when the laws of economics exert themselves. But many barriers remain in the differences in cultural, nationalistic ways of doing things, often expressed most positively in the most common of tools, language.

The enduring importance of language is signified by the ancients who wrote the Old Testament. Only ten chapters of Genesis had been disposed of before they addressed themselves to the question, "Why do people descended from the same source (Noah's family) speak different languages?" The story of the Tower of Babel was their answer.

That language barriers are coming down is seen in specialized fields and especially in our own field, graphic design.

Today there is truly international language in graphic design. We see it in this annual which is both a cause and an effect of the homogenizing of work being done around the globe.

The life of GRAPHIS, begun in 1944, parallels the most rapid advancement in the development of an international visual style; however, the process began significantly earlier.

A milestone was reached with the emigration to the United States of prominent Bauhauslers and eminent publication designers.

The United States was an emerging economic powerhouse in those days after World War I: a free-enterprise state of 150 million people, politically and culturally united and speaking, for the most part, the same language. US designers had a base of a gigantic gross national product and an unequalled media opportunity. Some other countries may have had more intensive media coverage than the US, but it is doubtful if any had the total mass of the United States, or the international influence.

It also was the time of Hollywood's greatest glory. American films, seen around the world, for better or for worse, were playing a significant role in the homogenization process. Today, the film-making art seems to be more celebrated outside the US than in it.

Not only have publications been an important factor, schools, travel and international advertising agency networks have played a part, also.

Consider the list of students who attended the Bauhaus. It was predominantly German, of course, but there was substantial representation from many other countries, including far-off Oriental nations. The tradition and cross-pollination continues, with students tracking around the world in search of design education.

In the art departments of branches of British, German and American advertising agencies located in Milan, for example, one finds an interesting jumble of nationalities, including a few Italians. If the designer does not speak the international language of design on arrival here, he probably will before he leaves. The same scene is found in Paris, London, New York and Tokyo.

Some observers will say that the international visual style is really Swiss design, and there is merit in that point of view. The idea of International Style, however, is that it comes from everywhere. Everyone can do it.

It makes no difference whether you are thinking of India, Bolivia, Bulgaria or, in America, the state of Montana, the top designers are completely tuned in to the international design style and are practising their art in similar fashion and at the same high quality levels. This certainly is to be seen in this book.

And it is to be observed as one travels internationally. Street graphics, signage in airports and in mass transit systems are testimony that the visual vocabulary has truly become international. This is not, however, in reference strictly to numbers, letterforms and symbology such as are sponsored by ICOGRADA and AIGA, but rather to creative approaches to all forms of graphics and advertising. There's more to it than Helvetica.
Clearly, all design has not reached the same level of competence. Of course, it never will, and untutored efforts in different countries will continue to reflect local cultures; however, the pattern is established indeed.

Design has risen to such a high state of play that good design often passes unnoticed.
A point that calls to mind the question posed by an internationally known designer who was making his way through a public car parking facility. He first asked, "Who was responsible for this work?" He thought the graphics to be outstanding.
None of the local people who were with him knew who had done the work.
"It's amazing," he said. "An unknown designer does this perfectly beautiful job.
It makes me wonder; what possibly can come next?"
Of course, something will.

Jerry Steimle

Vorwort

JERRY STEIMLE lebt in Kalifornien als freier Schriftsteller auf dem Gebiet der Media-Werbung und damit verbundener graphisch orientierter Aufgaben. Seine Karriere begann in der Agentur N.W. Ayer & Son, San Francisco. Er hat Artikel über Graphiker und die graphische Szene nicht nur in den Vereinigten Staaten, sondern auch in Kopenhagen, Hongkong, London, Mailand, Paris und Turin geschrieben.

Es wurde oft gesagt, dass eine wirkliche Zusammenarbeit der Menschen erst beim Auftauchen eines gemeinsamen Feindes, des lang erwarteten Besuchers von einem anderen Planeten, zustande kommen werde. Wirklichkeit gewordene Science Fiction also. Heute sieht es so aus, als wenn die Einigung der Menschen auf eine ganz andere Art stattfindet, nämlich auf wirtschaftlicher Ebene. Die sich dank der modernen Kommunikationsmöglichkeiten, Jets und Satelliten, auf unserem Planeten rapide ausbreitenden multinationalen Unternehmen haben die nationalen Interessen bereits so eng miteinander verflochten, dass eine Trennung kaum möglich erscheint. Eines der vielen Beispiele ist das Auftauchen der Sowjetunion als Unternehmer auf fremdem Boden. So ist sie unter anderem zusammen mit anderen Anlegern an einem Fischverarbeitungsbetrieb im US-Bundesstaat Washington beteiligt.

Wenn wirtschaftliche Kräfte ins Spiel kommen, gibt es kaum noch ideologische Barrieren. Diese bestehen vielmehr noch auf kulturellem Gebiet sowie durch die nationalen Eigenarten, die sich am deutlichsten durch die Sprache bemerkbar machen. Die Bedeutung der Sprache wird bereits im Alten Testament verzeichnet. Schon nach den ersten 10 Kapiteln des ersten Buches Moses wird die Frage gestellt, warum Menschen gleicher Abstammung (Noahs Familie) verschiedene Sprachen sprechen. Als Antwort wird die Geschichte des Turmes zu Babel erzählt.

Doch heute beginnen auch die Sprachbarrieren zu fallen, was auf Spezialgebieten und ganz besonders auf unserem Gebiet, dem Graphik-Design, deutlich wird. Man darf sagen, dass es heute eine wirklich internationale Sprache des Graphik-Designs gibt. Ein Beweis dafür ist das vorliegende Jahrbuch, das gleichzeitig als Ursache und Wirkung des einheitlichen Niveaus graphischer Arbeiten aus aller Welt gelten darf.

Die Entwicklung von GRAPHIS, das im Jahre 1944 erstmals erschien, entspricht der rapiden Entwicklung eines internationalen Stils, dessen Ursprung jedoch viel weiter zurückliegt: In der Emigration prominenter Bauhaus-Mitglieder und Zeitschriftengestalter in die Vereinigten Staaten. Nach dem ersten Weltkrieg entwickelten sich die USA rapide zu einer grossen Wirtschaftsmacht, ein Land des freien Unternehmertums mit 150 Millionen Einwohnern, politisch und kulturell vereinigt, mit zum grössten Teil einer gemeinsamen Sprache. Designer in den USA hatten die Grundlage eines gigantischen Bruttosozialproduktes und Möglichkeiten auf dem Gebiet der Medien, die in anderen Ländern unvorstellbar waren. Vielleicht war die Präsenz der Medien woanders intensiver, sie war jedoch nicht zu vergleichen mit der Masse und dem internationalen Einfluss der Medien in den Vereinigten Staaten. Das war auch die grosse Zeit Hollywoods. Amerikanische Filme, ob gut oder schlecht, wurden auf der ganzen Welt gesehen und spielten somit eine bedeutende Rolle im Prozess der internationalen Angleichung. Heute allerdings scheint die Filmkunst ausserhalb der Vereinigten Staaten grössere Anerkennung zu finden als im Lande selbst.

Auch wenn die Publikationen die bedeutendste Rolle spielten, so sollten auch die Schulen, Reisen und die internationalen Netze der Werbeagenturen erwähnt werden. Es genügt, sich an die Liste der Bauhaus-Schüler zu erinnern. Man fand hier natürlich vorwiegend Deutsche, aber auch viele andere Länder, einschliesslich jener des Fernen Ostens, waren hier vertreten. Diese Tradition der gegenseitigen Befruchtung wird durch die Studenten fortgesetzt, die weit reisen, um die bestmögliche Ausbildung auf dem Gebiet des Graphik-Designs zu erhalten. In den Niederlassungen britischer, deutscher und amerikanischer Werbeagenturen, z.B. in denen in Mailand, arbeiten Graphiker der verschiedensten Nationalitäten, darunter auch einige Italiener. Wenn ein Graphiker die internationale Sprache des Designs bei seiner Ankunft hier nicht beherrscht, so wird er sie vor seiner Abreise gelernt haben. Die gleiche Feststellung kann man in Paris, London, New York und Tokio machen.

Einige Fachleute bezeichnen den internationalen Stil als schweizerischen Ursprungs, und sie haben damit nicht ganz Unrecht. Internationaler Stil bedeutet jedoch, dass er an kein Land gebunden ist, sondern dass ein jedes dazu beiträgt. Es spielt keine Rolle, ob man an Indien,

Bolivien, Bulgarien oder an den Bundesstaat Montana in den USA denkt, für die Top-Designer an allen Orten gibt es nur den internationalen Stil, und sie arbeiten alle auf ähnliche Weise, mit gleich hohem Niveau. Dies findet man durch den vorliegenden Band bestätigt. Die gleiche Beobachtung macht man auf Reisen. Verkehrsschilder, Hinweisschilder auf Flughäfen und in öffentlichen Transportmitteln bestätigen die Internationalität des visuellen Vokabulars. Das betrifft jedoch nicht nur Zahlen, Buchstaben und Symbole, die durch die ICOGRADA und AIGA vereinheitlicht wurden, sondern vor allem auch das Handhaben aller Arten von Graphik und Werbung. Hier ist mehr im Spiel als nur die Helvetica. Natürlich hat das Design nicht überall einen gleich hohen Standard, und es ist kaum vorstellbar, dass dies je der Fall sein wird. In vielen Ländern wird es auch immer regional gefärbte, laienhafte Graphik geben, aber dessen ungeachtet besteht ein übernationaler Standard und Stil.

Graphik-Design hat ein so hohes Niveau erreicht, dass man es oft als selbstverständlich betrachtet. Dies erinnert mich an die Frage, die ein international bekannter Graphiker eines Tages stellte, als er das Orientierungssystem auf einem Parkplatz bewunderte. Seine erste Frage an seine Begleiter war: «Wer hat diese ausgezeichnete Arbeit gemacht?» Er war wirklich begeistert. Keiner konnte ihm jedoch eine Antwort geben. «Es ist erstaunlich,» sagte er, «ein unbekannter Designer, der eine wunderbare Arbeit geleistet hat. Ich frage mich, was danach noch kommen kann.» – Man kann sicher sein, es wird etwas kommen!

Jerry Steimle

Préface

JERRY STEIMLE est un écrivain californien spécialisé dans les problèmes de la publicité par les médias et du design, qui a débuté chez N.W. Ayer & Son à San Francisco. On lui doit des articles sur des designers et les grandes tendances du design à Copenhague, Hong-kong, Londres, Milan, Paris et Turin, ainsi qu'aux Etats-Unis.

On a souvent affirmé que la première coopération totale d'envergure entre humains ne verrait le jour que lorsqu'un ennemi commun unirait les peuples de la Terre dans un sursaut de révolte: le visiteur extra-terrestre tant redouté et attendu avec tant d'impatience, qui débarquerait de l'espace armes en mains. De la pure science-fiction, évidemment. L'unification de la Terre semble actuellement prendre une autre voie, économique cella-là. Un auteur contemporain nous rappelle que les multinationales disséminées sur la surface de la planète par la grâce des communications ultrarapides par jets et satellites sont en train de tisser un réseau d'intérêts tellement inextricable que les frontières entre nations paraissent de plus en plus floues. J'en veux pour exemple l'implantation de l'Union Soviétique en qualité d'employeur en terre étrangère—c'est ainsi que ce pays s'est associé à des investisseurs locaux pour gérer une usine de transformation du poisson dans l'Etat de Washington (USA).

Les barrières idéologiques s'effritent au contact des poussées économiques. Pourtant, il subsiste encore suffisamment de barrières sur le plan culturel, où les réactions nationalistes gouvernent nombre de nos attitudes, s'incarnant souvent à merveille dans ce prodigieux instrument social qu'est le langage. L'importance durable du langage est attestée depuis la rédaction de l'Ancien Testament. La première dizaine de chapitres élaborée, les anciens scribes n'eurent rien de mieux à faire que de s'occuper de savoir pourquoi les gens de même origine (la famille de Noé) parlaient des langues différentes. Et l'histoire de la Tour de Babel leur apporta la réponse.

Les barrières qu'érige la langue se mettent à leur tour à s'effriter dans tel domaine spécialisé, ainsi celui qui nous est propre, l'art graphique appliqué. On peut affirmer sans risque d'erreur qu'il existe aujourd'hui un véritable langage international du design graphique. Pour le constater, il suffit de se reporter au présent annuaire qui est à la fois l'origine et le résultat de l'homogénéisation des travaux réalisés tout autour de la planète. La croissance de GRAPHIS, qui a vu le jour en 1944, s'avère parallèle à la rapide éclosion d'un style visuel international, dont les origines sont à rechercher au lendemain de la Première Guerre mondiale, et qui s'accéléra par l'émigration en Amérique de nombreux représentants éminents du Bauhaus et de spécialistes hors pair du design de publications. Dans l'immédiat après-guerre, les Etats-Unis s'affirmaient comme une grande puissance économique, un pays de 150 millions d'habitants régi par la libre entreprise, unifié sur les plans politique et culturel et connaissant une langue dominante, l'anglais. Les designers américains avaient pour atouts l'utilisation d'un PNB proprement gigantesque et un accès aux médias inconnu ailleurs. Certains autres pays bénéficiaient peut-être d'une couverture médias plus intense que les Etats-Unis, sans toutefois atteindre l'effet de masse de l'Amérique, et certainement pas son influence au plan international. Ce fut aussi l'époque des grands triomphes d'Hollywood. Les films américains, projetés dans tous les pays du monde, ont joué un rôle essentiel dans le processus d'homogénéisation, quels que soient par ailleurs le mérite que l'on s'accorde à leur reconnaître ou les reproches qu'on est libre de leur adresser. De nos jours, le septième art semble être porté aux nues partout ailleurs qu'aux Etats-Unis.

Même si la part des publications a été prépondérante, celle des écoles, des voyages et des réseaux d'agences publicitaires de format international ne doit pas être négligée. Il suffit de reprendre la liste des étudiants du Bauhaus. On y trouve surtout des Allemands, c'est vrai, mais aussi un échantillon international représentatif de la Terre entière, jusque y compris les ressortissants de pays extrême-orientaux. La tradition de cette insémination croisée au plan mondial s'est maintenue, et l'on continue de voyager au loin pour puiser aux meilleures sources de la formation en matière de design. Parmi les graphistes œuvrant pour les filiales d'agences anglaises, allemandes et américaines à Milan, par exemple, on trouve un éventail de nationalités des plus intéressants, avec même quelques Italiens. L'artiste qui ne parlerait pas encore, à son arrivée, la langue internationale du design l'aura apprise avant de repartir. On peut faire les mêmes constatations à Paris, à Londres, à New York et à Tokyo.

Plus d'un observateur sera tenté d'attribuer le mérite du style visuel international aux Suisses, et il ne serait pas malaisé de défendre ce point de vue. Toutefois, l'idée même d'un style international implique qu'il a son origine dans tous les pays du monde, que chacun peut y contribuer et le mettre en œuvre.

Cela n'a en fait plus grande importance de distinguer l'Inde de la Bolivie, de la Bulgarie ou de l'Etat de Montana, aux USA — pour un designer figurant dans le peloton de tête, il n'existe qu'un seul style de création international, et tous ceux qui sont branchés sur ce courant unifié pratiquent leur art d'une manière analogue et opèrent au même niveau de qualité élevé. C'est ce que l'on constatera indubitablement en parcourant le présent ouvrage.

Le même constat s'impose lorsque l'on voyage dans le monde. La signalisation routière, celle employée dans les aéroports et dans les véhicules des transports publics attestent que le vocabulaire visuel s'est fait international. Je ne parle pas ici seulement des chiffres, lettres et symboles uniformisés par exemple sous l'impulsion de l'ICOGRADA et de l'AIGA, mais aussi et surtout des démarches créatives mises en œuvre pour la solution de tous problèmes de présentation graphique et de publicité. On est sur ce point bien au-delà du seul usage de l'Helvética.

Il faut bien admettre que tous les travaux qui se font à travers le monde ne dénotent pas le même niveau de compétence, et il serait bien difficile d'imaginer que cela sera jamais le cas. La création spontanée à l'échelle locale sera toujours imbibée de tradition vernaculaire, mais la structure transnationale est en place nonobstant tous les régionalismes.

La création graphique appliquée en est parvenue à un degré de perfection qui fait que les bons travaux passent plus d'une fois inaperçus. A cet égard, il me souvient d'une question posée par un graphiste de réputation internationale un jour qu'il admirait la signalisation d'un parking public. La première chose qu'il demanda à ses hôtes fut: «Qui a réalisé cet excellent travail?» Il était réellement ébloui de ce qu'il voyait. Consternation autour de lui: personne ne le savait. «Eh bien, dit-il, c'est vraiment extraordinaire. Voilà qu'un designer inconnu réalise une signalisation époustouflante. Je me demande ce qui pourra bien venir après.»

Quelque chose de plus parfait viendra après, soyons-en sûrs.

Index to Artists and Designers
Verzeichnis der Künstler und Gestalter
Index des artistes et maquettistes

Index to Art Directors
Verzeichnis der künstlerischen Leiter
Index des directeurs artistiques

Index to Agencies and Studios
Verzeichnis der Agenturen und Studios
Index des agences et studios

Index to Publishers
Verzeichnis der Verleger
Index des Editeurs

Index to Advertisers
Verzeichnis der Auftraggeber
Index des clients

ERRATUM – GRAPHIS ANNUAL 77/78

■ In the last volume of GRAPHIS ANNUAL no credits were given for the CCA-sponsored booklet on education shown as No. 181 on page 74. The booklet was conceived and designed by Jeff Barnes, who later joined CCA.

■ In der letzten Ausgabe von GRAPHIS ANNUAL zeigten wir auf Seite 74, unter der Nummer 181, eine Broschüre der CCA. Leider wurde der Name des Künstlers in den Credits nicht erwähnt; diesen Prospekt hat Jeff Barnes entworfen und ausgeführt, der erst später Mitarbeiter von CCA wurde.

■ Dans la dernière édition de GRAPHIS ANNUAL nous avons reproduit une brochure de CCA (no 181, p. 74) sans mentionner le nom de l'artiste. Elle a été conçue par Jeff Barnes qui est devenu plus tard l'un des collaborateurs de CCA.

■ Entry instructions will be mailed to anyone interested in submitting samples of outstanding graphics or photography for possible inclusion in our annuals. No fees involved. Closing dates for entries:
GRAPHIS ANNUAL (Advertising and editorial graphics): 15 December
PHOTOGRAPHIS (Advertising and editorial photography): 30 June
GRAPHIS POSTERS (International annual of poster art): 30 March
Write to: The Graphis Press, Dufourstr. 107, 8008 Zurich, Switzerland.

■ Einsendebedingungen können von jedermann angefordert werden, der uns Beispiele hervorragender Grafik oder Photographie zur Auswahl für unsere Jahrbücher unterbreiten möchte. Es werden keine Gebühren erhoben. Einsendetermine:
GRAPHIS ANNUAL (Werbe- und redaktionelle Graphik): 15. Dezember
PHOTOGRAPHIS (Werbe- und redaktionelle Photographie): 30. Juni
GRAPHIS POSTERS (Internationales Jahrbuch der Plakatkunst): 30. März
Adresse: Graphis Verlag, Dufourstr. 107, 8008 Zürich, Schweiz

■ Tout intéressé à la soumission de travaux graphiques et photographiques est prié de nous demander les informations nécessaires. Sans charge de participation. Dates limites:
GRAPHIS ANNUAL (art graphique publicitaire et rédactionnel): 15 décembre
PHOTOGRAPHIS (photographie publicitaire et rédactionnelle): 30 juin
GRAPHIS POSTERS (répertoire international de l'art de l'affiche): 30 mars
S'adresser à: Editions Graphis, Dufourstr. 107, 8008 Zurich, Suisse.

Editor, Art Director: Walter Herdeg
Assistant Editor: Stanley Mason
Project Manager: Heinke Jenssen
Designers: Ulrich Kemmner, Klaus Schröder
Art Assistants: Martin Byland, Willy Müller, Peter Wittwer

1

Magazine Advertisements

Newspaper Advertisements

Zeitschriften-Inserate

Zeitungs-Inserate

Annonces de revues

Annonces de presse

1

1 Artwork for an advertisement from a series for the airline *Air Bahama*. (USA)
2 Full-page advertisement to help popularize French *Pernod* in the USA. Pink faces, green bottle. (USA)
3, 4 Don't run away from it all, says this ad, subscribe to *Pardon*. Artwork and complete ad for a satirical magazine. (GER)
5 Double-spread ad for The Greyhound Corporation referring to their research facilities, which keep them "as much as ten years in the future". (USA)
6 Magazine ad for *Nastizil* nasal drops for children. (ARG)

1 Ausschnitt einer Anzeige aus einer Kampagne für die Fluggesellschaft *Air Bahama*. (USA)
2 «Wachsende Begeisterung» für den französischen *Pernod*. Rosa Gesichter mit grüner Flasche in ganzseitigem Inserat. (USA)
3, 4 Ausschnitt und Gesamtwiedergabe einer Abonnementswerbung der satirischen Monatszeitschrift *Pardon*. (GER)
5 Doppelseitige Anzeige einer Gesellschaft, deren Augenmerk dank neuer Forschungseinrichtungen auf die Zukunft der nächsten zehn Jahre gerichtet ist. (USA)
6 Zeitschrifteninserat für Kinder-Nasentropfen. (ARG)

1 Détail d'une annonce figurant dans une série publicitaire de la compagnie aérienne *Air Bahama*. (USA)
2 Annonce pleine page pour la promotion du *Pernod* français aux Etats-Unis. Visages roses, bouteille verte. (USA)
3, 4 Ne filez pas – abonnez-vous à *Pardon*. Détail et annonce complète pour un magazine satirique. (GER)
5 Annonce sur page double pour une société dont les nouveaux moyens de recherche permettent à s'orienter vers les prochaines dix années. (USA)
6 Annonce pour des gouttes nasales pour enfants. (ARG)

ARTIST / KÜNSTLER / ARTISTE:

1 Charles Santore
2 Bob Bidner
3, 4 Thomas M. Bunk
5 Sean Harrison/Gervasio Gallardio
6 Omar Tracogna

DESIGNER / GESTALTER / MAQUETTISTE:

1 Dave Bartels
3, 4 Jürgen-Horst Frickel
5 Ed Nussbaum
6 Eduardo A. Cánovas

ART DIRECTOR / DIRECTEUR ARTISTIQUE:

1 Dave Bartels
2 Bob Bidner
3, 4 Gerhard Kromschröder
5 Ed Nussbaum
6 Eduardo A. Cánovas

AGENCY / AGENTUR / AGENCE – STUDIO:

1 Clinton Frank Inc.
2 Ted Bates & Co., Inc.
5 Grey Advertising, Inc.
6 Estudio Cánovas

"Pernod. It grows on you."

Enjoy Pernod as a long drink with grapefruit juice, the "Pamplemousse." Also enjoyable with your favorite mixer, or with water and ice in a tall glass. Imported from France. 90 proof.

PERNOD

2

4

Advertisements
Inserate
Annonces

3

Here's where we keep our eye on the future.

5

6

7, 8 Page and complete double-spread magazine advertisement for *Decade,* a new low-tar cigarette that has taken ten years to develop. (USA)
9 Magazine advertisement in full colour for the mineral water *Evian* showing the cycle which finally produces the spring water. (FRA)
10 Large double-spread trade advertisement in full colour presenting the many popular sweets and snacks marketed by Standard Brands Confectionery. (USA)
11, 12 Painting and complete advertisement for imported *Courvoisier* cognac: "as long as there are people with taste". (NLD)

7, 8 Ganzseitige Illustration und Gesamtwiedergabe einer Zeitschriftenanzeige für *Decade,* eine neue leichte Zigarette, deren Entwicklung ein Jahrzehnt dauerte. (USA)
9 Farbiges Zeitschrifteninserat für das Mineralwasser *Evian.* Die Bildfolge zeigt die Entstehung dieses Wassers und seine Aufnahme im menschlichen Körper. (FRA)
10 Doppelseitiges Fachzeitschrifteninserat in Farbe, in welchem ein Grosshändler von ihm vertriebene bekannte Süsswarenmarken für sich aufmarschieren lässt. (USA)
11, 12 Ausschnitt mit Bildwiedergabe und Gesamtübersicht einer Anzeige für importierten *Courvoisier*-Cognac: «Solange es Menschen mit Geschmack gibt». (NLD)

ARTIST / KÜNSTLER / ARTISTE:

7, 8 Lemuel Line
9 Etienne Delessert
10 Alex Murawski
11, 12 M. van Malsen

DESIGNER / GESTALTER / MAQUETTISTE:

7, 8 Art Christy
9 Eliane Girard
10 Robert Qually
11, 12 Raymond van Geytenbeek

ART DIRECTOR / DIRECTEUR ARTISTIQUE:

7, 8 Art Christy
10 Robert Qually
11, 12 Raymond van Geytenbeek

AGENCY / AGENTUR / AGENCE – STUDIO:

7, 8 Della Femina, Travisano + Partners Inc.
9 TBWA
10 Lee King & Partners
11, 12 Jessurun/Bauduin/Foote, Cone & Belding B.V.

7

8

9

10

Advertisements / Inserate / Annonces

12

13

A votre service.

14

13, 14 Artwork and complete double-spread magazine advertisement for the airline *Air France* with letters and emblem formed by members of the staff. (USA)
15 Magazine advertisement for the fast Paris–New York flights of *Concorde*. (USA)
16 "Europeans rent *Europcars*." Colour ad from a series for a car hire service. (GER)
17 Small black-and-white ad for the New York City Ballet. (USA)
18 Magazine ad for a *Fender* electric guitar ("pick a live one"). Full colour. (USA)
19 Half-page full-colour magazine ad for a *Princess* tour to Alaska. (USA)

13, 14 Ausschnitt und vollständige Wiedergabe einer Zeitschriftenanzeige für die Fluggesellschaft *Air France*. Schriftzug und das Emblem der Linie sind durch Mitarbeiter dargestellt. (USA)
15 Zeitschriftenanzeige für die Überschallverbindung Paris–New York mit der *Concorde*. (USA)
16 Farbige Anzeige einer Werbekampagne für die europäische Autovermietung *Europcar*. (GER)
17 Kleine Schwarzweiss-Anzeige für das New York City Ballet. (USA)
18 Farbige Anzeige für elektrische Gitarren, vom Hersteller auch als Plakat erhältlich. (USA)
19 Halbseitige Anzeige in Farbe für spezielle Alaska-Reisen eines Reiseunternehmens. (USA)

13, 14 Détail et annonce de magazine sur page double pour la compagnie aérienne *Air France*. Logo et symbole sont représentés par les employés. (USA)
15 Annonce de magazine pour la promotion des vols Paris–New York de la *Concorde*. (USA)
16 Annonce d'une campagne publicitaire pour *Europcar*, un service de location de voitures. (GER)
17 Petite annonce en noir et blanc pour le New York City Ballet. (USA)
18 Annonce couleur pour des guitares électriques. Le même motif a paru sous forme d'affiche.(USA)
19 Annonce sur demi-page d'une agence de voyages pour des tours de l'Alaska. (USA)

ARTIST / KÜNSTLER / ARTISTE:

13, 14 Pierre Peyrolle
15 Etienne Delessert
16 Patrice Goichon
18, 19 James Endicott

DESIGNER / GESTALTER / MAQUETTISTE:

13, 14 Havas Conseil
15 Béat Brüsch
18 Talbert Smith/James Endicott
19 Jerry Regua/James Endicott

Advertisements / Inserate / Annonces

30

Paris-New York in 3½ Hours. Your daily Headstart.

Only Air France can give you a Headstart on the rest of the world every day of the week.
Each morning at 11 a.m., your Concorde flight departs Roissy Airport in Paris. And 3 1/2 supersonic hours later, you're in New York at 8:30 a.m. local time. You arrive at the start of a full business day, refreshed and relaxed, four valuable hours faster than by any other flight.
And at both ends of your journey, in Paris and New York, corresponding flights are con- veniently available to you from all of Europe and throughout all of North America.
Concorde is your Headstart. Only Air France makes it a daily event.

15

Europäer mieten Europcar

Wir sind der Meinung, daß Europäer mindestens so tüchtig sind wie alle anderen, und wenn es um Autovermietung geht, können wir das beweisen. Die Leute von Europcar sind erfahren und hilfsbereit. Unsere Methoden sind ausgesprochen leistungsfähig (die Europcar Super Service Kreditkarte zum Beispiel ist die einfachste und schnellste überhaupt).

Unsere Autos sind neueste Modelle und bestens gepflegt. Überall in Europa, in Afrika und dem mittleren Osten haben wir hunderte von einheitlichen, attraktiv gestalteten Niederlassungen*. Die Entwicklung unseres Unternehmens war die schnellste in der Branche.

Wenn Europcar heutzutage eine der bedeutendsten (wirklich internationalen) Autovermietungen ist, dann nur, weil wir überall hunderttausende zufriedene Kunden haben. Das ist der Beweis.

Information und Buchung auch über Ihr Reisebüro.

europcar ℮

DIRECT 20 A 508297 1277
BARTH PETER

SCHLEBUSCHWEG 19
2050 HAMBURG
301244 GE KASSEL
82095/62*050762*GE KASSEL

In USA, Lateinamerika und dem pazifischen Raum – National Car Rental.

16

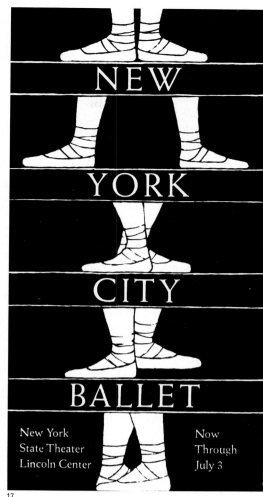

NEW YORK CITY BALLET

New York
State Theater
Lincoln Center

Now
Through
July 3

17

ART DIRECTOR:

13–15 Edouard Nicolas
16 Catherine Chevallier
18 Talbert Smith
19 Jerry Regua

AGENCY / AGENTUR:

13–15 Havas Conseil
16 Publicis Conseil
18 Wenger-Michael, Inc.
19 Cole & Weber

First heard emerging from the spectral depths of creation in 1976, Starcaster abandons the great, grey-green, greasy Limpopo and relentlessly climbs the charts. Its attack is heightened by a unique semi-hollow body and jaw-popping vocal range which make it a prized trophy among animusicologists.

When domesticated, Starcaster exhibits the most deceptive, chameleon-like vocal qualities. It not only bellows forth its own unique call but may emit musical tones associated with other members of the species Guitar Electrical as well.

A prolific mate, Starcaster couples boisterously in proximity to the Super Reverb and others of the family Amplifier Fender. Its excited cries when so engaged have been recorded voluminously.

For further reference, see Fender Authorized Dealer.

Pick a live one.

Fender
CBS Musical Instruments

For full-color poster of this ad, send $1 to Fender, Box 3410, Dept. 477, Fullerton, CA 92634

The Hard-Charging Sharp-Toothed Starcaster

(Astrogator Fender).

18

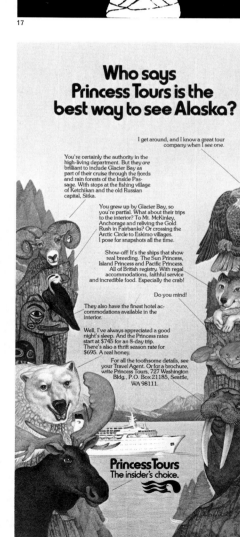

Who says Princess Tours is the best way to see Alaska?

I get around, and I know a great tour company when I see one.

You're certainly the authority in the high-living department. But they are brilliant to include Glacier Bay as part of their cruise through the fjords and rain forests of the Inside Passage. With stops at the fishing village of Ketchikan and the old Russian capital, Sitka.

You grew up by Glacier Bay, so you're partial. What about their trips to the interior? To Mt. McKinley, Anchorage and reliving the Gold Rush in Fairbanks? Or crossing the Arctic Circle to Eskimo villages. I pose for snapshots all the time.

Show-off! It's the ships that show real breeding. The Sun Princess, Island Princess and Pacific Princess. All of British registry. With regal accommodations, faithful service and incredible food. Especially the crab!

Do you mind!

They also have the finest hotel accommodations available in the interior.

Well, I've always appreciated a good night's sleep. And the Princess rates start at $745 for an 8-day trip. There's also a thrift season rate for $695. A real honey.

For all the toothsome details, see your Travel Agent. Or for a brochure, write Princess Tours, 727 Washington Bldg., P.O. Box 21185, Seattle, WA 98111.

Princess Tours
The insider's choice.

19

"I'm at the   end of my rope."

Blinded by depression, groping anxiously for meaning in what he sees as a hopeless, precarious existence, the depressed patient is often emotionally pulled in opposite directions. While his | depression is immobilizing him with feelings of withdrawal, lack of interest, and fatigue, the accompanying anxiety keeps him awake nights worrying about the future. | For these patients, there is no better tricyclic than Tofranil-PM. In a recent study of anxious depressed patients the quality of sleep and rising time was significantly better with imipramine | pamoate group than in an amitriptyline [Elavil] treated group. Other measures of relief were not significantly different. | **Tofranil-PM** imipramine **pamoate** | Unsurpassed effectiveness among tricyclics in relieving anxiety, sleep disturbances and other symptoms of depression.

20

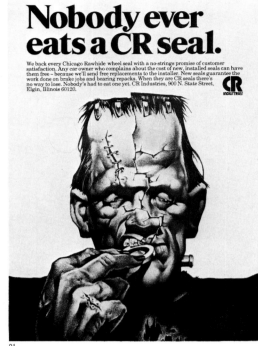

Nobody ever eats a CR seal.

We back every Chicago Rawhide wheel seal with a no-strings promise of customer satisfaction. Any car owner who complains about the cost of new, installed seals can have them free – because we'll send free replacements to the installer. New seals guarantee the work done on brake jobs and bearing repacks. When they are CR seals there's no way to lose. Nobody's had to eat one yet. CR Industries, 900 N. State Street, Elgin, Illinois 60120.

21

Dean's **All Your Ice Cream Dreams Come True**

22

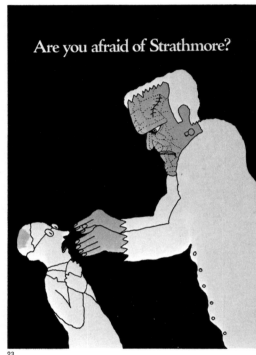

Are you afraid of Strathmore?

23

ARTIST / KÜNSTLER / ARTISTE:

20 Eugene Mihaesco
21 Graphicsgroup
22 Bruce Wolfe
23 Simms Taback
24 Braldt Bralds

DESIGNER / GESTALTER / MAQUETTISTE:

20 John DeCesare
22 Bruce Wolfe
23 Simms Taback
24 Robert Pütz

ART DIRECTOR / DIRECTEUR ARTISTIQUE:

20 John DeCesare
21 Robert Sherman
22 David Bartels
23 Norman Siegal

AGENCY / AGENTUR / AGENCE – STUDIO:

20 Ciba-Geigy
21 Brand Advertising
22 Clinton E. Frank, Inc.
23 The Lampert Agency
24 Robert Pütz

Advertisements / Inserate / Annonces

20 Double-spread black-and-white advertisement for *Tofranil* for the treatment of depression. (USA)
21 Trade ad from a colour campaign for wheel seals made by CR Industries ("Nobody's had to eat one yet"). (USA)
22 Full-page newspaper ad in full colour for *Dean's* ice-cream specialities, here presented as treasure. (USA)
23 Page of magazine insert on tinted stock for *Strathmore* papers. Pink and yellow Frankenstein figure. (USA)
24 Illustration from a double-spread advertisement for *Siegwerk* printing inks, whose symbol is the rainbow. (GER)

20 Doppelseitige Schwarzweiss-Anzeige für ein Medikament gegen Depressionen. (USA)
21 Farbiges Fachzeitschrifteninserat aus einer Kampagne für Raddichtungen («Niemand frisst CR-Dichtungen»). (USA)
22 Doppelseitiges Zeitungsinserat in Farbe für Speiseeisspezialitäten, hier der Inhalt einer Schatztruhe. (USA)
23 Vorderseite einer Zeitschriftenbeilage auf Spezialpapier für einen Papierhersteller. Frankenstein-Figur rosa und grün. (USA)
24 Illustration eines doppelseitigen Inserats für Druckfarben von *Siegwerk*, deren Symbol der Regenbogen ist. (GER)

20 Annonce sur page double en noir-blanc en faveur d'un produit pharmaceutique pour le traitement de dépressions. (USA)
21 Annonce professionnelle en couleurs d'une campagne pour des joints de roues («personne ne bouffe les joints CR»). (USA)
22 Annonce de journal pleine page (en couleurs) pour des spécialités de glaces, présentées ici comme trésor. (USA)
23 Page d'un encart publicitaire imprimé sur papier teint pour une papeterie. Monstre de Frankenstein en rose et vert. (USA)
24 Illustration d'une annonce double page pour les encres d'imprimerie *Siegwerk*, dont le symbole est l'arc-en-ciel (GER)

32

25–27 "Siegwerk are colour specialists for anything that has to be packed." —"It's good to be prepared for periods of drought." Two complete ads with detail of artwork from a campaign for *Siegwerk* printing inks, whose symbol is the rainbow. (GER)
28 Magazine advertisement in full colour for wines from the vineyards of New York State. (USA)
29–31 Two medallions and complete magazine advertisement from a colour campaign for *Marantz* stereo receivers. (USA)

25–27 Zwei Inserate und ein Ausschnitt einer Werbekampagne der Siegwerk-Farbenfabrik, bekannt «wie eine bunte Kuh», mit dem Regenbogensymbol für ihre Druckfarben. (GER)
28 Farbiges Zeitschrifteninserat für die Weine aus dem nördlichen Teil des amerikanischen Bundesstaates New York. (USA)
29–31 Zwei Ausschnitte von Zeitschrifteninseraten mit einer Gesamtwiedergabe aus einer farbigen Werbekampagne für *Marantz*-Stereoanlagen. «Wir klingen besser.» (USA)

25–27 «Siegwerk, les spécialistes des couleurs, pour tout ce qu'il faut emballer.» – «Il faut tout prévoir pour des périodes difficiles.» Annonces complètes et détail de l'illustration figurant dans une campagne pour les encres d'imprimerie Siegwerk, avec l'arc-en-ciel comme symbole. (GER)
28 Annonce de magazine en couleurs pour des vins provenant des vignobles de l'état de New York. (USA)
29–31 Médaillons et annonce de magazine complète tirés d'une campagne publicitaire en couleurs pour des récepteurs stéréophoniques. (USA)

Advertisements
Inserate
Annonces

29

27

28

30

ARTIST / KÜNSTLER / ARTISTE:

25–27 Tomi Ungerer
28 Em. Schongut
29–31 Abe Gurvin

DESIGNER / GESTALTER / MAQUETTISTE:

25–27 Robert Pütz
29–31 Abe Gurvin

ART DIRECTOR / DIRECTEUR ARTISTIQUE:

29–31 Norm Galston

AGENCY / AGENTUR / AGENCE – STUDIO:

25–27 Robert Pütz
29–31 Sanford & Charles

31

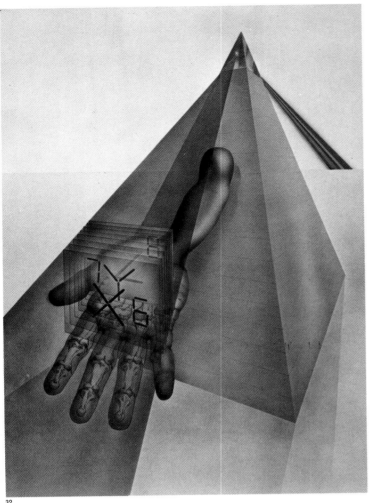

32

34

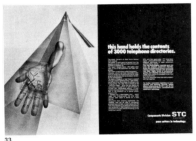

33

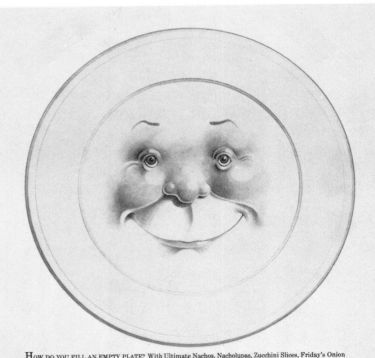

HOW DO YOU FILL AN EMPTY PLATE? With Ultimate Nachos, Nacholupas, Zucchini Slices, Friday's Onion Rings, Friday's Mushrooms, Guacamole Y Tostados Con Queso, French Fries, Baked Potatoes, Peel & Eat Spiced Shrimp, Homemade Soup Du Jour Et De La Nuit, Corn on the Cob, Friday's Chef Salad, Spinach Salad, Avocado and Crabmeat Louis, Omelettes Grand' Mére, Spanish Omelettes, Crabmeat Artichoke Omelettes, Roadrunner Omelettes, Bacon and Cheese Omelettes, Strawberry Omelettes, "We'll Try Anything Once" Omelettes, Eggs to Order, Western Omelettes, Monday, Tuesday, Wednesday, Thursday, Friday, and Saturday Burgers, Bacon Cheeseburgers, Western Burgers, Mexican Burgers, Cheddar Burgers, Bacon Cheddar Burgers, Peking Burgers, Mushroom Burgers, California Burgers, Pizza Burgers, Great American Cheeseburgers, Name Your Own Burgers, Friday's London Broil, Club Steaks, Chopped Steaks, New York Strips, Steak on a Stick, Filets, Chicken Friday, Steak Fingers, Shrimp Friday, Steak Stick and Shrimp, Shrimp & Fingers, Crabmeat/Shrimp Mornay, Shrimp on a Stick, Friday's Club Sandwiches, Mushrooms-Steak and Mushrooms, Friday's Ham & Cheese, California Gold, Friday's Stew on a Biscuit, Friday's Steak Sandwiches, The Pocket, Hot Corned Beef Sandwiches, Texas Style Red Chili and Tostados, Coney Island Platters, Great American Hot Dog Platters, Cheesecake, "Outrageous" Desserts, Carrot Cake, Hot Apple Pie, Homemade Grasshopper Pie, Friday's Sundays, Ice Cream, Sherbet, or a Friday's Tin Roof.

At T.G.I. Friday's you'll find over 100 delicious dishes. And some very contented plates.
120 Texas Street / 221-8596 / Open everyday from 11:30 a.m. to 2:00 a.m. except Sunday.

37

Advertisements / Inserate / Annonces

35

38

32, 33 Illustration and complete double-spread magazine advertisement in full colour featuring holography and offering the technical services of STC, makers of electronic equipment. (SAF)
34–36 Two illustrations (full colour) and complete ad from a series to promote *Municaps* for combating the symptoms of anxiety, stress and overwork. (GER)
37 Black-and-white advertisement listing the dishes served at *T.G.I. Friday's*, a restaurant in Dallas. (USA)
38, 39 Illustration and complete trade magazine advertisement for *Ciba-Geigy* dyes for use with acrylics. (GBR)

32, 33 Illustration und Gesamtwiedergabe einer farbigen doppelseitigen Zeitschriftenanzeige, die sich auf die zukunftsweisende Technik der Holographie bezieht. Die Anzeige wirbt für einen Hersteller elektronischen Zubehörs. (SAF)
34–36 Zwei farbige Illustrationen und Gesamtwiedergabe aus einer Anzeigenkampagne für *Municaps*, ein Medikament gegen Zeitsymptome wie Lebensangst, Stress und Überforderung: «*Municaps* schafft Lebenskraft». (GER)
37 Schwarzweiss-Anzeige eines Restaurants in Texas mit einer Aufzählung der über hundert Gerichte, die dort serviert werden. (USA)
38, 39 Illustration und Gesamtwiedergabe eines Fachzeitschrifteninserats für *Ciba-Geigy*-Farbstoffe *Maxilom M* für Acrylfasern. Die Markenbezeichnung *M* wird hier von Zugvögeln dargestellt. (GBR)

32, 33 Illustration et annonce de magazine sur page double (en couleurs) se référant à la nouvelle technique de l'holographie. Elément publicitaire pour un fabricant d'équipements électroniques. (SAF)
34–36 Deux illustrations en couleurs et annonce complète figurant dans une série pour la promotion de *Municaps*, un produit pharmaceutique pour le traitement d'états d'anxiété, de stress et de surménage. (GER)
37 Annonce en noir et blanc présentant les mets servis dans un restaurant à Dallas, Texas. (USA)
38, 39 Illustration et annonce de revue professionnelle en faveur des matières colorantes de *Ciba-Geigy* pour les fibres acryliques. (GBR)

40

42

ARTIST / KÜNSTLER / ARTISTE:

40, 41 Abe Gurvin
42, 43 Ken Laidlaw
44 Wally Neibart

DESIGNER / GESTALTER / MAQUETTISTE:

40, 41 Abe Gurvin
44 Marty Kendrick
45 Bill Bonnell
46 Jeff A. Barnes
47 Wim Verboven

ART DIRECTOR / DIRECTEUR ARTISTIQUE:

40, 41 Norm Galston
42, 43 Neil Fazakerley
44 Roger Raymor
45 Bill Bonnell
46 Jeff A. Barnes

43

Oh, we've known about Chilly Things frozen novelties for some time now. And we openly accept the full responsibility for not bringing them to you sooner. You won't have to wait any longer. Wilson Dairy now stocks the entire Chilly Things line. Pops, Fudge Bars, Rounds, Sandwiches, Cones, Slices, Snowmen, Gingerbread Men, Giant Amazing Things, seasonal and special promotion products. Just wait til you see the packaging! The Chilly Things brand is backed by the most aggressive marketing program in the country. Sales aids for each product and merchandising effectiveness programs are yours for the asking. The Chilly Things line has a proven ability to maintain sales and profits throughout the winter! Call your Wilson Dairy rep today. He'll show you this exciting line. And while you have his attention, ask about our "Heads Up" discounts. It's our way of saying "Forgive us for waiting so long."

WILSON DAIRY CO.
5255 Tillman Avenue
Detroit, Michigan 48208
313-895-6000

We're . . . uh . . . sorry for the . . . er . . . delay.

44

41

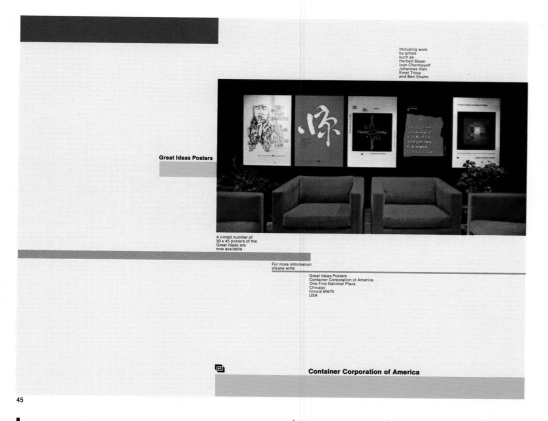

Great Ideas Posters

Including work
by artists
such as
Herbert Bayer
Ivan Chermayeff
Johannes Itten
Ernst Trova
and Ben Shahn

A limited number of
30 x 45 posters of the
Great Ideas are
now available

For more information
please write

Great Ideas Posters
Container Corporation of America
One First National Plaza
Chicago
Illinois 60670
USA

Container Corporation of America

45

Depend on the package that we build

When you work with a single-source packaging supplier, you can expect quality all the way around.

And CCA grows the trees, produces the paperboard, and makes the cartons frozen food processors rely on. All this and more: materials research, structural and graphic design, mechanical packaging, transportation.

J. R. Simplot Company uses CCA paperboard to make cartons in its own converting operation. CCA supplies Simplot cartons, too. Institutional and retail. We've also helped with corporate identity and package design. It's an ongoing relationship we're proud of.

We build packaging programs for frozen food processors.

Container Corporation of America
Carton Division
Mill Division

46

Boston road, 1974 / 294 x 294 cm

Richard Serra in het Stedelijk

De eerste grote museumpresentatie van de tekeningen van de Amerikaanse beeldhouwer Serra, wiens 'Sight Point' (1971-1975) al enkele jaren in de tuin van het Stedelijk prijkt.
20 tekeningen van monumentale omvang uit de periode 1971-1977.

Tot 2 januari 1978

47

Stedelijk Museum Amsterdam

Open:
dagelijks, 9.30-17.00 uur
zon- en feestdagen,
13.00-17.00 uur

Stedelijk Museum
Paulus Potterstraat 13
Amsterdam
Tel. 020-73 21 66

Overige tentoonstellingen:

Daniel Graffin
textielskulpturen
t/m 27 november

Paper for Space
tekeningen van Nederlandse
beeldhouwers
t/m 27 november

Images of an Era
het Amerikaanse affiche
1945/75
t/m 11 december

Harold Cohen
computer tekeningen
van 25 november t/m
8 januari

De tentoonstellingen

Dat zijn er nog al wat in het Stedelijk Museum: zo'n dertig per jaar. Je hoeft je er nooit te vervelen. Meestal kan er in het Stedelijk gekozen worden uit 4 à 5 verschillende exposities. En dan rekenen we de eigen kollektie nog niet eens mee. Hard werken dus voor die timmermannen, elektriciens, sekretaresses, konservators enz. enz. Allemaal bezig om u goed op de hoogte te houden van de moderne kunst.
Tot uw dienst…

AGENCY / AGENTUR / AGENCE – STUDIO:

40, 41 Sanford & Charles
42, 43 T. Richard Johnson Ltd.
44 Tailford Associates, Inc.
45, 46 Container Corporation of America
47 Total Design

40, 41 Complete trade magazine ad and illustration (Humphrey Bogart) for *Superscope* broadcasting equipment. (USA)
42, 43 Complete advertisement and colour illustration of a "lame duck" for *Taylor* process control equipment. (GBR)
44 Trade magazine ad for *Three Rivers* apologizing for delay in introducing a new line of frozen confectionery. (USA)
45 Ad for the Container Corporation of America offering posters from their *Great Ideas* series. (USA)
46 Black-and-white trade ad for CCA packages. (USA)
47 Black-and-white announcement of exhibitions in the Stedelijk Museum, Amsterdam. (NLD)

40, 41 Illustration (Humphrey Bogart) und vollständiges Fachzeitschrifteninserat für *Aircommand*-Sendeanlagen. (USA)
42, 43 Gesamtwiedergabe und farbige Illustration einer «lahmen Ente» aus einer Anzeige für Überwachungssysteme. (GBR)
44 Fachzeitschriftenanzeige für eine neue Marke tiefgekühlter Lebensmittel, auf die der Handel schon lange gewartet hat. (USA)
45 Zeitschriftenanzeige einer Verpackungsfirma für Künstlerplakate, die in begrenzter Auflage erhältlich sind. (USA)
46 Schwarzweiss-Fachzeitschrifteninserat für Verpackungen. (USA)
47 Schwarzweiss-Anzeige für Ausstellungen im Stedelijk-Museum Amsterdam mit Abbildung aus der laufenden Ausstellung. (NLD)

40, 41 Annonce de la presse professionnelle et illustration (Humphrey Bogart) pour des installations de télévision. (USA)
42, 43 Annonce complète et illustration couleur d'un canard boiteux pour les équipements de contrôle *Taylor*. (GBR)
44 Annonce professionnelle présentant l'excuse d'une compagnie alimentaire pour l'introduction tardive d'une nouvelle marque de produits surgelés. (USA)
45 Annonce de magazine présentant les affiches de divers artistes d'une série parue à tirage limité. (USA)
46 Annonce en noir et blanc pour les emballages CCA. (USA)
47 Annonce en noir et blanc pour une exposition présentée au Musée Stedelijk à Amsterdam. (NLD)

Advertisements / Inserate / Annonces

50

51

52

49

48, 49 Illustration in actual size and complete double-spread advertisement for a new *Saupiquet* mustard dressing for mackerel. (FRA)
50, 51 Two full-page advertisements in full colour for a *Deinhard* German champagne. (GER)
52 Double-spread trade magazine advertisement with a black-and-white illustration for *Fastin* capsules to control appetite. (USA)

48, 49 Illustration in Originalgrösse und Gesamtwiedergabe einer doppelseitigen Anzeige für Makrelen in Senfsauce und elf weitere Fischspezialitäten. (FRA)
50, 51 Zwei ganzseitige farbige Inserate für *Deinhard Lila* Sekt, angelehnt an den Surrealismus und die naive Malerei. (GER)
52 Doppelseitiges Fachzeitschrifteninserat mit Schwarzweiss-Illustration für *Fastin*-Kapseln zur Eindämmung des Hungergefühls. (USA)

48, 49 Illustration en grandeur nature et annonce complète sur double page pour les maquereaux à la sauce moutarde et douze autres entrées de poisson de *Saupiquet*. (FRA)
50, 51 Deux annonces pleines pages (en couleurs) pour une marque de champagne. (GER)
52 Annonce professionnelle sur page double avec illustration en noir et blanc en faveur des capsules *Fastin* pour inhiber l'appétit. (USA)

ARTIST / KÜNSTLER / ARTISTE:

48, 49 Rick Meyerowitz
50, 51 Dorothee Walter
52 Lee M. Cuggan

DESIGNER / GESTALTER / MAQUETTISTE:

50, 51 Dorothee Walter
52 Dave Meade

ART DIRECTOR / DIRECTEUR ARTISTIQUE:

48, 49 Gérard Jean
52 Dave Meade

AGENCY / AGENTUR / AGENCE – STUDIO:

48, 49 Chevalier, Le Forestier, Michel & BBDO
50, 51 Deinhard & Co., Marketing Service
52 Frank J. Corbett

Advertisements
Inserate
Annonces

53

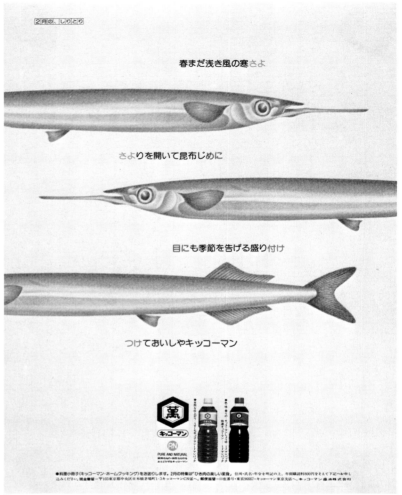

54

ARTIST / KÜNSTLER / ARTISTE:

53, 54, 56–58 Tadashi Ohashi
55 Mike Golding

DESIGNER / GESTALTER / MAQUETTISTE:

53, 54, 56–58 Tadashi Ohashi
55 Hans Goedicke/Rob Floor

ART DIRECTOR / DIRECTEUR ARTISTIQUE:

53, 54, 56–58 Tadashi Ohashi
55 Hans Goedicke

AGENCY / AGENTUR / AGENCE – STUDIO:

55 J. Walter Thompson

53, 54, 56, 57 Four full-page magazine advertisements from a long and continuing series showing vegetables and fish, for the soy sauces made by Kikkoman Shoyu Co. Ltd. (JPN)
55 Full-page black-and-white newspaper advertisement suggesting day trips with Netherlands Railways, with a *Kodak* film to snap the sights. (NLD)
58 Small black-and-white advertisement for the soy sauces of Kikkoman Shoyu Co. Ltd. in which the artist of this long series for once allows himself a dash of humour. (JPN)

53, 54, 56, 57 Ganzseitige Zeitschrifteninserate aus einer lang andauernden Werbekampagne für *Kikkoman*-Soya-Saucen unter dem Slogan «rein und natürlich» mit Abbildungen von Gemüsearten und Fischen. (JPN)
55 Ganzseitiges Schwarzweiss-Zeitungsinserat, das für *Kodak*-Farbfilme wirbt. Beschrieben werden die von der Niederländischen Eisenbahn angebotenen Tagesausflüge, deren Eindrücke dank *Kodak* festgehalten werden können. (NLD)
58 Kleine Schwarzweiss-Anzeige für die Saucen von *Kikkoman*, in welcher sich der Künstler dieser langen Serie von Anzeigen einmal ein bisschen Humor erlaubt. (JPN)

53, 54, 56, 57 Quatre annonces de magazines pleines pages figurant dans une longue série avec des illustrations de légumes et de poissons pour les sauces soja de *Kikkoman Shoyu*. (JPN)
55 Annonce de presse pleine page en noir et blanc présentant des propositions pour des excursions d'une journée avec la société des chemins de fer néerlandais et les pellicules couleur *Kodak* pour les prises de vues. (NLD)
58 Petite annonce en noir et blanc pour les sauces *Kikkoman*. Cette fois-ci, l'artiste de cette longue série a su donner à l'annonce un air humoristique. (JPN)

55

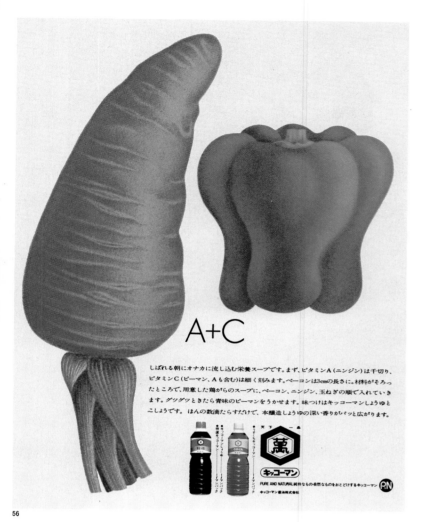

A+C

しばれる朝にオナカに流し込む栄養スープです。まず、ビタミンA（ニンジン）は千切り、ビタミンC（ピーマン、Aも含む）は細く刻みます。ベーコンは3cmの長さに。材料がそろったところで、用意した鶏がらのスープに、ベーコン、ニンジン、玉ねぎの順で入れていきます。グツグツときたら青味のピーマンをうかせます。味つけはキッコーマンしょうゆとこしょうです。ほんの数滴たらすだけで、本醸造しょうゆの深い香りがむッと広がります。

PURE AND NATURAL 純粋なもの・自然なものをおとどけするキッコーマン
キッコーマン醤油株式会社

56

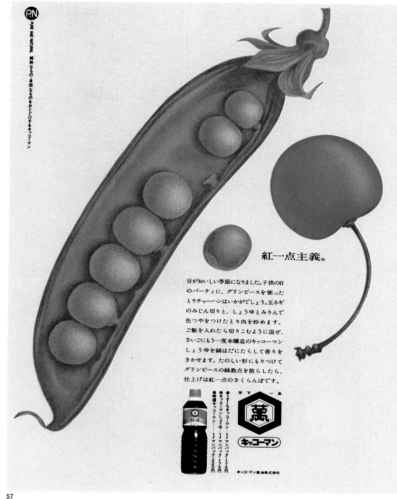

PN PURE AND NATURAL 純粋なもの・自然なものをおとどけする キッコーマン

紅一点主義。

豆がおいしい季節になりました。子供の日のパーティに、グリンピースを使ったとりチャーハンはいかがでしょう。玉ネギのみじん切りと、しょうゆとみりんで色つやをつけたとり肉を炒めます。ご飯を入れたら切りこむように混ぜ、さいごにもう一度本醸造のキッコーマンしょうゆを鍋はだにたらして香りをきかせます。たのしい形にもりつけてグリンピースの緑数点を散らしたら、仕上げは紅一点のきくらんぼです。

キッコーマン醤油株式会社

57

拝啓、旦那さま

遅くなるのはお仕事のため
ええ、信じております
でもお電話の一本ぐらい

それは、もう、私たちのために額に汗して働いてくださっているのですもの。残業なんてことになると、どんなに遅くなろうとも、三つ指ついてお迎えしたいぐらい。

おつきあいだって、リッパなお仕事のひとつと考えておりますことよ。食卓の前で女房がツノを出している様など、美観上も美容上もよろしくありませんわ。

でも、せっかく用意したお料理がムダになるっていうこと、ちょっともったいない気がするのです。

お電話一本くだされば、ご予定によって、軽い夜食に変えてお待ち申しあげてもいいし冷蔵庫にしまって明日のおそうざいに再利用してもいいし。

お肉ひとつ、お魚ひとつ、旦那さまの収入から出たもの。ゆめゆめおろそかにてきません、わ。

愛情という、2名の調味料
キッコーマンしょうゆ

色にも、ゼイタクな料理ばかりつくっていも、味つけひとつに、味の変化ひとつに、お金では買えない愛情をつけ加える、大切な心のお児。確かなふものを選びましょう。キッコーマンは、たっぷりと時間をかけて、丹念に育てられる本醸造・特級のしょうゆです。愛情という名にふさわしい調味料です。惚愛のカゲにはいつも、いい味が。

COOK BOOK PRESENT
ふたりのためのクック・ブック プレゼント
（お料理が102種226点）

ふたり用に選びぬいたさまざまな料理

58

43

The Gottex Cult

From the Mediterranean to the South Seas, wherever you find bronzed sunworshippers, white sands and sparkling blue oceans, you'll find Gottex swimwear. Because beautiful people love beautiful places and beautiful things. Like Gottex. Here we illustrate just one gorgeous Gottex print to show you why. Stunning in the brilliance and purity of its colour and the primitive power of its design, you'll recognize it as a modern interpretation of the sun-inspired artwork of the ancient Aztecs. The caftan is equally at ease on the beach or for home entertaining. Cotton in small, medium or large, 145.00. The sleek maillot swimsuits slip on like a second skin in silky smooth nylon/spandex. Sizes 30 to 36, 52.00 each. Predominately red print. Personal Shopping Only. Downtown (Third Floor), Pointe Claire, Anjou, Cavendish Mall, Carrefour Laval. Dept. 246. Why not use your Eaton Account Card?

EATON

59 Full-page newspaper advertisement in full colour for *Gottex* beachwear sold by *Eaton's* department stores—here a caftan and swimsuits with patterns inspired by the art of the Aztecs. (CAN)
60 Full-page newspaper ad in full colour from a Christmas series for *Eaton's* department stores, here for *Highland Queen* skirts and blazers in ice-cream colours. (CAN)
61 Full-page newspaper ad in sepia and blue announcing the reopening of a traditional market, this time with a new fashion section. (USA)

59 Ganzseitiges Zeitungsinserat eines Kaufhauses für *Gottex*-Strandkleidung, unter dem Titel «Der *Gottex*-Kult». Wie auch das abgebildete Muster, spielt dieser Titel auf die Kultur des alten Sonnenreiches der Azteken an. (CAN)
60 Ganzseitiges farbiges Zeitungsinserat für Damenoberbekleidung. Das ganze Inserat ist in den «Eiscreme-Farben» der Kleidung gedruckt. Die Farben heissen entsprechend, z. B. Vanille, Pistazie usw. (CAN)
61 Ganzseitiges Zeitungsinserat für einen traditionsreichen Markt. Text und Skizze des Ortes sind blau gedruckt, die Abbildungen mit Schlagzeile sind braun. (USA)

59 Annonce de presse pleine page d'un grand magasin présentant sous le titre «Le culte *Gottex*» la nouvelle mode de plage. Ce titre, ainsi que le motif représenté, font allusion à la culture des Aztèques. (CAN)
60 Annonce de presse en couleurs pour la nouvelle mode féminine dans une gamme de couleurs «ice cream», p. ex. vanille, pistache, etc. (CAN)
61 Annonce de presse pleine page en faveur du marché Faneuil Hall. Le texte ainsi que le plan du lieu sont imprimés en bleu, l'illustration et le slogan en brun. (USA)

ARTIST / KÜNSTLER / ARTISTE:

59 Ugenie Groh
60 Gail Krouse
61 Dick Mitchell/Don Grimes/David Kent/
   Mary Keck/Mike Washlesky

DESIGNER / GESTALTER / MAQUETTISTE:

59 Ginny Poisson
60 Linda DaCosta
61 Bob Dennard/Dick Mitchell

ART DIRECTOR / DIRECTEUR ARTISTIQUE:

59, 60 Harriet Golfos Santroch
61 Bob Dennard

AGENCY / AGENTUR / AGENCE – STUDIO:

59, 60 T. Eaton Co.
61 The Richards Group

Advertisements / Inserate / Annonces

62

GET YOUR BACK LEGS INTO RAM JEANS.

63

64

65

ARTIST / KÜNSTLER / ARTISTE:

62 Joseph Sellars
63 Nicholas Price
64, 65 Aldo Lanfranco
66, 67 Lars Melander
68 Roy Ellsworth
69 John Deerotyne
70 Rick Meyerowitz

DESIGNER / GESTALTER / MAQUETTISTE:

62 Joseph Sellars
63 Colin Craig
64, 65 Aldo Lanfranco
66, 67 Lars Melander
68 Ton Vergouw
69 Douglas Hoppe Stone
70 Bill Sweney

ART DIRECTOR / DIRECTEUR ARTISTIQUE:

62 Joseph Sellars/Karen Brown
64, 65 Aldo Lanfranco
66, 67 Lars Melander
68 Ton Vergouw
69 Douglas Hoppe Stone
70 Bill Sweney

AGENCY / AGENTUR / AGENCE – STUDIO:

62 Dayton's Adv.
64, 65 Aldo Lanfranco
66, 67 Hera Annonsbyrå
68 J. Walter Thompson Company B.V.
69 Rose & Stone
70 Cole, Henderson & Drake, Inc.

TILL ALLA GODSHANTERARE
SOM VILL ÅKA SNÅLSKJUTS

6 gånger till under 1974 har Dagens Nyheter en gul halvsida för annonsering av produkter och tjänster inom områdena Lager, Transport och Spedition.

Den dag du tröttnat på räckvidden i landets sju-åtta fackpresstidningar på området kan du göra prova DN.

Facktidningarna är ju visserligen både selektiva och bra, dvs dom når inte fel slags människor. Kruxet är bara att dom är så små att dom inte når så förfärligt många av rätt slags människor heller. Vilket också framgår av jämförelsen med en stor branschfacktidning i debatten på andra sidan.

Det fina med DN är ju att den inte bara handlar om godshantering. Därför når DN också en massa människor utanför din avgränsade målgrupp, alla dom andra i företaget som brukar ha ett ord med i laget när det gäller att välja produkter och tjänster inom det här området.

Godshanterarna som vill åka snålskjuts på sporten, politiken och TV-programmet gör nog klokt i att inte gå förbi DN nästa gång det blir tal om att annonsera.

66

Konsten att handplocka besökare
till "gör-det-själv"-mässan

Det bör en snickare, murare eller målare i nästan varje människa. Därför reserverar vi en helsida i DN den 29 mars under annonsrubriken "Bygga om till nytt". Ett fint tillfälle för den som säljer verktyg och annan utrustning som behövs för "gör-det-självarna".

Mer än 20 000 nyfikna, händiga människor — både fackfolk och amatörer — räknar man med ska komma till årets "gör-det-själv"-utställning i S:t Eriksmässans lokaler i Älvsjö den 29 mars—7 april. Men hur ska dom veta att just du finns med där. Och vad du tänker visa för nyheter.

Ett bra sätt att handplocka besökare till just din monter är att annonsera på den specialsida DN reserverar för utställare. Samma dag som mässan öppnar, den 29 mars.

Tänk på det bör en snickare, målare eller murare i nästan varje människa.

67

"Mehari's zijn klein. Mehari's zijn groot."
(ARABISCH RAADSEL)

Uit Afrika komen Mehari's. Gerold uit de pure tabakken van Cameroun.
In karavanen van Tamanrasset. Door gloeiend zand en koele oases. Mehari's. En Extra Mehari's.
Er is voor beide 'n moment.

68

Advertisements / Inserate / Annonces

62 Full-page newspaper advertisement in full colour for Levi's shirts in the "pale, dry colours of the desert", sold by Dayton's, men's clothiers. (USA)
63 Double-spread trade magazine advertisement in colour for Ram jeans, with a romantic fairy-tale illustration. (GBR)
64, 65 Detail and complete magazine advertisement in colour for a Turin jeweller: gold designed "with the eye and the hand of the artist". (ITA)
66, 67 Black-and-white space promotion ads placed in trade magazines by the newspaper Dagens Nyheter. (SWE)
68 Full-colour magazine ad for the two sizes of Mehari's cigars, made of tobacco from Cameroon. (NLD)
69 Double-spread trade ad with colour illustration for a new Fairchild computerized testing system. (USA)
70 Trade ad with colour illustration for the pilot insurance system of Aviation Insurance Agency. (USA)

62 Ganzseitiges Inserat für Levi's-Kleidung in «gezähmten» blassen, trockenen Farben der Wüste. (USA)
63 Doppelseitiges Fachzeitschrifteninserat in Farbe für Ram-Jeans, illustriert wie ein Märchen. (GBR)
64, 65 Ausschnitt und Gesamtwiedergabe einer farbigen Zeitschriftenanzeige für Schmuck. Dargestellt sind die gestalteten Werkzeuge des Künstlers, Auge und Hand. (ITA)
66, 67 Ganzseitige Schwarzweiss-Anzeigen aus einer Fachzeitschrift mit Informationen über die Inserierungsmöglichkeiten in einer Tageszeitung. (SWE)
68 Ganzseitige farbige Zeitschriftenanzeige für zwei Sorten von Mehari's-Zigarillos. (NLD)
69 Doppelseitiges farbiges Fachzeitschrifteninserat für Computer-Kontrollsysteme von Fairchild. (USA)
70 Ganzseitiges farbiges Inserat aus einer Pilotenzeitschrift für eine Arbeitsunfähigkeits-Versicherung. (USA)

62 Annonce pleine page pour les vêtements Levi's, dont les couleurs atténuées évoquent le désert. (USA)
63 Annonce professionnelle en couleurs pour les jeans Ram, avec une illustration évoquant un conte de fées. (GBR)
64, 65 Détail et annonce correspondante (en couleurs) pour les bijoux de Franco Rutigliano. On y représente les outils de l'artiste — la main et l'œil. (ITA)
66, 67 Annonces pleines pages publiées dans une revue professionnelle. Elément promotionnel d'un journal avec des informations concernant l'insertion d'annonces. (SWE)
68 Annonce de magazine pleine page (en couleurs) pour deux sortes de cigarillos Mehari. (NLD)
69 Annonce professionnelle sur page double pour les systèmes électroniques de contrôle Fairchild. (USA)
70 Annonce pleine page (en couleurs) tirée d'une revue pour pilotes pour une assurance d'invalidité. (USA)

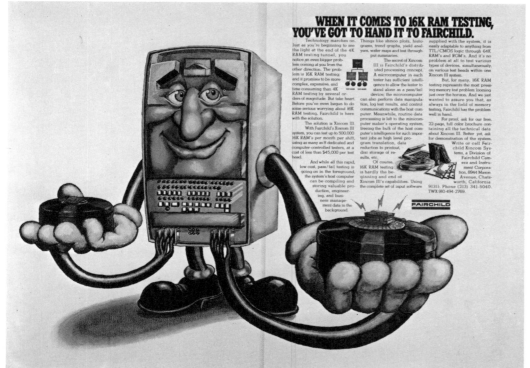

WHEN IT COMES TO 16K RAM TESTING,
YOU'VE GOT TO HAND IT TO FAIRCHILD.

69

When your body needs
a helping hand.

If there's a way to help you back in the air, our full-time Aerospace Medical Director will find it.

Aviation Insurance Agency

70

De computer en de oude Leidse.

SNA spaart tijd, geld en ergernis.
Oók in de kaasfabriek.

IBM

ARTIST / KÜNSTLER / ARTISTE:

71 Jan Abbing/Mariet Numan/Jos van Uytreght
72–74 Erich Sokol
75, 76 Kunio Hagio
77 Cathy Bennett
78 Luc LeBon

DESIGNER / GESTALTER / MAQUETTISTE:

72–74 Atelier Brunner
75, 76 Don Moravick
77 Denis Robert
78 Luc Le Bon

ART DIRECTOR / DIRECTEUR ARTISTIQUE:

71 Joop Smit
75, 76 Don Moravick
77 Harriet Santroch
78 Luc LeBon

AGENCY / AGENTUR / AGENCE – STUDIO:

71 Prad B.V.
72–74 Gould, Cargill & Cie. KG
75, 76 Don Moravick & Assoc.
77 T. Eaton Co.
78 Ned Tieche

Vollendet

AUSTRIAN AIRLINES
Was sonst

**Advertisements / Inserate
Annonces**

48

73   74

75

76

71 Full-page newspaper ad from a series for the Dutch IBM about "the unknown possibilities of the computer"—here in cheese dairies. Yellow cheese. (NLD)
72–74 Illustrations and complete advertisement from a series in which famous composers praise *Austrian Airlines* in their own individual styles. Here Beethoven and Schubert. Black and white. (AUT)
75, 76 Illustration and complete ad for cheap groceries from *Shop and Save* stores. (USA)
77 Christmas ad (full-page newspaper) for toys from the toy department of *Eaton's* stores. (CAN)
78 Colour newspaper ad appearing on St. Patrick's Day for *Dayton's* men's clothing store. (USA)

71 Ganzseitige Anzeige für IBM über die «unbekannten Möglichkeiten des Computers». (NLD)
72–74 Illustration und eine Gesamtwiedergabe von Schwarzweiss-Anzeigen der *Austrian Airlines*, mit Anspielung auf die Werke und Zeit von Schubert und Beethoven. (AUT)
75, 76 Illustration und Gesamtwiedergabe eines Inserates für günstige Lebensmittel. (USA)
77 Anzeige des Kaufhauses *Eaton's* für seine Spielwarenabteilung. (CAN)
78 Anzeige von *Dayton's* Kaufhaus anlässlich des irischen Nationalfeiertages «St. Patrick's Day», mit guten Ratschlägen, wie man irisch sein kann, wenn man es nicht ist. (USA)

71 Annonce pleine page pour IBM se référant aux "possibilités inconnues de l'ordinateur". (NLD)
72–74 Illustrations et annonce correspondante en noir et blanc de la compagnie aérienne autrichienne faisant allusion aux œuvres et à l'époque de Schubert et Beethoven. (AUT)
75, 76 Illustration et annonce en faveur de produits alimentaires bon marché. (USA)
77 Annonce du grand magasin *Eaton's* en faveur de son département de jouets. (CAN)
78 Annonce d'un grand magasin publiée à l'occasion du jour de St-Patrick, fête nationale irlandaise. «Comment être irlandais si vous ne l'êtes pas.» (USA)

77

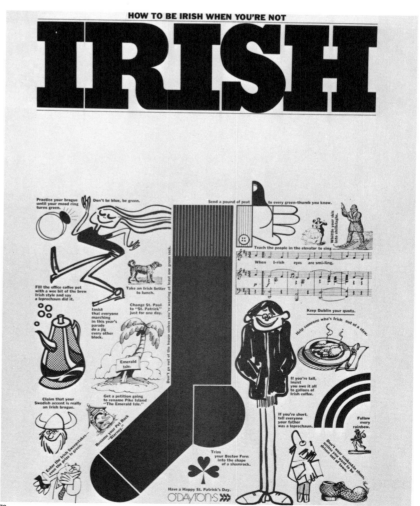

78

79 Full-page advertisement with black-and-white illustrations for the *Omni* catering services. (USA)
80 Institutional newspaper ad for the Container Corporation's facilities in Anderson, Indiana. (USA)
81 Newspaper ad for *Sting-Kill* swabs for the treatment of painful and itching bites and stings. (USA)
82 Newspaper ad for energy-giving dextrose tablets. (NLD)
83 "Our daily bread." Colour newspaper ad for Swedish Railways as an efficient means of transport—here for bread. (SWE)
84–88 Black-and-white illustrations and one complete newspaper advertisement from two series for Suntory Ltd., suppliers of wines and spirits. The ads feature stories and essays by well-known authors. (JPN)

79 Ganzseitiges Inserat eines Hotels für Service-Leistungen bei Banketts und ähnlichen Anlässen. (USA)
80 Schwarzweiss-Zeitungsanzeige für Verpackungen. (USA)
81 Schwarzweiss-Anzeige für ein Mittel, das bei Insektenstichen und ähnlichem Linderung verspricht. (USA)
82 Anzeige für energiespendendes *Dextro-Energen*. (NLD)
83 Zeitungsinserat der Schwedischen Eisenbahn in Brotfarben, mit dem Titel «unser täglich Brot». (SWE)
84, 87 Schwarzweiss-Illustrationen aus einer Zeitungswerbekampagne für alkoholische Getränke, verpackt in einer Serie von Geschichten, den «*Suntory*-Fabeln vom Trinken». (JPN)
85, 86, 88 Illustrationen und Gesamtwiedergabe einer Anzeige aus der Serie «*Suntory*-Dichtungen und Essays». Für Getränke. (JPN)

79 Annonce double page d'un hôtel qui offre ses services pour des banquets et des fêtes. (USA)
80 Annonce noir-blanc pour les emballages CCA. (USA)
81 Annonce noir-blanc en faveur d'un produit pour le traitement de piqûres d'insecte. (USA)
82 Pour *Dextro-Energen* pour économiser l'énergie. (NLD)
83 «Notre pain quotidien.» Annonce de presse en teintes brunes pour la société des chemins de fer suédois. (SWE)
84, 87 Illustrations en noir et blanc figurant dans une campagne publicitaire pour des boissons alcooliques, emballées dans une série de «contes *Suntory* de la boisson». (JPN)
85, 86, 88 Illustrations et annonce complète de la série «œuvres poétiques et essais *Suntory*». (JPN)

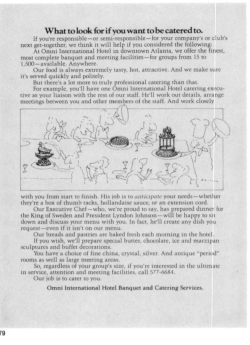

79

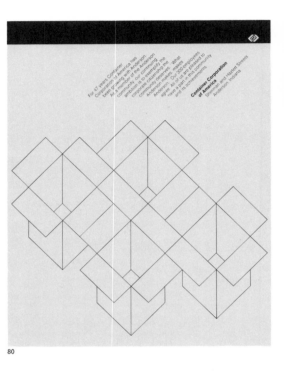

80

81

ARTIST / KÜNSTLER / ARTISTE:

79 Robert Blechman
81 Corey Christensen
82 Picha
83 Birgitta Laurell/Nicola Amandonico
84 Shiro Tatsumi
85, 86 Kazuo Watanabe
87 Mitsuru Gotsuji
88 Juzo Itami

Advertisements
Inserate
Annonces

82

83

DESIGNER / GESTALTER / MAQUETTISTE:

80 Jeff A. Barnes
82 Marien de Goffau
84, 87 Hiroyuki Okumura
85, 86, 88 Yoshio Namba

ART DIRECTOR / DIRECTEUR ARTISTIQUE:

79 Jerry Sullivan
80 Jeff A. Barnes
81 Denis Johnson
82 Marien De Goffau
83 Johan Sten
84–88 Shohei Shinada

AGENCY / AGENTUR / AGENCE – STUDIO:

79 Cole, Henderson & Drake
80 Container Corporation of America
81 Bernstein Rein & Boasberg
82 McCann-Erickson BV
83 Arbman
84–88 Sun-ad Co. Ltd.

86

84

85

87

88

51

2

Booklets

Folders

Catalogues

Invitations

Programmes

Broschüren

Faltprospekte

Kataloge

Einladungen

Programme

Brochures

Dépliants

Catalogues

Invitations

Programmes

omissi n

which is why some things are better
left unsaid. Sins of omission may
be grave indeed---as in buildings
that omit amenities for the people
who live and work in them---but
omission is often a virtue in design.
"Less is more," Mies said, and he
was right---more or less. Yet, when
you consider that both Samuel Goldwyn
and John Keats were concerned with

From
Notes on Omission
by Ralph Caplan.
For a copy send two
dollars to Omission
Herman Miller, Inc.
Zeeland, Michigan 49464

Herman Miller leaves some things to be desired

89

connection

Herman Miller, a highly connective company

, but there are worse things in life
than missing connections. For instance,
not having any connections to miss---
being unconnected or disconnected, cut
off, alienated, out of touch. Making
connections is the basis of poetry, in-
vention, crime detection and air travel.
It is no accident that the Boy Scout knot

From
Notes on Connection
by Ralph Caplan.
For a copy send two
dollars to Connection
Herman Miller, Inc.
Zeeland, Michigan 49464

90

atten tion

so that people are free to attend to what they care
about. Ironically, though, the freest societies invar-
iably create environments that militate against
attention. Visual pollution is harmful not just because it is ugly but because it is distractive. And
therefore destructive. Like other pollution, it de-
stroys the balance of nature---in this case, human
nature. A climate loaded with designs clamoring for
your attention is a climate in which you end up
paying attention to nothing. For example,

From
Notes on Attention
by Ralph Caplan.
For a copy send two
dollars to Attention
Herman Miller, Inc
Zeeland, Michigan 49464

Herman Miller tries to pay attention

91

89–91 From a series of seven notebook covers, also used (with modifications) as posters for Herman Miller, Inc., suppliers of office furniture, office services and systems. The irregular shapes are in strong colours. (USA)
92, 93 Cover and page illustrations (in orange, brown, grey and black) from a brochure on sources of electric power issued by Southern California Edison Co. (USA)
94 Inside spread (full colour) of a large folder on the new *Martex* line of towels. The "towels" actually hang free on a real line, with name and size printed on the back. (USA)
95 One side of a folder about IBM systems networks. (USA)
96, 97 "The right nose... for the right computer." Folder promoting the CS/40 computer system for a Zurich company. The snout of an orange fox springs forwards when folder is opened. (SWI)

89–91 Umschlagseiten von «Notizbüchern», die Gedanken zu den Begriffen «Weglassen», «Verbindung» und «Aufmerksamkeit» enthalten und Teil eines Kommunikations- und Werbeprogramms der Herman Miller Inc. sind. (USA)
92, 93 Umschlag- und Seitenillustration einer Broschüre in Braun/Orange/Schwarz, mit Akzentsetzung in Weiss, zu dem Thema «Quellen elektrischer Energie». (USA)
94 Farbige Doppelseite aus einem Werbeprospekt für Handtücher. Die Wäscheleine ist montiert, die Rückseite der «Wäsche» enthält Referenzangaben. (USA)
95 Aussenseite eines IBM-Faltprospektes mit dem Titel «Architektur der Systemnetze». (USA)
96, 97 Innenseite eines Faltprospektes für CS/40-Computersysteme von *Data General*. «Die richtige Nase... für den richtigen Computer». (SWI)

89–91 Couvertures d'une série de carnets de notes, dont chacun est consacré à l'explication d'un mot particulier, comme p. ex. «omission», «relation» et «attention». Ils font partie d'un programme de communication et de publicité de la Herman Miller, Inc., meubles et services de bureau. (USA)
92, 93 Couverture et page illustrée (orange, brun, gris et noir) d'une brochure traitant des sources d'énergie électrique. (USA)
94 Page double (en couleurs) d'un dépliant grand format présentant la nouvelle gamme des linges *Martex*. Les «linges» sont étendus sur une vraie corde avec des spécifications imprimées au verso. (USA)
95 Dépliant pour les systèmes électroniques IBM. (USA)
96, 97 «Avoir du flair...» Dépliant pour la promotion des systèmes électroniques CS/40 de *Data General*. Lorsqu'on ouvre le dépliant, le museau du renard s'avance. (SWI)

94

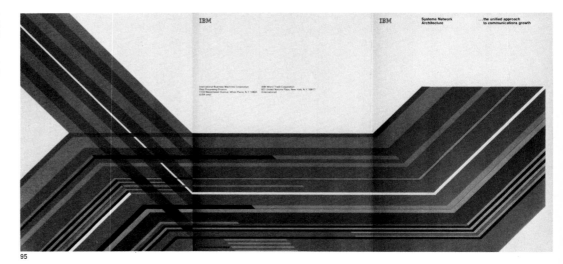

95

Booklets / Prospekte / Brochures

92

93

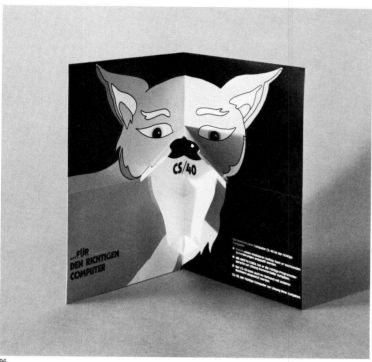

96

97

ARTIST / KÜNSTLER / ARTISTE:

89–91 John Massey
92, 93 Don Weller
94 Jerry Cosgrove
95 Ine Wijtvliet
96, 97 Claude Luyet

DESIGNER / GESTALTER / MAQUETTISTE:

89–91 John Massey
92, 93 Don Weller
94 B. Martin Pedersen
95 Ine Wijtvliet
96, 97 Claude Luyet

ART DIRECTOR / DIRECTEUR ARTISTIQUE:

89–91 John Massey
92, 93 Don Weller
94 B. Martin Pedersen
95 Ine Wijtvliet
96, 97 Carlo Bonaccorsi

AGENCY / AGENTUR / AGENCE – STUDIO:

89–91 John Massey, Inc.
92, 93 The Weller Institute for the Cure of Design
94 Jonson, Pedersen, Hinrichs
95 IBM Corp.
96, 97 Edelta SA

T.W. BECKETT. HOW DO THEY WEIGH-UP?

98

Acute
Streptococcal
Pharyngitis

You can rely on oral medication to
prevent serious sequelae, but can you
rely on the patient to take it?

99

If local markets are few—the total globe might do.

CHEMIMPO
INTERNATIONAL BV

100

If local markets are few—the total globe might do.

CHEMIMPO
INTERNATIONAL BV

101

56

102

ARTIST / KÜNSTLER / ARTISTE:

98 Danie Vermeulen
99 Mueller & Wister Studio
100, 101 Josse Goffin
102 Heather Cooper/Roger Hill
103 Krishna Das/Navroz Contractor/Sunil Sen

DESIGNER / GESTALTER / MAQUETTISTE:

98 Ian Coetser
99 Mueller & Wister Studio
102 Jim Donoahue
103 V. V. Dukle

98 One of a series of mailers for *Philips* electronic weighing equipment, here used in coffee making. (SAF)
99 Cover (full colour) of a folder about a *Wyeth* single-injection treatment for streptococcal pharyngitis. (USA)
100, 101 Covers (in full colour) for two folders issued by *Chemimpo.* marketers of chemical products. (NLD)
102 One side of a large concertina-type folder dealing with a CTS satellite. (CAN)
103 Page from a booklet about Suhrid Geigy Ltd., Bombay, makers of pharmaceuticals and dyestuffs, with a diagram showing the organization of the company. (IND)

98 Deckblatt eines Prospektes mit brauner Kaffeekanne aus einer Serie für elektronische Wägesysteme von *Philips.* (SAF)
99 Farbige Titelseite eines medizinischen Prospektes der Firma *Wyeth* für die Behandlung von Rachenkatarrh durch eine einmalige Injektion anstelle von oraler Medikamenteinnahme. (USA)
100, 101 Farbige Umschlagseiten von Werbeprospekten einer Firma, die sich als Brücke zwischen Herstellern von chemischen Produkten und dem Markt sieht. (NLD)
102 Seite eines Leporello-Prospektes für CTS-Satelliten. (CAN)
103 Organigramm der Suhrid Geigy Ltd., Bombay, Hersteller von Pharmazeutika und Farbstoffen, aus Firmenprospekt. (IND)

98 D'une série de dépliants pour des systèmes électroniques de pesage, utilisés ici pour la production du café. (SAF)
99 Couverture (en couleurs) d'un dépliant de la compagnie *Wyeth* en faveur d'un nouveau traitement de la pharyngite par moyen d'une seule piqûre. (USA)
100, 101 Couvertures en couleurs de deux dépliants publiés par une organisation de vente de produits chimiques. (NLD)
102 D'un dépliant en accordéon pour les satellites CTS. (CAN)
103 Page d'une brochure publiée par une compagnie de produits pharmaceutiques et de colorants présentant un diagramme sur l'organisation de cette compagnie. (IND)

ART DIRECTOR / DIRECTEUR ARTISTIQUE:

98 Ian Coetser
100, 101 Bart Van Mierop/Fred Bosboom
102 Robert Burns/Don Hewson
103 Sunil Sen

AGENCY / AGENTUR / AGENCE – STUDIO:

98 Ian Coetser Assoc.
99 Mueller & Wister Studio
100, 101 Data-Doorn
102 Don Hewson & Associates
103 Shilpi Advertising Ltd.

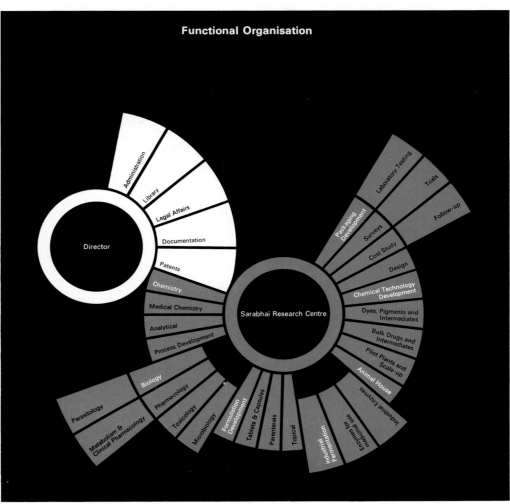

Functional Organisation

103

ARTIST / KÜNSTLER / ARTISTE:

109 Barrie Tucker
110 Ernie James
111–113 Eugène Mihaesco

DESIGNER / GESTALTER / MAQUETTISTE:

104 Gene Grossman/Vern Ford
105 Rolf Harder
106–108 Arie J. Geurts
109, 110 Barrie Tucker/Ernie James
111–113 John DeCesare

ART DIRECTOR / DIRECTEUR ARTISTIQUE:

104 Gene Grossman
105 Rolf Harder
106–108 Arie J. Geurts
109, 110 Barrie Tucker/Ernie James
111–113 John DeCesare

AGENCY / AGENTUR / AGENCE – STUDIO:

104 Anspach, Grossman, Portugal, Inc.
105 Rolf Harder & Assoc.
106–108 Carton y Papel de Mexico SA,
    Laboratorio de Diseño y Mercadotecnica
109, 110 Tucker & James
111–113 Geigy Pharmaceuticals

104

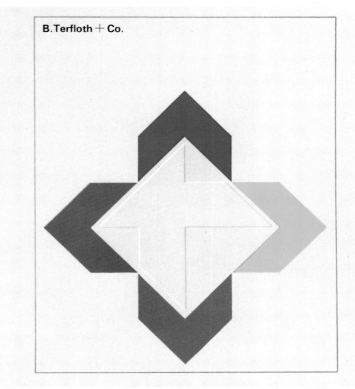

B. Terfloth + Co.

105

106

107

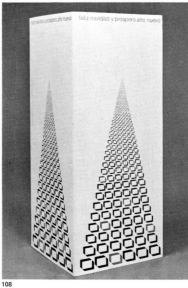

108

Booklets
Prospekte
Brochures

111

104 Cover design of a quarterly report issued in the form of a folder by Aero-Flow Dynamics, Inc. Grey and dark blue. (USA)
105 Cover of a folder intended to hold various mailings, for B. Terfloth & Co., Montreal. Blind embossed "t". (CAN)
106–108 Three-dimensional folding Christmas and New Year's cards for the Mexico City branch of Container Corporation of America. All in red, white and green. (MEX)
109, 110 Illustrations (full colour) from a *Sandoz* book on hypertension. Fig. 109 refers to Richard Bright and his work on renal mechanisms, Fig. 110 to blood pressure variability. (AUS)
111–113 Double spread, cover and full-page illustration from a *Geigy* booklet on depression and its treatment. Black and white. (USA)

109

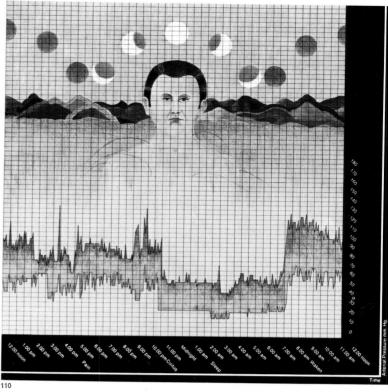

110

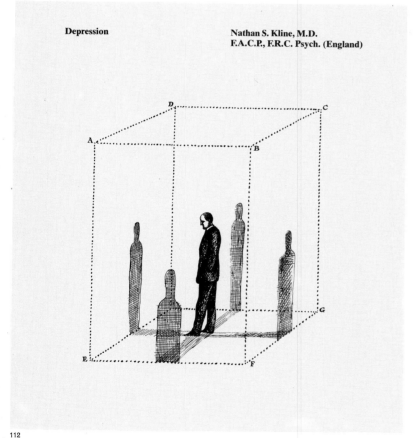

Depression

Nathan S. Kline, M.D.
F.A.C.P., F.R.C. Psych. (England)

112

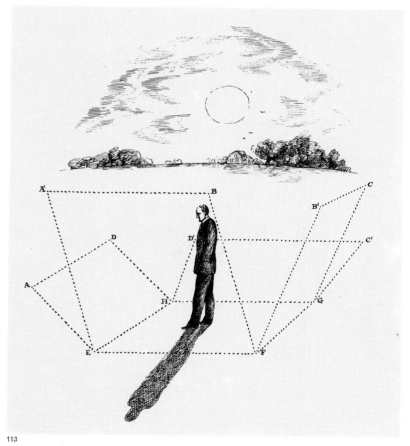

113

114

116

115

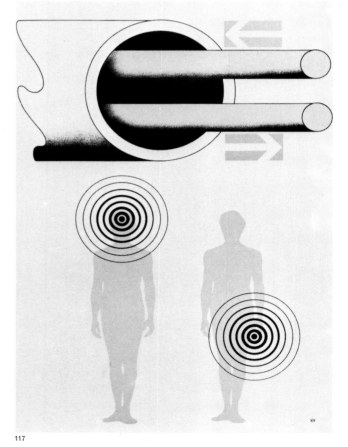

117

ARTIST / KÜNSTLER / ARTISTE:

114, 115 Alexander Kamenz
116–118 David Hornblow/Csaba Banki
119–121 Fernando Puig Rosado

DESIGNER / GESTALTER / MAQUETTISTE:

114, 115 Alexander Kamenz
116–118 David Hornblow
119–121 Bernard Duparc

ART DIRECTOR / DIRECTEUR ARTISTIQUE:

114, 115 Alexander Kamenz
119–121 Aldo Bernardo

AGENCY / AGENTUR / AGENCE – STUDIO:

114, 115 Dr. Schweers Werbung
116–118 Hornblow Grainger Design Partnership Ltd.
119–121 Expand Conseil

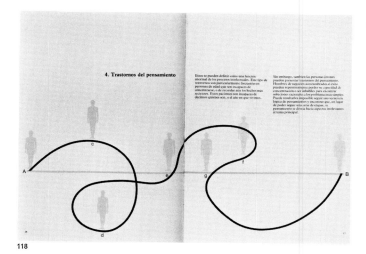

118

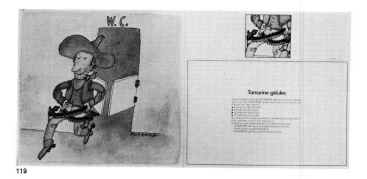

119

120

114, 115 Covers (full colour) of two folders from a series under the general title of "Even the great have weaknesses". Each folder deals with the shortcomings of a great man (here Einstein and Picasso) while advertising the tranquillizer *Adumbran*. (GER)
116–118 Two full-page illustrations (black and one colour) and double-page spread (black and two colours) from a book issued by the pharmaceutical firm Organon International BV to introduce sales representatives to psychotherapy and psychotropic drugs. (NLD)
119–121 Spread and illustrations in a humorous vein from a booklet about *Tamarine* capsules against constipation. (FRA)

114, 115 Farbige Umschlagseiten von Faltprospekten der Firma *Thomae* als Werbung für das Beruhigungsmittel *Adumbran*. Abb. 114 bezieht sich auf Einstein, Abb. 115 auf Picasso. Die Broschüren enthalten u. a. Anekdoten über die Schwächen dieser Persönlichkeiten. (GER)
116–118 Farbige Illustrationen aus einem Buch, welches zur Schulung des Verkaufspersonals eines Herstellers von Pharmazeutika dienen soll. Es geht um die Psychotherapie und die damit verbundenen Medikamente. (NLD)
119–121 Doppelseite und Illustrationen aus einer medizinischen Broschüre für *Tamarine*, ein Mittel gegen Verdauungsstörungen. Diese Kapseln sind in jede der Illustrationen auf humoristische Weise integriert. (FRA)

114, 115 Couvertures (en couleurs) de deux dépliants figurant dans une série intitulée «Même les grands hommes ont leurs faiblesses». Chaque dépliant est consacré aux imperfections d'un grand homme (ici Einstein et Picasso) tout en promouvant le tranquillisant *Adumbran*. (GER)
116–118 Deux illustrations pleines pages (noir et une couleur) et page double (noir et deux couleurs) figurant dans un livre publié par une compagnie de produits pharmaceutiques. Il est destiné à la formation des représentants dans le domaine de la psychothérapie et des médicaments psychotropiques. (NLD)
119–121 Page double et illustration d'une brochure présentant de façon humoristique les effets des capsules *Tamarine* contre la constipation. (FRA)

121

122

125

122–124 Cover illustration (actual size), complete cover and double spread (black on tinted paper) from a booklet in a *Geigy* series on creative psychiatry; Arthur Koestler here writes on creativity. (USA)
125, 126 Double spread and illustration in actual size published in an *Abbott* folder about a treatment for epilepsy. The illustration shows a child in normal health and the same child during an epileptic attack. (USA)

122–124 Illustration (Originalgrösse) und Gesamtwiedergabe des Umschlags sowie Doppelseite (schwarz auf farbigem Papier) aus einer Broschüre, die zu einer *Geigy*-Reihe über kreative Psychiatrie gehört. Hier ist das Thema Kreativität. (USA)
125, 126 Doppelseite und Illustration in Originalgrösse aus einem Prospekt für ein Mittel gegen epileptische Anfälle. Die Illustration zeigt ein Kind in gesundem Zustand und während eines epileptischen Anfalls. (USA)

122–124 Illustration (grandeur nature), couverture complète et pages doubles (noir sur papier teint) d'une brochure faisant partie de la série *Geigy* sur la «psychiatrie créative». Ici c'est Arthur Koestler qui écrit sur la créativité. (USA)
125, 126 Page double et illustration en grandeur nature d'un dépliant sur le traitement de l'épilepsie. L'illustration présente un enfant dans un état de santé normal et pendant une crise épileptique. (USA)

ARTIST / KÜNSTLER / ARTISTE:
122–124 Alice Brickner
125, 126 Mark English

DESIGNER / GESTALTER / MAQUETTISTE:
122–124 Ron Vareltzis

ART DIRECTOR / DIRECTEUR ARTISTIQUE:
122–124 Ron Vareltzis
125, 126 Charles A. Walz

AGENCY / AGENTUR / AGENCE – STUDIO:
125, 126 Abbott Laboratories

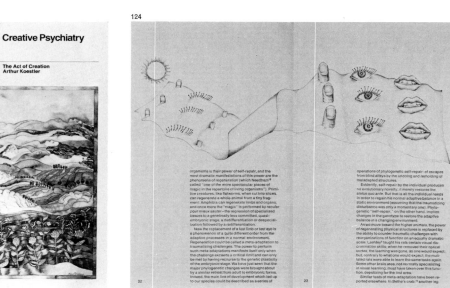

123

Creative Psychiatry

12 The Act of Creation
Arthur Koestler

124

Booklets / Prospekte / Brochures

128

127, 128 Complete cover and illustration in nearly actual size from a folder about a *Squibb* treatment for vaginal infection. (AUS)
129 Catalogue cover for Silverwood & Beck, manufacturers. (AUS)
130 Cover in beige and white of a brochure issued by Refined Syrups & Sugars, Inc., who are modifying their production range. (USA)
131 Inside of a folder about a medicine for poor appetite and tiredness in children, manufactured by Elmu S.A. Colour illustrations. (SPA)
132 Page of a folder (blue, white and mauve) about a *Roche* pharmaceutical for use against bronchitis. (CAN)
133 From a concertina-type folder announcing a move of the designers Skidmore Sahratian Inc. Black-and-white illustrations as examples of the work of individual artists. (USA)

127–128 Gesamtwiedergabe und Illustration des Umschlags eines medizinischen Prospektes über die Behandlung von Infektionen der Vagina. (AUS)
129 Katalog-Umschlagseite mit dem Markenzeichen der Firma. (AUS)
130 Umschlag (weisse Linien auf beigem Karton) der Broschüre einer Zucker-Raffinerie, die ihr Produktionsprogramm umstellt. (USA)
131 Farbige Innenseite eines Faltprospektes für ein Medikament gegen Appetit-losigkeit und Müdigkeitserscheinungen bei Kindern. (SPA)
132 Seite aus einem Prospekt (blau, weiss und violett) für ein *Roche*-Medikament gegen Bronchitis. (CAN)
133 Aus einem Leporello-Prospekt der Designer Skidmore Sahratian Inc., mit welchem die neue Adresse der Firma bekanntgegeben wird. Hier Schwarzweiss-Illustrationen von verschiedenen Künstlern des Studios. (USA)

127, 128 Couverture complète et illustration (approx. grandeur nature) d'un dépliant sur le traitement d'infections vaginales. (AUS)
129 Couverture d'un catalogue avec le symbole de l'entreprise. (AUS)
130 Couverture (beige et blanc) de la brochure d'une raffinerie de sucre qui modifie son programme de production. (USA)
131 Page intérieure d'un dépliant consacré à un médicament contre le manque d'appétit et la fatigue chez les enfants. Illustrations en couleurs. (SPA)
132 Page d'un dépliant (bleu, blanc et mauve) consacré à un produit pharma-ceutique *Roche* contre la bronchite. (CAN)
133 D'un dépliant en accordéon annonçant le changement d'adresse des de-signers Skidmore Sahratian Inc. Les illustrations noir-blanc présentent les travaux de plusieurs artistes du studio. (USA)

Booklets
Prospekte
Brochures

129

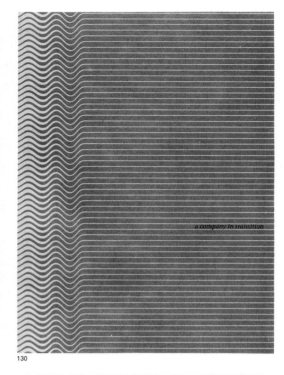

a company in transition

130

131

ASTENOLIT

Una fórmula completa para el tratamiento racional de ...

•Anorexia
ASTENOLIT produce su rápida regresión por la acción orexígena directa de la carnitina y complementaria de la vitamina B₁₂.

•Fatiga y estados de agotamiento
La presencia en ASTENOLIT del ácido acetilaspártico y de aspartato de Mg-K, permite una economía energética con mantenimiento de la reserva de ATP.

•Astenia
El aporte de aminoácidos (acetilglutamina, citrulina, fosforilserina) y vitaminas B₁, B₆ y B₁₂, que realiza ASTENOLIT permite restablecer el equilibrio metabólico y corregir las deficiencias vitamínicas objetivadas a través de la astenia.

... con todas las ventajas

-Fácil administración en ampollas bebibles de sabor agradable
-Sin efectos secundarios (no produce excitación ni insomnio)

ASTENOLIT

-Restaura el apetito
-Corrige los déficits vitamínicos
-Posee acción antianémica
-Aporta energía al paciente fatigado
-Revitaliza y tonifica al paciente asténico

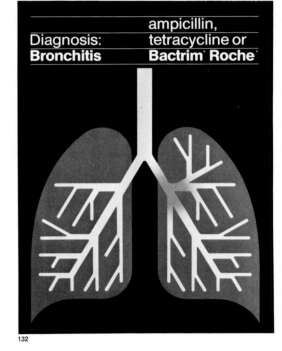

Diagnosis: **Bronchitis**

ampicillin, tetracycline or **Bactrim Roche**

132

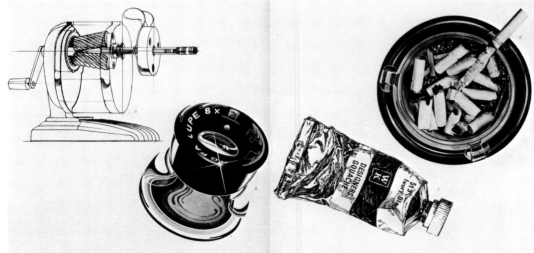

133

Booklets / Prospekte / Brochures

ARTIST / KÜNSTLER / ARTISTE:
138 David Palladini
139, 140 Sue Coe

DESIGNER / GESTALTER / MAQUETTISTE:
136, 137 Garry Emery
138 Joseph J. Fazio
139, 140 John DeCesare

ART DIRECTOR / DIRECTEUR ARTISTIQUE:
136, 137 Garry Emery
138 Joseph J. Fazio
139, 140 John DeCesare

AGENCY / AGENTUR / AGENCE – STUDIO:
134, 135 Ford, Byrne & Associates
136, 137 Interact Communications
138–140 Geigy Pharmaceuticals

134

135

136

137

138

134, 135 Folder (wheel in black, white and grey on purple ground) and leaflet (dark green design on lighter green) about an RCA headwheel reworking service. (USA)
136, 137 Cover (red and yellow lettering, blind embossed syringe) and central spread (red, blue and ochre in black syringe) of a small brochure on a *Glaxo* anaesthetic. The diagram in Fig. 137 compares the after-effects of five anaesthetics. (AUS)
138–140 Covers of two folders in the *PharmaScan* series, with one illustration in actual size. The folders contain medical reports and are mailed by *Geigy* to pharmacists. (USA)

134, 135 Faltprospekt (Rad in Schwarz, Weiss und Grau auf violettem Grund) und Deckblatt (in Grüntönen) eines Prospektes über einen RCA-Aufarbeitungs-Service für Magneträder. (USA)
136, 137 Umschlag (Schrift in Rot und Gelb, Spritze in Blindprägung) und Doppelseite (Blau, Rot und Ocker in schwarzer Spritze) einer Broschüre über ein *Glaxo*-Betäubungsmittel. Das Diagramm in Abb. 137 vergleicht Nachwirkungen verschiedener Mittel. (AUS)
138–140 Titelseiten von zwei Prospekten der *PharmaScan*-Reihe von *Geigy*, mit einer Illustration in Originalgrösse. Die an Apotheker gerichteten Prospekte enthalten medizinische Berichte. (USA)

139

140

134, 135 Dépliant (roue en noir, blanc et gris sur fond violet) et prospectus (design en vert foncé sur fond vert clair) en faveur du service de reconditionnement RCA de roues magnétiques. (USA)
136, 137 Couverture (typo rouge et jaune, seringue en gaufrage à sec) et page double (rouge, bleu et ocre dans seringue noire) d'une petite brochure sur un anesthésique *Glaxo*. Le diagramme sous fig. 137 compare les effets ultérieurs de cinq anesthésiques. (AUS)
138–140 Couvertures de deux dépliants de la série *PharmaScan* avec une illustration en grandeur nature. Les dépliants, destinés aux pharmaciens, contiennent des rapports médicaux. (USA)

ARTIST / KÜNSTLER / ARTISTE:

141 Richard Hess
142, 143 Eugène Mihaesco
144 Geoffrey Moss
145 Milton Glaser

DESIGNER / GESTALTER / MAQUETTISTE:

141–144 John DeCesare
145 Joseph J. Fazio

ART DIRECTOR / DIRECTEUR ARTISTIQUE:

141–144 John DeCesare
145 Joseph J. Fazio

AGENCY / AGENTUR / AGENCE – STUDIO:

142–145 Geigy Pharmaceuticals

142

141 Composition (actual size) from a *Ciba-Geigy* portfolio on depression. See next spread. (USA)
142, 143 Complete leaflet about a *Geigy* antidepressive drug, and detail of the black-and-white drawing. (USA)
144 Illustration from a folder mailed to doctors on a *Geigy* antidepressant. (USA)
145 Newspaper-like *Geigy* publication on arthritis, here with quotations from Shakespeare. (USA)

141 Abbildung (Originalgrösse) aus einer *Ciba-Geigy*-Mappe zu dem Thema Depression. (USA)
142, 143 Komplette Seite und Ausschnitt mit Schwarzweiss-Zeichnung, aus einem von *Geigy* herausgegeben Prospekt für ein Medikament gegen neurotische Depressionen. (USA)
144 Illustration aus einer Mappe für Ärzte über ein *Geigy*-Medikament gegen Depressionen. (USA)
145 Titelseite einer zeitungsähnlichen Publikation von *Geigy* über arthritische Erkrankungen. Der Text enthält Zitate zum Rheumatismus aus Shakespeares Werken. (USA)

141 Composition (grandeur originale) figurant dans un portfolio de *Ciba-Geigy* sur la dépression mentale. Voir aussi la page double suivante. (USA)
142, 143 Prospectus consacré à un antidépresseur *Geigy* et détail de l'illustration noir-blanc. (USA)
144 Illustration d'un portfolio pour un antidépresseur *Geigy*, destiné au corps médical. (USA)
145 Couverture d'une publication *Geigy* évoquant un quotidien. Elle est consacrée à l'arthrite et contient des citations de Shakespeare au sujet du rhumatisme. (USA)

143

144

CLINICAL FORUM ON ARTHRITIS

Geigy

The raw rheumatic days of Shakespeare linger on

In Elizabethan England, one of the most terrible curses one could possibly utter was to wish upon an enemy the eternal tortures of rheumatism. A cruel curse of this type was penned by William Shakespeare for his eloquent Prospero. The wrongfully deposed Duke of *The Tempest* had magical powers putting him in a good position to make his curse come true:

I'll rack thee with old cramps, Fill all thy bones with aches and make thee roar.

Prospero in The Tempest, I, ii

This was a particularly terrible curse, since, although Prospero may not have known it, he was wishing degenerative joint disease (osteoarthrosis) upon his enemy. Later in *The Tempest*, Prospero unleashes yet another curse, worse than the first:

Go charge my goblins that they grind their joints With dry convulsions, shorten up their sinews With aged cramps,...

Prospero in The Tempest, IV, i

Shakespearian rheumatology is not far different from the modern lay notions of rheumatology. The Elizabethans, for instance, believed that wet weather and dampness were causes of rheumatism. Rheumatism-provoking weather is poetically described by Titania:

The winds...have suck'd up from the sea Contagious fogs;... Therefore the moon (the governess of floods) Pale in her

enemy, washes all the air, That rheumatic diseases do abound.

Titania in A Midsummer Night's Dream, I, ii

Shakespeare's characters frequently associate old age with rheumatoid deformities, stiffness, aches, and pains. The geriatric and the rheumatic must have been virtually synonymous in Elizabethan times:

And thy unkindness be like crooked age.

Gaunt in Richard II, II, i

If quiet life be best;...well corresponding with your stiff age.

Guiderius in Cymbeline, III, iii

(continued on page 5)

145

146–150 Double spread and compositions from a large *Ciba-Geigy* presentation portfolio containing works by well-known artists on various aspects of depression. Here Wilson McLean on disturbed sleep, Mark English on loss of libido, Jean-Michel Folon on loss of self-esteem and Eugene Mihaesco on fear of insanity. Figs. 146–149 are in colour. (USA)

146–150 Gesamtwiedergabe der Innenseiten und Illustrationen aus einer umfangreichen *Ciba-Geigy*-Präsentationsmappe, welche Arbeiten bekannter Künstler zu den verschiedenen Erscheinungsformen der Depression enthält. Hier Wilson McLean zu «Schlafstörungen», Mark English zu «Libidoverlust», Jean-Michel Folon zu «Selbstverachtung» und Eugene Mihaesco zu «Furcht vor Wahnsinn». Die Illustrationen der Abb. 146–149 sind farbig. (USA)

146–150 Page double et compositions d'un portfolio grand format de *Ciba-Geigy* présentant des œuvres d'art d'artistes de renom illustrant divers aspects de dépressions mentales. Nos illustrations: Wilson McLean au sujet de l'insomnie, Mark English au sujet du manque de la libido, Jean-Michel Folon au sujet du mépris de soi-même et Eugène Mihaesco au sujet de la peur de l'aliénation mentale. Les fig. 146–149 sont en couleurs. (USA)

ARTIST / KÜNSTLER / ARTISTE:

146, 147 Wilson Mc Lean
148 Mark English
149 Jean-Michel Folon
150 Eugène Mihaesco

DESIGNER / GESTALTER / MAQUETTISTE:

146–150 John DeCesare

ART DIRECTOR / DIRECTEUR ARTISTIQUE:

146–150 John DeCesare

146

148

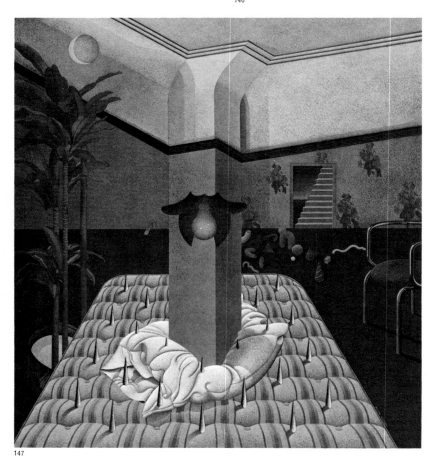

147

149

Booklets / Prospekte / Brochures

151

151 Invitation to an exhibition of furniture by the designer Shigeru Uchida. Pale blue on beige ground. (JPN)
152 Artwork used in a folder about the *Roche* product *Dalmane*. (USA)
153, 154 Double spread from a booklet sent to the medical profession about *Beconase* nasal spray against allergic rhinitis, showing the results of a double blind cross-over trial, and detail (Fig. 154) of the cover illustration of the booklet. (AUS)
155 Illustration from a booklet about the printing of securities issued by the Egmont H. Petersen printing house in Copenhagen. (DEN)
156 Cover of a small brochure about a programme intended to create an interface between the Massachusetts Institute of Technology's research activities and industrial companies that can benefit by them. Design in blue and white. (USA)

151 Einladung zu einer Ausstellung von Möbeln des Designers Shigeru Uchida. (JPN)
152 Illustration aus einem Prospekt über das *Roche*-Medikament *Dalmane*. (USA)
153, 154 Doppelseite aus einer an Ärzte gerichteten Broschüre über *Beconase*-Nasenspray gegen Heuschnupfen, mit Darstellung der Ergebnisse eines blinden Vergleichstests, und Illustration des Umschlags dieser Broschüre. (AUS)
155 Illustration aus einem Prospekt über das Drucken von Wertpapieren, herausgegeben von der Druckerei Egmont H. Petersen in Kopenhagen. (DEN)
156 Blaue Linien auf weissem Grund, übergehend in weisse Linien auf blauem Grund. Umschlagseite einer Broschüre des Massachusetts Institute of Technology über das Industrie-Verbindungsprogramm, welches den Mitgliedsfirmen des Instituts den Zugang zu den personellen und wissenschaftlichen Forschungsmöglichkeiten erleichtern soll. (USA)

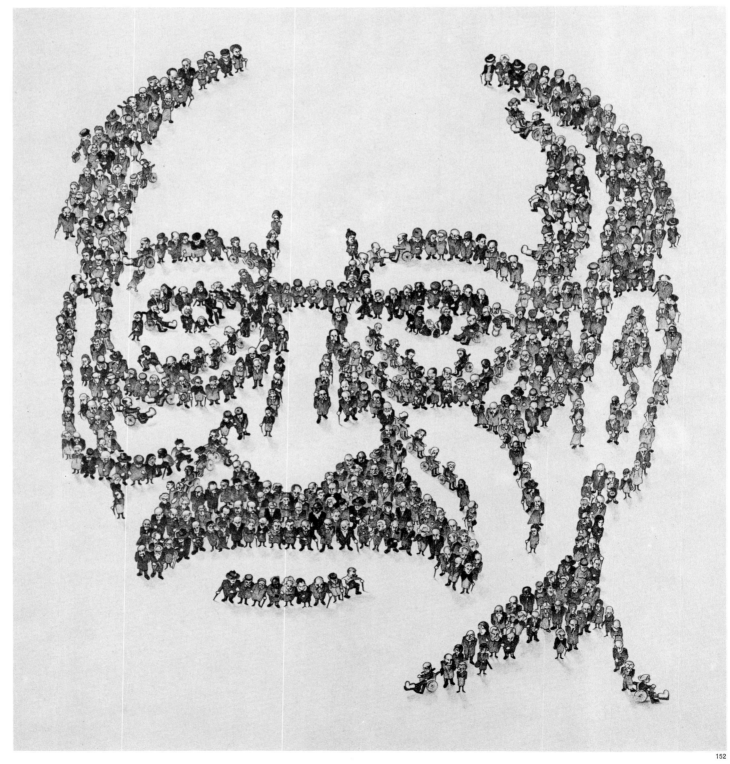

152

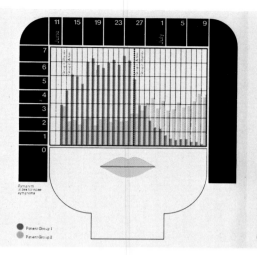
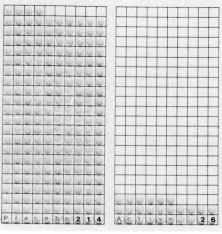

A double blind crossover trial in 29 patients with hayfever comparing the effect on nasal symptoms of a daily dose of 400 mcg Beclomethasone dipropionate aerosol intranasally with placebo.

Right: Average daily symptom scores from 29 patient diary cards
Nasal blocking, nasal secretion and sneezing all evaluated 0-3 semi-quantitatively.
This figure shows the effectiveness of Beconase Nasal Spray as compared to a placebo aerosol in the control of nasal symptoms in patients with seasonal allergic rhinitis. (Mygind N. Brit. Med. J., 1973, 4, 464).
Urinary excretion of 17-ketogenic steroids was measured in 12 patients during the active and placebo periods, and no significant effect on adrenal function was demonstrated at recommended doses. This lack of significant effect on adrenal function, or on eye symptoms, together are felt to indicate minimal systemic activity.

Far right: Total intake of antihistamine tablets during the last week of the trial in 29 patients
Altogether, the placebo groups took 214 antihistamine tablets during the last week of treatment, whereas the active aerosol groups took only 26. In 25 of the 29 patients, the effect of Beconase was so pronounced that their total intake of antihistamine tablets in the same week was two, as against 203 for the placebo group. (After Mygind N. Brit. Med. J., 1973, 4, 464).

153

154

ARTIST / KÜNSTLER / ARTISTE:
151 Takenobu Igarashi
152 John Trull
153 Garry Emery
154 Wes Walters

DESIGNER / GESTALTER / MAQUETTISTE:
151 Takenobu Igarashi
153, 154 Garry Emery
155 Erik Pelt
156 Betsy Hacker

ART DIRECTOR / DIRECTEUR ARTISTIQUE:
151 Takenobu Igarashi
152 Stan Dornfest
153, 154 Garry Emery
155 Erik Pelt/Hans Nielsen

AGENCY / AGENTUR / AGENCE – STUDIO:
151 Takenobu Igarashi Design
152 Wesson & Warhaftig
153, 154 Interact Communications
156 MIT Design Services

151 Invitation à une exposition de meubles du designer Shigeru Uchida. (JPN)
152 Illustration d'un dépliant consacré au médicament *Dalmane* de *Roche*. (USA)
153, 154 Page double d'un prospectus, destiné au corps médical, pour *Beconase*, un spray nasal contre la rhinite allergique, avec les résultats d'un test de comparaison. Fig. 154: détail de l'illustration de couverture. (AUS)
155 Illustration d'une brochure sur l'impression de valeurs, publiée par l'imprimerie Egmont H. Petersen à Copenhague. (DEN)
156 Couverture d'une petite brochure consacrée à un programme de communication entre le Massachusetts Institute of Technology et des entreprises industrielles pouvant profiter ainsi des activités de recherches scientifiques de celui-ci. (USA)

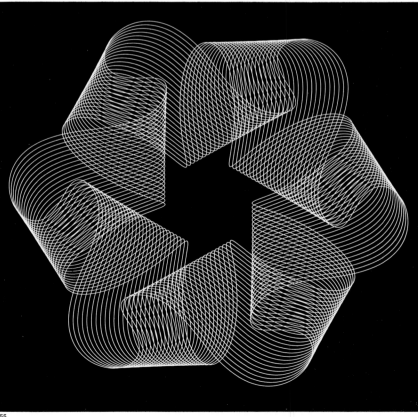

155

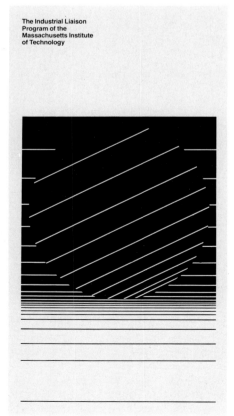

The Industrial Liaison Program of the Massachusetts Institute of Technology

156

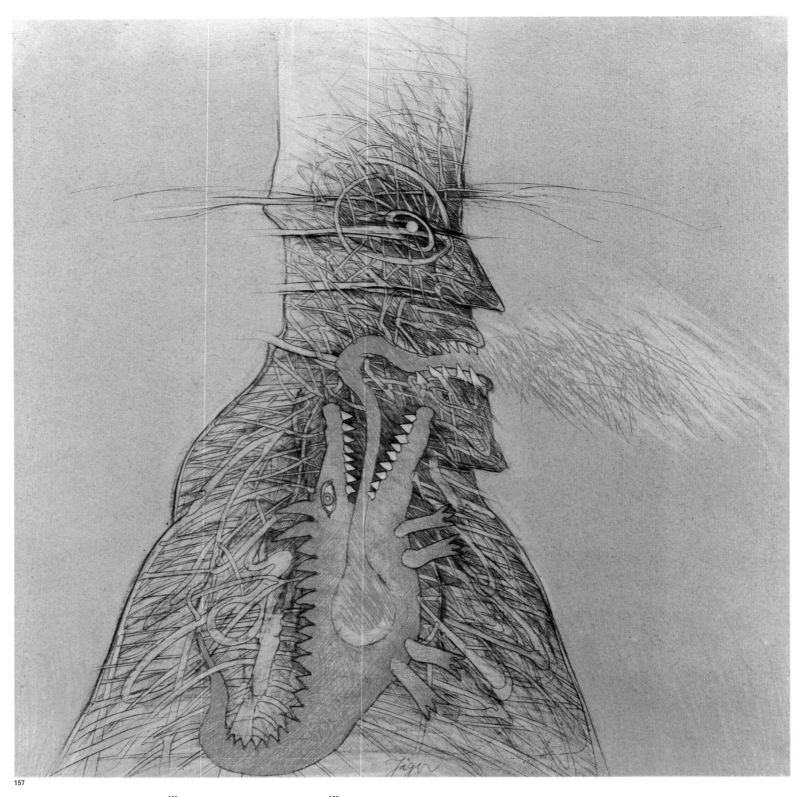

157

158

Bronchitis in Wissenschaft und Kunst Prof. Dr. W. T. Ulmer B. Jäger

1

Soziale Bedeutung Ursachen für die Entstehung Erscheinungsformen Wahl des Antibiotikums

Informationen über eine große Volkskrankheit.

Hostacyclin 500 Hoechst

159

25 Jahre Diogenes

Andersch • Sempé • Molière • Lawrence
Simenon • Maupassant • Faulkner • Busch
Melville • Flora • O'Casey • Gorey • Wells
Čechov • Wilde • McCullers • Brambach
O'Faolain • Shakespeare • Hammett
Kinder • Steger • Widmer
Wollschläger • Zimnik
Schopenhauer • Balzac
Traven • Marcuse • Ambler
Heine • Millar • Topor • O'Connor
Baudelaire • O'Flaherty • Macdonald
Flaubert • Slesar • Bosc • Tschukowskaja
Lodemann • Hottinger • Fellini • Sillitoe
Ungerer • Poe • Thoreau • Gogol • Verne
Orwell • Highsmith • Murschetz • Conrad
Morweiser • Chaval • Jiménez • Sendak
Jägersberg • Goya • Chandler • Richartz
Carroll • Fitzgerald • Loriot • Maugham

ARTIST / KÜNSTLER / ARTISTE:

157, 158 Bernhard Jäger
159, 160 Tomi Ungerer
161, 162 Jerry Cosgrove/Robert Dale
163, 164 Sandi Glass

DESIGNER / GESTALTER / MAQUETTISTE:

157, 158 Bengt Fosshag
159, 160 Hans Höfliger
161, 162 Jerry Cosgrove
163, 164 Don Trousdell

ART DIRECTOR / DIRECTEUR ARTISTIQUE:

157, 158 Karl W. Henschel
161, 162 John Vise

AGENCY / AGENTUR / AGENCE – STUDIO:

157, 158 Sign Studio
159, 160 Diogenes Verlag
161, 162 Cosgrove Assoc. Inc.
163, 164 Don Trousdell

160

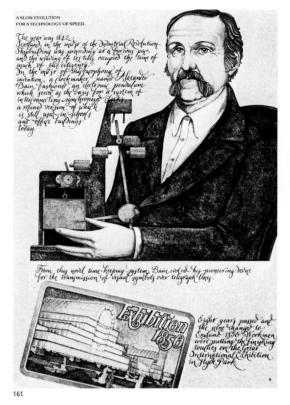

161

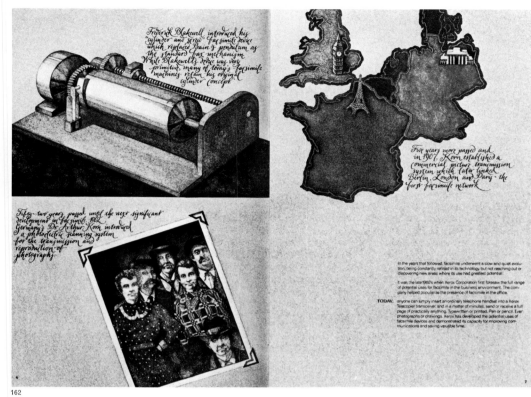

162

163

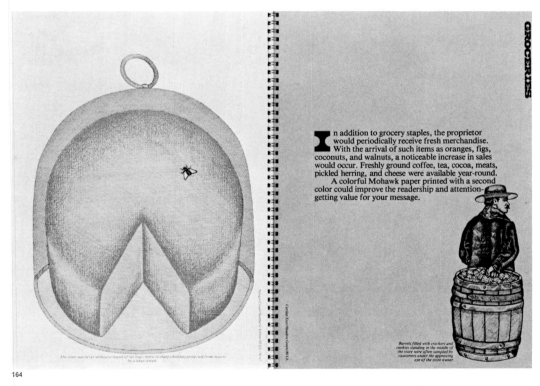

164

Booklets / Prospekte / Brochures

157, 158 Illustration in roughly actual size and complete cover of a *Hoechst* brochure from a series on bronchitis. (GER)
159, 160 Cover of a small catalogue marking a jubilee of the publishing house *Diogenes*, and detail of the vignette. (SWI)
161, 162 Colour page and spread from a brochure entitled *The Age of Facsimile* issued by *Xerox*, here dealing with the early inventions for facsimile reproduction. (USA)
163, 164 Cover and double spread, both in colour, from a spirally bound booklet about the old country store (the spread shows a cheddar cheese and a biscuit barrel) designed to present the various qualities of *Mohawk* papers. (USA)

157, 158 Illustration und Gesamtwiedergabe des Umschlags eines *Hoechst*-Prospektes für das Medikament *Hostacyclin 500*, aus einer Serie über Bronchitis. (GER)
159, 160 Titelseite eines kleinen Jubiläumsprospektes des *Diogenes*-Verlags und Vignette daraus. (SWI)
161, 162 Farbige Seiten aus einer *Xerox*-Broschüre über die Entwicklung der telephonischen Bildübermittlung, hier die frühen Anfänge der Faksimile-Reproduktion. (USA)
163, 164 Titel- und Doppelseite eines nostalgisch gestalteten Katalogs eines Papierherstellers, um die Druckmöglichkeiten auf farbigem Papier zu demonstrieren. (USA)

157, 158 Illustration (approx. grandeur nature) et couverture d'une brochure *Hoechst* faisant partie d'une série consacrée à la bronchite. (GER)
159, 160 Couverture d'un petit catalogue publié lors du 25e anniversaire des Editions *Diogenes*, avec vignette. (SWI)
161, 162 Page couleur et page double d'une brochure intitulée *L'âge du fac-similé*, publiée par *Xerox*: référence aux premières inventions dans la reproduction de fac-similés. (USA)
163, 164 Couverture et page double (en couleurs) d'une brochure à reliure spirale évoquant «le bon vieux temps». Elément de promotion pour les papiers *Mohawk*. (USA)

165

166

Booklets
Prospekte
Brochures

168-173

165 Cover of a spirally bound catalogue of *Ullstein* special papers. The cut-away arcs reveal numerous coloured samples. (GER)
166, 167 Board cover (imitating leather) and composite spread from an issue of the *Champion Papers* publication *Imagination* devoted to Ireland. These monographs also present paper qualities. (USA)
168–173 Sequence of cartoons from a folder used as a mailer to advertise a children's cartoon film about a dog. (CSR)
174 Large newspaper-like folder announcing the resurgence of the publishing house *Le Sagittaire*. Black and white. (FRA)
175 Folder to take printed matter relating to the business magazine *Fortune*. (USA)

165 Umschlag eines grossen Katalogs, mit Spiralbindung, für Spezialpapiere von *Ullstein*. Durch Ausschnitte werden die zahlreichen farbigen Muster sichtbar. (GER)
166, 167 Karton-Umschlagseite, die wie Leder aussieht, und Innenseiten aus einer Publikation von *Champion Papers*, welche Irland gewidmet ist. (USA)
168–173 Folge von Cartoons aus einem Prospekt, der für einen Zeichentrickfilm für Kinder wirbt. (CSR)
174 Grosse zeitungsähnliche Publikation, mit welcher die Rückkehr des Verlags *Le Sagittaire* bekanntgemacht wird. (FRA)
175 Kartonmappe für lose Werbeblätter des Wirtschaftsmagazins *Fortune*. (USA)

165 Couverture d'un grand catalogue à reliure spirale pour les papiers spéciaux de *Ullstein*. Les découpes à l'emporte-pièce révèlent la gamme des papiers teints. (GER)
166, 167 Couverture cartonnée (imitation de cuir) et page double d'un numéro de la publication *Imagination* de *Champion Papers*. Celui-ci est consacré à l'Irlande. (USA)
168–173 Séquence de dessins animés présentés dans un dépliant pour la promotion d'un dessin animé pour enfants. (CSR)
174 Dépliant grand format évoquant un quotidien pour annoncer le retour des Editions *Le Sagittaire*. (FRA)
175 Portfolio contenant des éléments publicitaires en faveur du périodique économique *Fortune*. (USA)

167

ARTIST / KÜNSTLER / ARTISTE:

165 CR-Graphik Service GmbH
168–173 Jiří Šalamoun
174 Jean Alessandrini
175 Richard Walukanis

DESIGNER / GESTALTER / MAQUETTISTE:

165 CR-Graphik Service GmbH
166, 167 James N. Miho
168–173 Jiří Šalamoun
174 Jean Alessandrini
175 Richard Walukanis

ART DIRECTOR / DIRECTEUR ARTISTIQUE:

166, 167 Edward Russel
168–173 Zdena Křivanová
174 Jean Alessandrini
175 Richard Walukanis

AGENCY / AGENTUR / AGENCE – STUDIO:

165 CR-Graphik Service GmbH
166, 167 Champion Papers
168–173 Pressfoto

174

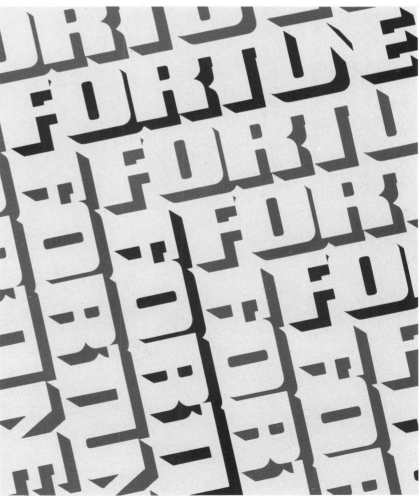

175

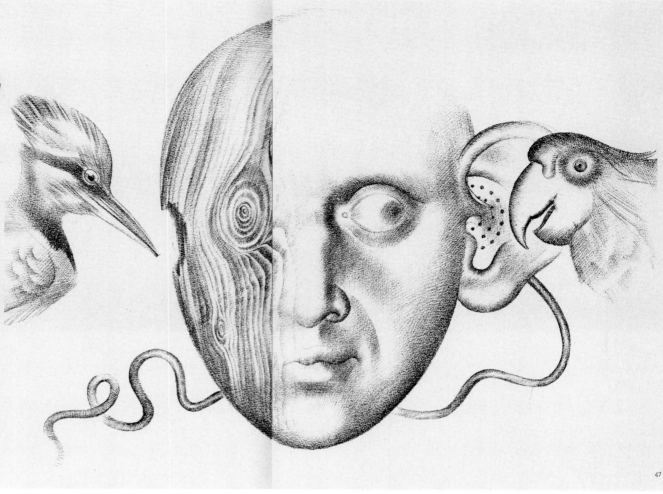

ENDURING TIMIDITY ON THE WIRE SERVICES

By JOHN M. PEARCE

The two major American wire services have only two wares to sell: the 24-hour flow of news on their vast Teletype networks, and a reputation for utter objectivity—for the type of story that will be judged acceptable and printed by newspapers as diverse as *The New York Times* and the *Arizona Republic*.

But it is just this 1950s sort of objectivity—the "just the facts, ma'am" approach—that breeds excessive caution. Combined with a healthy respect for authority figures (both services are in fact an integral part of the press establishment), such caution can so get in the way of full reporting that the meaning of an event is obscured or lost entirely.

In its most subtle and insidious form, that is one type of self-censorship. It is unconscious censorship of one institution by another. An overheated critic of the news agencies, which I am not, might call it rape by consent.

At its outer limit, this sort of attitude leads to unwillingness by editors to allow on the wire any assertion that can't be pinned directly on someone—preferably someone of authority. And in the trenches, it leads reporters to bring that most omniscient and readily quotable source, the "observer," into play. When a wire service story relates that "observers believe" something, you can be reasonably certain the observers are the reporters involved and their pressroom colleagues. There's usually nothing unsound about the observation, and where politics is concerned, it may be the most

John M. Pearce worked for newspapers in Texas before joining the Associated Press in the mid-1960s. He is now a stockbroker in Washington.

46

47

MIDDELHAUVE KINDERBÜCHER

Frederick

15 JAHRE

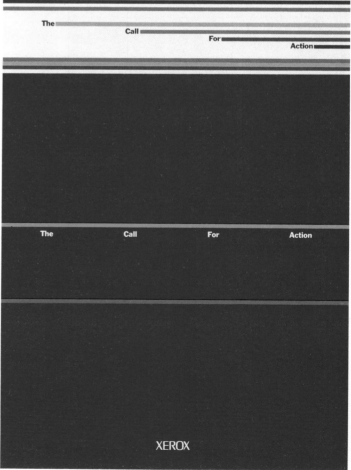

The Call For Action

The   Call   For   Action

XEROX

176–178 Double spreads, all in black and white, from the publication *Dateline 75*. They deal with the question of self-censorship hitherto practised in the news services, newspapers and news magazines. (USA)
179 Sticker marking the 15th anniversary of a children's book publisher. The mouse is the hero of one of Lionni's books. (GER)
180 Cover of a brochure about *Xerox* telecopiers for the speedy transmission of facsimiles by telephone. (USA)
181 Inside of an invitation issued by *Meitetsu*. Pins in full colour. (JPN)
182 Cover of a publisher's folder promoting a book of stories about a cat. Black, white and various shades of pink. (SWI)

176–178 Doppelseiten (schwarzweiss) aus der Publikation *Dateline 75*. Es geht um die Frage der bis anhin praktizierten Selbstzensur der Nachrichtendienste, Zeitungen und Magazine. (USA)
179 Kleber zum 15jährigen Jubiläum des *Middelhauve* Kinderbuchverlags. Die Maus Frederick ist der Held aus einem der Bücher von Leo Lionni. (GER)
180 «Der Ruf nach Taten», Umschlag einer farbigen Broschüre über *Xerox*-Telekopiergeräte für die telephonische Übermittlung von Faksimiles. (USA)
181 Einladungskarte der japanischen Firma *Meitetsu*. Die Nadeln sind farbig. (JPN)
182 Farbiger Umschlag eines Katalogs des *Benteli*-Verlags. Bei dem Kater handelt es sich um Jakob, den Helden einer Serie von Katzengeschichten. Im Katalog wird unter anderem ein weiterer Band dieser Reihe angekündigt. (SWI)

176–178 Pages doubles (toutes en noir et blanc) figurant dans la publication *Dateline 75*. Elles se réfèrent au problème de l'autocensure effectuée jusqu'à présent par les agences d'informations, les journaux et les magazines d'informations. (USA)
179 Sticker qui marque le 15e anniversaire d'une maison d'édition de livres d'enfant. Le souris s'appelant Frédéric est le héro d'un livre réalisé par Leo Lionni. (GER)
180 Couverture d'une brochure présentant les télécopieurs *Xerox* qui permettent de transmettre des fac-similés par téléphone. (USA)
181 Invitation d'une entreprise japonaise. Les épingles sont en couleurs. (JPN)
182 Couverture du dépliant d'une maison d'éditions pour la promotion d'une série d'histoires de chats. Noir, blanc et diverses teintes lilas. (SWI)

ARTIST / KÜNSTLER / ARTISTE:

176 Robert Pryor
177, 178 Carol Wald
179 Leo Lionni
181 Shigeo Okamoto
182 Sven Hartmann

177

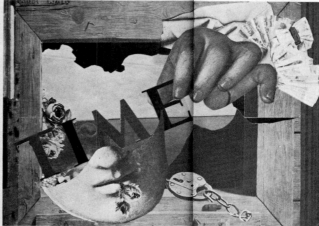

178

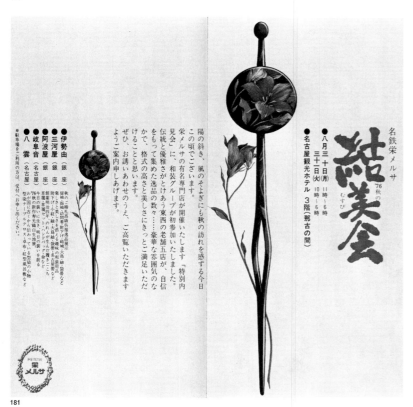

181

182

DESIGNER / GESTALTER / MAQUETTISTE:

176–178 Hector Marrero
179 Leo Lionni
180 Jerry Cosgrove/Vicki Navratil
181 Shigeo Okamoto
182 Benteli-Team

ART DIRECTOR / DIRECTEUR ARTISTIQUE:

176–178 Ahmad Sadiq
179 Leo Lionni
180 John Vise
181 Shigeo Okamoto
182 Ted Scapa

AGENCY / AGENTUR / AGENCE – STUDIO:

180 Cosgrove Assoc. Inc.
181 Shigeo Okamoto Design Center
182 Benteli-Verlag

Booklets
Prospekte
Brochures

183

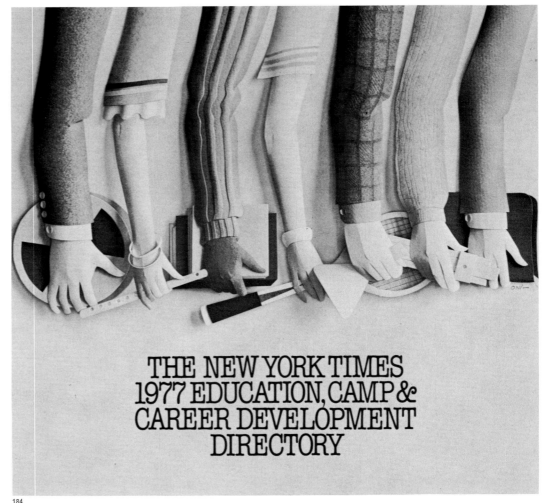

THE NEW YORK TIMES
1977 EDUCATION, CAMP &
CAREER DEVELOPMENT
DIRECTORY

184

183 Embossed cover of a booklet about the insurance company Lobell & Nalven Inc. (USA)
184 Cover of a *New York Times* directory. Monochrome with red lettering. (USA)
185 Folder with colour illustration about *Xerox* facsimile transmitting equipment. (USA)
186 Cover of a concertina-type mailer for space promotion in *TV Guide* magazine. (USA)
187 Cover illustration in full colour for a type specimen catalogue issued by the typographers Alphabet Innovations AB. (SWE)
188, 189 Mailing piece (shown closed, with red heart) and concertina-type folder contained in it (consisting of cut-out men and women) as space promotion for the magazine *TV Guide*. (USA)

183 Umschlag einer Broschüre der *Lobell-Nalven*-Versicherung mit Blindprägung. (USA)
184 Umschlag eines Verzeichnisses der *New York Times* über Weiterbildungsprogramme. (USA)
185 Prospekt mit farbiger Illustration über *Xerox*-Faksimile-Übermittlungsgeräte. (USA)
186 Deckblatt eines Leporello-Prospektes als Inserentenwerbung einer TV-Programmzeitschrift. (USA)
187 Farbige Illustration der Umschlagseite eines Katalogs von Alphabet Innovations AB über verschiedene Schrifttypen und Ornamente. (SWE)
188, 189 Aufklappbares Deckblatt mit rotem Herz und leporello-artiger Inhalt (bestehend aus Männern und Frauen) als Inserentenwerbung für eine Fernsehzeitschrift, mit Angaben über den Einfluss von Männern beim Kauf von Konsumgütern. (USA)

183 Couverture (gaufrage à sec) de la brochure d'une compagnie d'assurances. (USA)
184 Couverture d'un répertoire du *New York Times* contenant des programmes de formation. (USA)
185 Dépliant avec illustration couleur pour les appareils de transmission de fac-similés de *Xerox*. (USA)
186 Couverture d'un dépliant en accordéon pour la promotion du magazine *TV Guide*. (USA)
187 Illustration de couverture (en couleurs) pour un catalogue présentant les divers caractères d'Alphabet Innovations AB. (SWE)
188, 189 Elément publicitaire (fermé, avec cœur rouge) et dépliant en accordéon y contenu (composé d'hommes et de femmes découpés) pour la promotion du magazine *TV Guide*. (USA)

How
to
send
an
Action
Document
from
New
York
to
Los
Angeles
in
two
minutes
or
less...

185

186

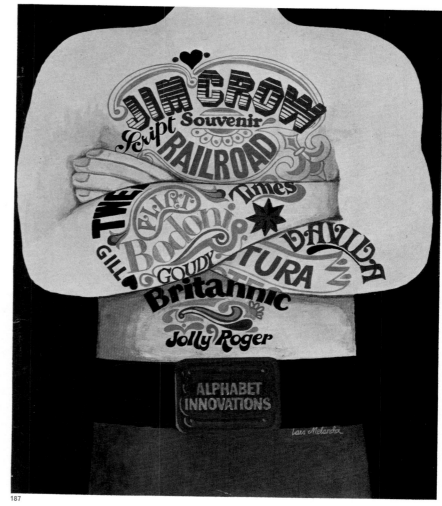

187

188

189

ARTIST / KÜNSTLER / ARTISTE:

183 Sondra Mayer
184 Oni
185 Jerry Cosgrove
187 Lars Melander

DESIGNER / GESTALTER / MAQUETTISTE:

183 Sondra Mayer
184 Arnold Kushner
185 Jerry Cosgrove
186, 188, 189 Bobbi Adair
187 Lars Melander

ART DIRECTOR / DIRECTEUR ARTISTIQUE:

184 Andrew Kner
185 John Vise
186, 188, 189 John William Brown

AGENCY / AGENTUR / AGENCE – STUDIO:

185 Cosgrove Assoc. Inc.
186, 188, 189 TV Guide – Triangle Publications, Inc.

190

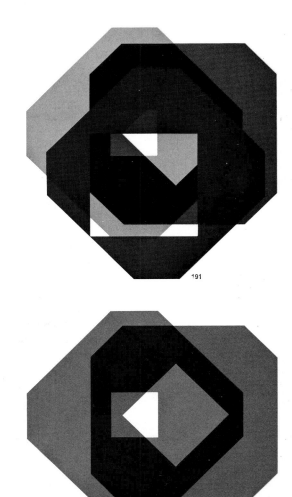

191

192

190 Cover design in flat colours for a folder to take printed matter about Bullen and Partners, consulting engineers. (GBR)
191–194 Design in flat, overlapping colours and complete folder, from the printed matter relating to the Swiss Federal government's selection of the best commissioned films of the year. (SWI)
195 Cover of a booklet about Fujairah International Airport, issued by the Ministry of Public Works. Title in white and pale green on green. (UAE)
196 Cover of a folder containing information on sailing terms and signals, issued to demonstrate several qualities of *Abitibi* papers. (CAN)
197 Cover of a promotional record cover with the songs of migratory birds, for *Swissair*. (SWI)
198 Two panels of a folder issued by a publisher about a Swiss writer. Brown stock. (SWI)

190 Farbige Illustration einer Mappe für lose Werbeblätter einer Ingenieursfirma. (GBR)
191–194 Graphiken in ungebrochenen, sich überschneidenden Farben und Gesamtwiedergabe einer Mappe für Unterlagen des Eidgenössischen Departements des Innern über die besten Auftragsfilme des Jahres 1977. (SWI)
195 Umschlagseite einer Broschüre über den internationalen Flughafen Fujairah, herausgegeben vom Ministerium für öffentliche Bauten. Titel in Weiss und Hellgrün auf Grün. (UAE)
196 Deckblatt einer Mappe mit Informationen über Begriffe und Signale aus der Schiffahrt, von einem Papierhersteller als Werbung für seine Erzeugnisse verwendet. (CAN)
197 Hülle für eine Schallplatte mit Vogelstimmen, herausgegeben von der *Swissair*. (SWI)
198 Zwei Textblocks aus einem Verlagsprospekt über den Schriftsteller Clemens Mettler. (SWI)

Fujairah
International
Airport

مطار الفجيرة الدولى

195

Tar Talk.
No. 3 in a series exploring the world of man under sail.
Presented on Paragon Offset and Paragon Cover.

196

ART DIRECTOR / DIRECTEUR ARTISTIQUE:
191–194 Kurt Wirth
195 Fritz Gottschalk
196 Robert Burns
197 Bernard B. Sanders
198 Michael Baviera

AGENCY / AGENTUR / AGENCE – STUDIO:
190 Bloy Eldridge Ltd.
191–194 Kurt Wirth
195 Gottschalk & Ash Ltd.
196 Burns, Cooper, Hynes Ltd.
197 Sanders & Noe, Inc.
198 M. + M. Baviera

ARTIST / KÜNSTLER / ARTISTE:

190 Robert Custance
191–194 Kurt Wirth
196 Heather Cooper/Roger Hill
197 David M. Seager

DESIGNER / GESTALTER / MAQUETTISTE:

191–194 Kurt Wirth
195 Don Kindschi
196 Robert Burns/Roger Hill
197 David M. Seager
198 Michael Baviera

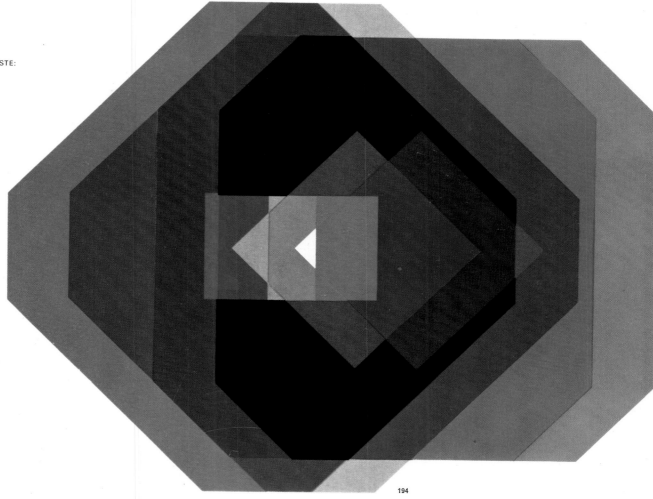

193

194

190 Illustration de couverture (en teintes atténuées) d'un portfolio contenant des éléments de publicité d'un bureau d'ingénieurs. (GBR)

191–194 Illustrations en tons atténués, s'entrecoupant, et portfolio contenant des informations du Département fédéral de l'intérieur concernant les meilleurs films de commande de l'année. (SWI)

195 Couverture d'une brochure sur l'aéroport international Fujairah, publiée par le Ministère des travaux publics. Titre en blanc sur fond vert atténué. (UAE)

196 Couverture d'un portfolio contenant des informations sur le «langage des marins». Elément de publicité en faveur des papiers *Abitibi*. (CAN)

197 Pochette d'un disque promotionnel de *Swissair* avec les cris des oiseaux migrateurs. (SWI)

198 Deux panneaux d'un dépliant consacré à un écrivain suisse. Papier brun. (SWI)

Booklets
Prospekte
Brochures

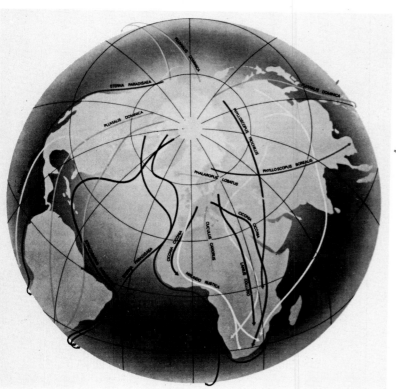

197

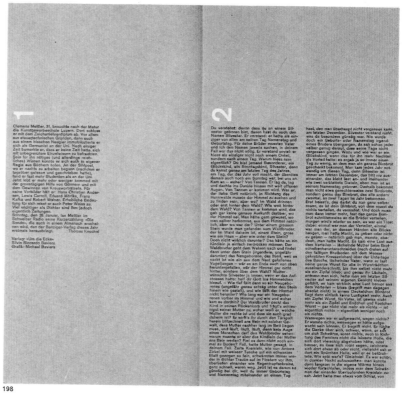

198

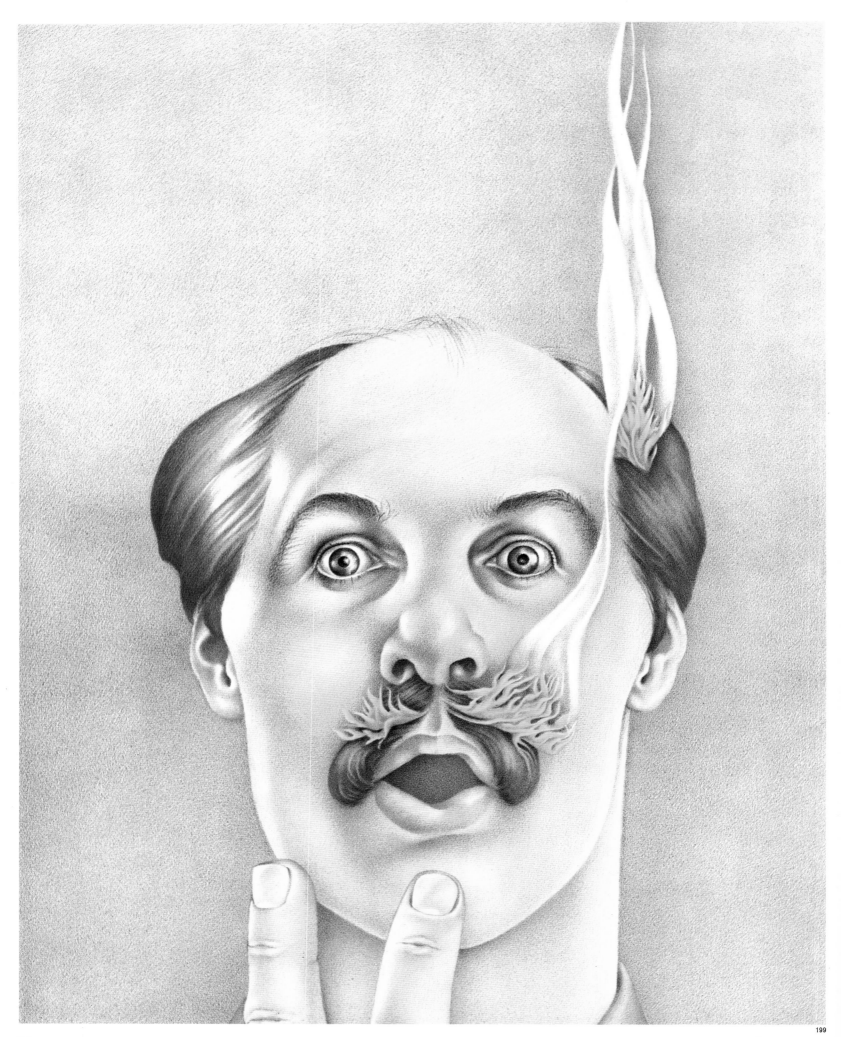

199

200

ARTIST / KÜNSTLER / ARTISTE:

199, 200 Maire Smith
201 Walter Tafelmaier
203, 204 N. Hoefig/E. Lord/S. Glass/
D. Trousdell

DESIGNER / GESTALTER / MAQUETTISTE:

199, 200 Garry Emery
201 Walter Tafelmaier
202 Helmut Schmid
203, 204 Don Trousdell

ART DIRECTOR / DIRECTEUR ARTISTIQUE:

199, 200 Garry Emery
202 Helmut Schmid
203, 204 Don Trousdell

AGENCY / AGENTUR / AGENCE – STUDIO:

199, 200 Garry Emery Designer
202 Nippon International Agency
203, 204 Shoestring Studio

199, 200 Page in actual size and complete double spread from a public relations booklet published by the Melbourne Board of Works. The reference here is to forest fires. (AUS)
201 Cover of the Bavarian radio's programme for the first six months of 1978. Flower vignettes in full colour. (GER)
202 Spread from the prospectus of a kindergarten in Osaka, using children's drawings. Blue and red on grey stock. (JPN)
203, 204 Double spreads from a programme of summer courses at Syracuse University. (USA)

199, 200 Illustration in Originalgrösse und komplette Doppelseite einer Public-Relations-Broschüre des Bauamtes von Melbourne, hier im Zusammenhang mit Waldbränden. (AUS)
201 Titelseite des Programms des Bayerischen Rundfunks für das 1. Halbjahr 1978. Blumen in Gelb-, Orange- und Grüntönen. (GER)
202 Doppelseite aus einem japanischen Kindergarten-Prospekt, in dem Kinderzeichnungen als Illustrationen verwendet werden. Hier ein Beispiel (einfarbig) mit Ortsskizze. (JPN)
203, 204 Doppelseiten aus dem Programm der Sommerkurse an der Syracuse University. (USA)

199, 200 Page en grandeur nature et page double figurant dans une brochure promotionnelle publiée par le service de l'urbanisme de Melbourne. Référence aux incendies de forêts. (AUS)
201 Couverture du programme réunissant les émissions de la radiodiffusion bavaroise pour les premiers six mois de l'année 1978. Fleurs en teintes jaunes, orange et vertes. (GER)
202 Page double du prospectus d'un jardin d'enfant à Osaka illustré de dessins d'enfant. Bleu et rouge sur papier gris. (JPN)
203, 204 Pages doubles du programme des cours d'été de l'Université de Syracuse (USA).

Booklets / Prospekte / Brochures

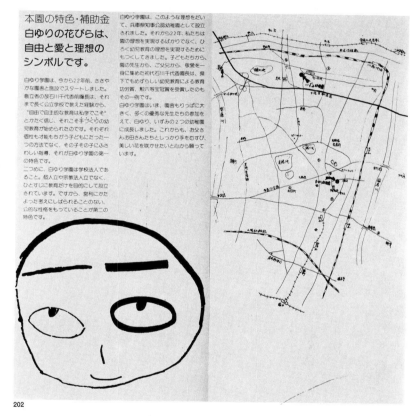

201

202

203

204

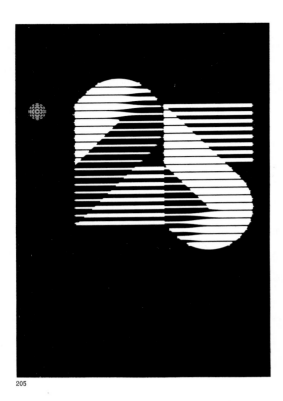

205

206

207

Booklets
Prospekte
Brochures

ARTIST / KÜNSTLER / ARTISTE:
212, 213 Erhard Göttlicher

DESIGNER / GESTALTER / MAQUETTISTE:
205–207 Ueli Dietiker/Yvon Laroche/
Alain Leduc/André Théroux
208 Myrtle McNulty
209–211 Mario Furtado
212, 213 Borek Sipek

ART DIRECTOR / DIRECTEUR ARTISTIQUE:
208 Kristina Jorgensen
209–211 Mario Furtado

AGENCY / AGENTUR / AGENCE – STUDIO:
205–207 Société Radio-Canada,
Service de la Publicité
209–211 MIT Press Design Department

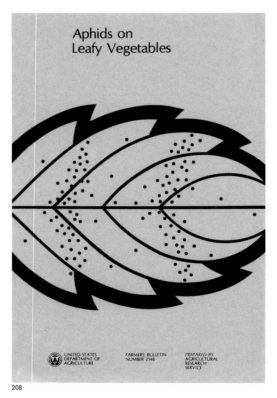

208

209

205–207 Folder (silver on black), programme (brownish shades) and invitation (blue cut-out boards) for the jubilee of Canadian Television. (CAN)
208 Cover of a brochure from a series issued by the US Department of Agriculture. (USA)
209–211 Covers of catalogues of books published by MIT Press in the various fields of knowledge. Each booklet black and white on a code colour. (USA)
212, 213 Front and complete cover of a catalogue for an exhibition of the drawings of Erhard Göttlicher in Berlin. (GER)

205–207 Kartonmappe (Silber auf Schwarz), Programm (Brauntöne) und Einladung (blaue Kartonstreifen auf Sand) zum Jubiläum des kanadischen Fernsehens. (CAN)
208 Umschlag einer Broschüre, die zu einer Reihe von Publikationen des Landwirtschaftsministeriums der USA gehört. (USA)
209–211 Umschlagseiten von Buchkatalogen des MIT-Verlags auf verschiedenen Gebieten der Wissenschaft. Alle Umschlagseiten in einer Code-Farbe (USA)
212, 213 Ausschnitt und ganzer Umschlag eines Ausstellungskatalogs der Zeichnungen von E. Göttlicher in Berlin. (GER)

205–207 Dépliant (argent sur noir), programme (teintes brunâtres) et invitation (bandes en carton bleu) pour le jubilé de la télévision de Radio-Canada. (CAN)
208 Couverture d'une brochure figurant dans une série publiée par le Département de l'agriculture des Etats-Unis. (USA)
209–211 Couvertures de catalogues de livres publiés par MIT Press dans les divers domaines scientifiques. Typo noir-blanc sur fond couleur défini par un code-couleur. (USA)
212, 213 Recto et couverture complète du catalogue pour une exposition des dessins de Erhard Göttlicher à Berlin. (GER)

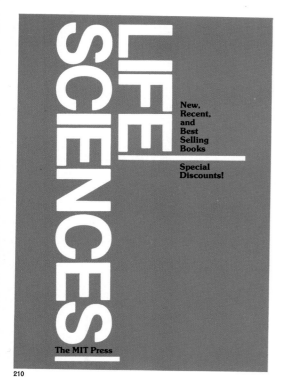

210

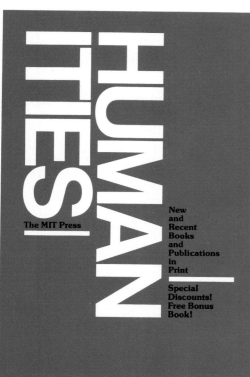

211

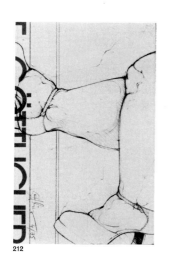

212

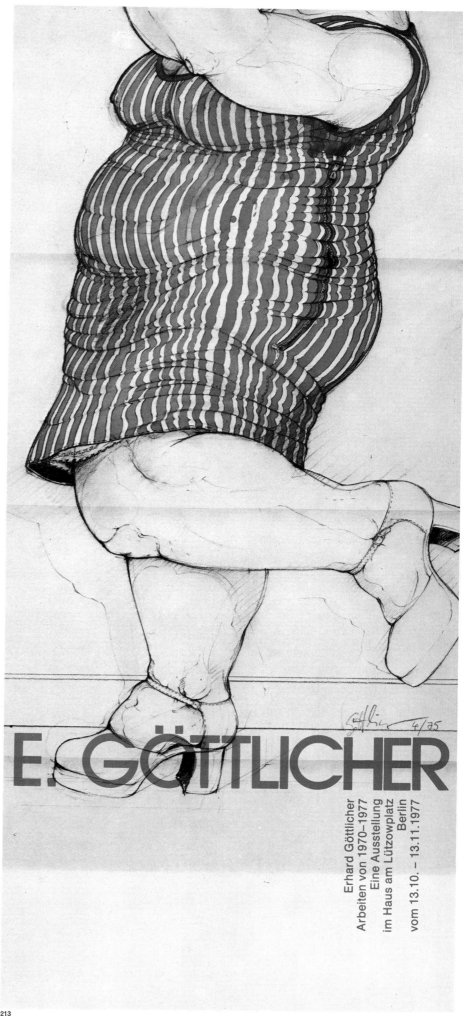

213

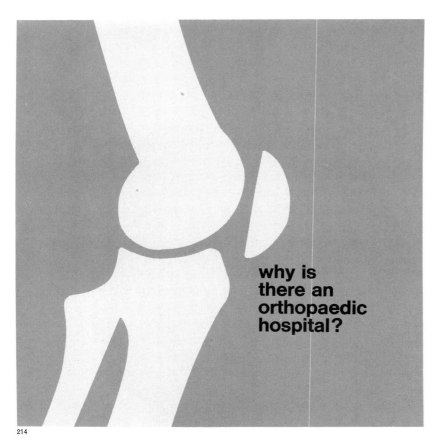

why is
there an
orthopaedic
hospital?

214

214 Brochure on an orthopaedic hospital in Los Angeles. White and black on sand. (USA)
215 "Sebastian the bear wants to marry." Cover of a booklet with a children's story issued by the Swiss Bank Corporation. (SWI)
216, 217 Call for entries for an arts festival in Pennsylvania; illustration in actual size. (USA)
218 Folder (shown open) for a "museum of ancient sculpture" in Frankfurt. (GER)
219 Complete cover of a prospectus of The Berkeley Schools. Red "B" on olive. (USA)

214 Umschlag einer Public-Relations-Broschüre einer orthopädischen Klinik. (USA)
215 Umschlag einer Broschüre des Schweizerischen Bankvereins für Kinder. (SWI)
216, 217 Gesamtwiedergabe und Illustration einer Einladung der Pennsylvania-Universität zur Teilnahme an einer Kunstausstellung. (USA)
218 Innenseite einer Mappe für Informationsmaterial des «Museums alter Plastik». (GER)
219 Kompletter Umschlag mit rotem B für eine Broschüre der *Berkeley*-Schulen. (USA)

214 Couverture de la brochure promotionnelle d'une clinique orthopédique. (USA)
215 «L'ours Sébastien se marie.» D'une brochure avec des contes illustrés pour enfants, publiée par la Société de Banque Suisse. (SWI)
216, 217 Invitation à participer à un festival des beaux-arts en Pennsylvanie. (USA)
218 Dépliant (ouvert) d'un Musée de sculpture ancienne à Francfort. (GER)
219 Couverture complète d'un prospectus des écoles *Berkeley*. «B» rouge sur fond olive. (USA)

216

215

88

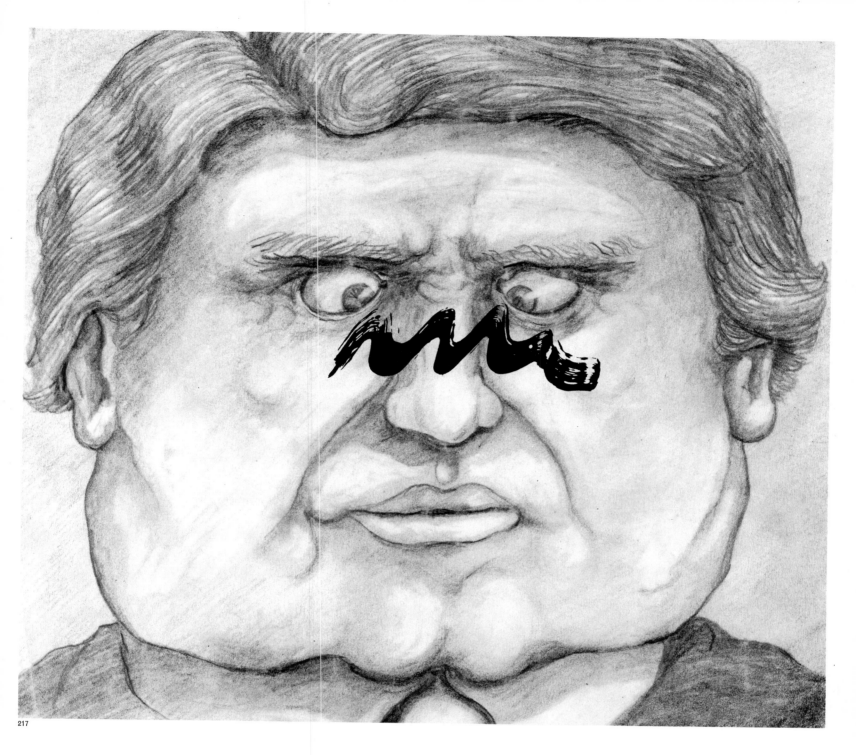

217

ARTIST / KÜNSTLER / ARTISTE:

215 Heinz Looser-Brenner
216, 217 Lanny Sommese

DESIGNER / GESTALTER / MAQUETTISTE:

214 Gerry Rosentswieg
215 Heinz Looser-Brenner
216, 217 Lanny Sommese
218 Kristian Roth
219 Claude Skelton

ART DIRECTOR / DIRECTEUR ARTISTIQUE:

214 Gerry Rosentswieg
215 Heinz Looser-Brenner
216, 217 Lanny Sommese
218 Kristian Roth
219 Claude Skelton

AGENCY / AGENTUR / AGENCE – STUDIO:

214 The Graphics Studio
215 Heinz Looser-Brenner
216, 217 Lanny Sommese
219 The North Charles Street
Design Organization

218

219

220

221

224

225

220 Cover of a booklet about Canadian Industries Ltd., manufacturers of chemicals and related products. Each letter is in a different colour. (CAN)
221 "Watch out for unpleasant surprises!" Envelope (bright colours) containing the brochure of an insurance company. On the front of the brochure, a wolf emerges from the sheepskin. (SWE)
222 Brochure with die-cut pages about a national women's organization. (GER)
223 Programme of a Gershwin concert broadcast from Berlin. White and purple on wine red. (GER)
224, 225 Typical article on a parental problem and folder (orange and grey) containing a number of such articles, issued by the National PTA, a parents' and teachers' organization. (USA)
226 Page from a brochure about a *Citicorp* stock purchase plan. Black and white, grey tone. (USA)
227 Brochure on a contest for the handsomest books of the year, issued by Design Canada. (CAN)

220 Umschlag einer Broschüre der Canadian Industries Ltd., Hersteller von Chemikalien und verwandten Produkten. Jeder Buchstabe hat eine andere Farbe. (CAN)
221 «Hüte Dich vor unangenehmen Überraschungen!» Farbige Hülle für die Broschüre einer Versicherungsgesellschaft. Auf dem Umschlag der Broschüre entsteigt ein Wolf dem Schafspelz. (SWE)
222 Umschlag einer Informationsbroschüre des Deutschen Frauenrats. Ausgestanzte Profile. (GER)
223 Programm eines vom SFB übertragenen Gershwin-Konzerts. (GER)
224, 225 Beispiel eines als Erziehungshilfe gedachten Artikels und Mappe (orange und grau), die eine Reihe solcher Artikel unter dem Titel «Die heutige Familie im Brennpunkt» enthält. Herausgeber ist die PTA, eine amerikanische Eltern-Lehrer-Organisation. (USA)
226 Seite aus einer Broschüre für ein Anlage-Programm. Die Angst vor dem Börsenmarkt wird dem Kunden genommen, nicht aber die vor grossen Mädchen, Tieren und Topfpflanzen. (USA)
227 Katalog zu dem Wettbewerb «Die schönsten kanadischen Bücher des Jahres», herausgegeben von Design Canada. (CAN)

220 Couverture d'un prospectus de Canadian Industries Ltd., fabricant de produits chimiques et de produits connexes. Chaque caractère est d'une couleur différente. (CAN)
221 «Méfiez-vous de surprises désagréables!» Enveloppe (couleurs vives) contenant la brochure d'une compagnie d'assurances. Couverture: un loup enlève sa peau de mouton. (SWE)
222 Brochure d'informations avec pages découpées à l'emporte-pièce sur une organisation nationale de femmes. (GER)
223 Programme d'un concert de Gershwin diffusé par la radiodiffusion berlinoise. Blanc et violet sur fond rouge bordeaux. (GER)
224, 225 Article typique traitant de problèmes familiaux et portfolio (orange et gris) contenant un nombre d'articles réunis sous le titre «La famille d'aujourd'hui, notre point de mire». Ils ont été publiés par une organisation américaine de parents et de professeurs. (USA)
226 Page d'une brochure contenant un programme de placement. Noir et blanc, ton gris. (USA)
227 Catalogue du concours des plus beaux livres canadiens de l'année. (CAN)

Deutscher Frauenrat

Informationen für die Frau

222

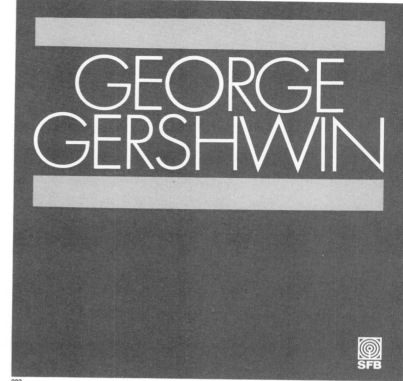

GEORGE GERSHWIN

SFB

223

Now, if I could just figure out what to do about tall girls, fuzzy animals and potted plants. Maybe I'll ask my mother.

226

1 9 7 7

The look of books
Les plus beaux livres
Design Canada

227

Booklets / Prospekte / Brochures

228

229

Booklets
Prospekte
Brochures

228 Illustration from a brochure about starting to work. Here the picture symbolizes leaving the egg. (GER)
229 Promotional mailer for WABC Television, underlining its popularity with women. Pages with cut-out edges. (USA)
230 Diagram from a booklet about the rural district authorities of Hesse. Coloured bars on silver ground. (GER)
231 Folder to recruit members for the American Library Trustee Association. Pink lines, white dots on blue. (USA)
232, 233 Invitation to a lecture on audio-visual systems, with detail of the eye symbol. Blue on grey stock. (USA)
234 Cover of a programme for a showing of French films of the seventies in Trieste. Blue on white. (ITA)
235 Booklet on the uses of data processing in broadcasting. Green, blue and white on black. (GER)
236 Brochure about music for pre-school children, issued by Kingston College of Advanced Education. Red ground. (AUS)
237 Black-and-white cover of a theatre programme. (BEL)

228 Illustration aus der Broschüre *Berufsanfang.* Hier ist das Thema «Szenenwechsel». (GER)
229 Direktwerbung, mit der die Popularität eines bestimmten US-Fernsehsenders bei Frauen hervorgehoben wird. (USA)
230 Diagramm aus einer Broschüre über die hessischen Landkreise. Farbig auf silbernem Grund. (GER)
231 Mitgliederwerbung einer amerikanischen Bibliotheks-Vereinigung. Rosa Linien, weisse Punkte, auf Blau. (USA)
232, 233 Einladung zu einer Präsentation über audio-visuelle Systeme, mit Detail des Symbols. Blau auf Grau. (USA)
234 Umschlag eines Vorführprogramms über französische Filmen aus den 70er Jahren in Triest. Blau auf Weiss. (ITA)
235 Umschlag einer Informationsschrift über EDV im Rundfunk. Grün, blau und weiss auf Schwarz. (GER)
236 Broschüre über Musik für Kinder im Vorschulalter. In der Broschüre werden Kinderzeichnungen verwendet. (AUS)
237 Schwarzweisser Umschlag eines Theaterprogramms. (BEL)

228 Illustration d'une brochure sur l'entrée dans le monde du travail, ici l'éclatement de la coquille. (GER)
229 Elément promotionnel d'une station de TV soulignant sa popularité chez les femmes. (USA)
230 Diagramme d'une brochure sur les districts ruraux de la Hesse. Traits colorés sur fond argenté. (GER)
231 Dépliant déstiné au recrutement de membres d'une association de bibliothèques américaines. Rose, blanc, bleu. (USA)
232, 233 Invitation à un discours sur les systèmes audio-visuels avec détail du symbole. Bleu sur papier gris. (USA)
234 Couverture du programme pour une présentation de films français des années 70 à Trieste. Bleu sur blanc. (ITA)
235 Brochure d'information sur l'utilisation d'ordinateurs dans le domaine de la radiodiffusion. (GER)
236 Brochure consacrée à la musique destinée aux enfants à l'âge préscolaire, illustrée de dessins d'enfant. (AUS)
237 Couverture noir-blanc d'un programme de théâtre. (BEL)

230

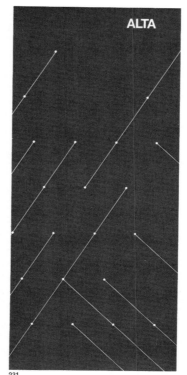

231

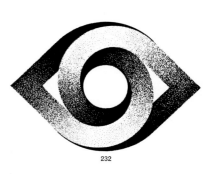

232

233

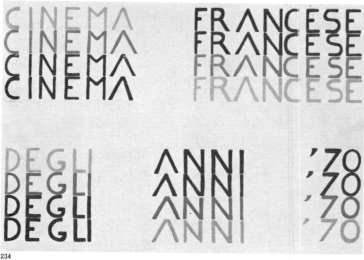

234

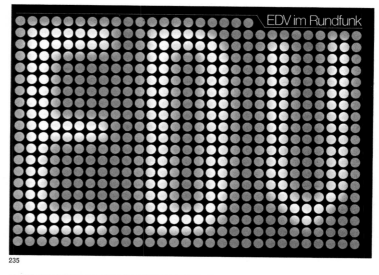

235

236

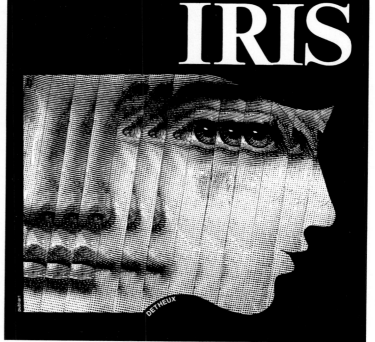

237

238 Double spread from an issue of the *Push Pin* house organ devoted to the kiss. (USA)
239 Covers and panels of folders issued by Sleeping International System Italia. (ITA)
240 Cover of a government guide to courses in native studies offered in Ontario. Blue and orange design on a brown ground. (CAN)
241 Inside of a large folder about new address groups offered by the address register of the Post Office. Vignettes in full colour. (SWE)
242 Full-page colour illustration (the ladder of success) from a recruitment brochure issued by Deloitte, Haskins and Sells, chartered accountants. (CAN)
243 Cover of a catalogue of signs made by W. R. Grace & Co. Black and white on dark grey. (USA)

238 Doppelseite aus der *Push-Pin*-Hauszeitschrift, hier dem Kuss gewidmet. (USA)
239 Umschlag- und Innenseiten von Katalogen eines Lieferanten von Betten. (ITA)
240 Umschlag einer Regierungs-Broschüre über die in Ontario vorhandenen Studienmöglichkeiten der Eingeborenenkultur und -geschichte. Blau und orange auf Braun. (CAN)
241 Innenseite eines grossen Prospektes über neue Berufsgruppen im Adressenregister der Post. Farbige Darstellung der neuen Gruppen mit Zahlenangaben. (SWE)
242 Illustration aus einem Prospekt für Personalwerbung einer Buchhaltungsfirma. (USA)
243 Deckblatt eines Kataloges mit Preisangaben für freistehende Schilder. Schwarzweiss auf grauem Grund. (USA)

Uses of the Mouth: The Kiss

Nicolas J. Perella

Anthropologists, physiologists, and psychologists who have concerned themselves with the problem have put forth the theory that the kiss may very well be a vestigial remainder or a carry-over of a primitive habit of eating and thereby assimilating into the self any object felt to be "good" or desirable. If this is so, then it is all the more curious and significant that the labial kiss, which is so much taken for granted in Western societies, is not at all a universally practiced custom, for it was unknown to the majority of primitive peoples as well as to large segments of Asiatic cultures until introduced into them by Westerners. In 1897 the French anthropologist Paul d'Enjoy pointed out that the Chinese felt a kind of horror, as at some cannibalistic act, when confronted with the Western custom of mouth-to-mouth kissing. It was d'Enjoy's view that the basic elements or activities connected with the European kiss are biting and sucking. This relationship seems to have occurred to Sigmund Freud, who apparently, however, did not suspect its full anthropophagous implications. Discussing the preliminary and excitatory sexual activities, he wrote: "The kiss between the

238

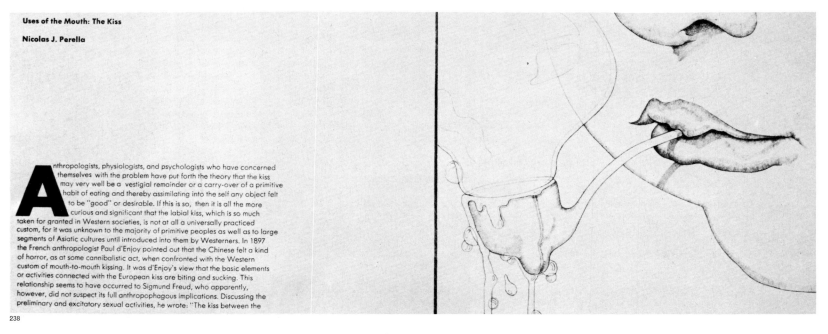

35 nya adressgrupper. 25 123 nya adresser. 5 619 nya namn.

241

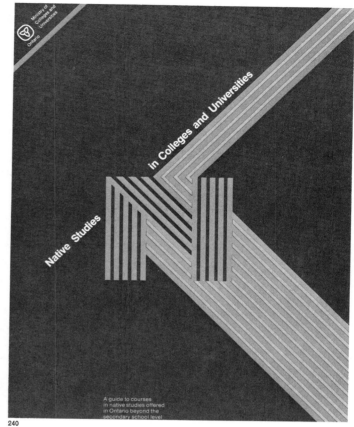

240

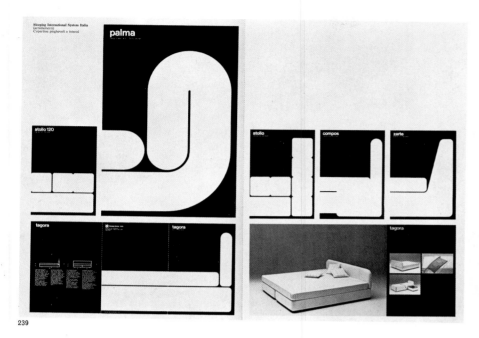

239

242

243

ARTIST / KÜNSTLER / ARTISTE:
238 Joyce McDonald
239 Rinaldo del Sordo/
    Giuseppe Berlinghieri
241 Lars Melander
242 Heather Cooper

DESIGNER / GESTALTER:
238 Seymour Chwast
239 Rinaldo del Sordo/
    Giuseppe Berlinghieri
240 Peter Adam
241 Lars Melander
242 Dawn Cooper Tennant
243 George Tscherny

ART DIRECTOR / DIRECTEUR ARTISTIQUE:
238 Seymour Chwast
239 Rinaldo del Sordo/
    Giuseppe Berlinghieri
240 Gottschalk & Ash
242 Robert Burns
243 George Tscherny

AGENCY / AGENTUR / AGENCE – STUDIO:
238 Push Pin Studios
239 Studio Giob
240 Gottschalk & Ash Ltd.
242 Burns, Cooper, Hynes Ltd.
243 George Tscherny, Inc.

Booklets
Prospekte
Brochures

244

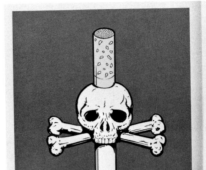

247

245

249

ARTIST / KÜNSTLER / ARTISTE:

244 Tim Lewis
245 Guy Billout
246 Dave Bhang
247 John Van Hamersveld
248 Glen Iwasaki
249 Thomas Kovacs

DESIGNER / GESTALTER / MAQUETTISTE:

244, 245 Kit Hinrichs/Linda Hinrichs
246–248 Takenobu Igarashi/Yoshitsuyo Noma
249 Thomas Kovacs
250–252 Jim Lienhart

ART DIRECTOR / DIRECTEUR ARTISTIQUE:

244, 245 Kit Hinrichs
246–248 Takenobu Igarashi
249 Thomas Kovacs
250–252 Jim Lienhart

96

248

244, 245 Page and double spread from a large self-promotion brochure (the second in a series) issued by the design studio Jonson Pedersen Hinrichs, which operates two offices in New York and San Francisco. (USA)
246—248 Double spreads, all in full colour, from a self-promotion booklet for Zen Environmental Design, containing illustrations by a number of Californian artists. (JPN)
249 Cover illustration from a booklet about a union of professional employees formed at the University of Illinois. Black and white. (USA)
250—252 Covers and double spread from small brochures about management workshops and recruitment services offered by Management Organization Inc. Symbols and type matter in colour. (USA)

244, 245 Seite und Doppelseite (zweifarbig) aus dem Eigenwerbungsprospekt eines Design-Studios mit zwei Niederlassungen. Daher wurde die Zwei als Thema gewählt. (USA)
246—248 Farbige Doppelseiten aus einem Eigenwerbungskatalog der Umweltgestaltungsfirma *Zen* mit Beispielen der Arbeiten verschiedener kalifornischer Künstler. (JPN)
249 Schwarzweisse Illustration des Umschlags einer Gewerkschaftsbroschüre für Hochschulpersonal an der Universität von Illinois. (USA)
250—252 Umschlagseiten und Doppelseite von Prospekten einer Personalvermittlungsgesellschaft auf Management-Ebene. Abb. 252 ist eine Wiederholung des in Abb. 251 in Blindprägung gezeigten Symbols, mit Bogen in Violett, Rot und Gelb. (USA)

244, 245 Page et page double d'une brochure auto-promotionnelle (la deuxième dans une série) publiée par le studio de design Jonson Pedersen Hinrichs qui ont des studios à New York et San Francisco, ce qui évoque le chiffre. (USA)
246—248 Pages doubles, en couleurs, d'une brochure autopromotionnelle d'un bureau spécialisé dans le design appliqué à l'environnement; illustrations de divers artistes californiens. (JPN)
249 Illustration de couverture d'une brochure sur un syndicat des employés de faculté de l'Université de l'Illinois. Noir et blanc. (USA)
250—252 Couvertures et page double d'une petite brochure d'un service de placement et de formation pour managers. Symboles et typographie en couleurs. (USA)

AGENCY / AGENTUR / AGENCE – STUDIO:

244, 245 Jonson Pedersen Hinrichs
246—248 Takenobu Igarashi Design
249 TGK Design

Booklets
Prospekte
Brochures

250

ACTION PERSPECTIVES
WORKSHOP

251

RESULTS AT THE TOP
A FRESH APPROACH
TO EXECUTIVE SEARCH

252

WHY CHOOSE US?

BECAUSE WE COMBINE A SEARCH DISCIPLINE THAT IS AS PROFESSIONAL AND RESOURCEFUL AS ANYBODY'S WITH A DESIRE TO BE PART OF YOUR CORPORATE FAMILY.

In other words, we want to (1) care about your business (2) be in association with you for the long pull (3) help you think through and act on your organizational needs while (4) gaining for ourselves a solid sense of accomplishment and professional satisfaction.

We invite you to compare our approach with those of much larger firms. If you do, we think you'll conclude that benefits of size turn out to be imaginary, and that apart from rhetoric, we provide an added margin on performance.

Some things to consider:

ONE-TO-ONE RELATIONSHIP

Good executive search is a one-to-one affair between client and consultant. A large search firm can't offer more than that, but it can offer a whole lot less. For example, one-to-three or four. You may have been through the routine: the partner books the assignment, then turns it over to a junior who turns it over to another junior. To say the least, accountability gets hazy.

We're strictly one-to-one.

FILES

Ah, those mythical, wondrous files! Those vast treasure chests, laden with top executive talent, simply waiting to be pried open. Frankly, it's time for de-bunking.

Extensive resume files contain information on job-seekers. They're of little use to you.

Corporate files of great use to search consultants aren't files at all, but directories; directories published by such firms as Standard & Poor's, Standard Rate and Data Service, Dun & Bradstreet and Moody's. As you well know, they're available to anyone for the price of a subscription. We have these directories in our research library along with numerous business periodicals.

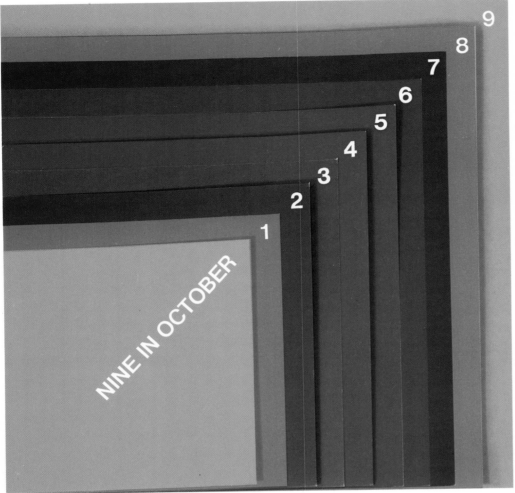

253

ARTIST / KÜNSTLER:

254 Josse Goffin
255 Ph. Langlois
256 Zélio Alves Pinto
257 Oswaldo Miranda
258 Marina Langer-Rosa
259 Rolf Iseli

DESIGNER / GESTALTER:

253 Louise Casselman
254 Max Marsily
256 Zélio Alves Pinto
257 Oswaldo Miranda
258 Helmut Langer
259 Rolf Iseli
260 Peter Proto/Jon Bodsworth

ART DIRECTOR:

253 John William Brown
254 Josse Goffin
257 Oswaldo Miranda
258 Helmut Langer
260 Peter Proto

AGENCY / AGENTUR:

253 TV Guide – Triangle Publications, Inc.
257 P.A.Z.
260 Peter Proto Associates

254

255

98

Ilustrações para um conto
de Julio Cesar Monteiro Martins
revista Viaje-Bem

256

**Booklets
Prospekte
Brochures**

QUE NOSSAS REALIZAÇÕES DO ANO QUE VEM TENHAM O TAMANHO EXATO DE NOSSAS ESPERANÇAS. O TAMANHO DO FUTURO.

257

258

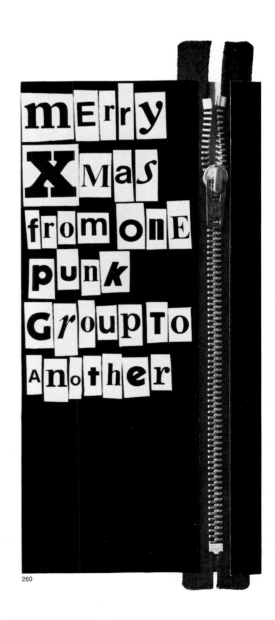

259

260

ARTIST / KÜNSTLER / ARTISTE:

261–264 Jan Lenica
267, 268 Gerhard C. Schulz
269 Alain Gauthier
270 Barrie Tucker

DESIGNER / GESTALTER / MAQUETTISTE:

261–264 Alain Le Quernec
265, 266 René Gauch
267, 268 Gerhard C. Schulz
270 Barrie Tucker

ART DIRECTOR / DIRECTEUR ARTISTIQUE:

261–264 Alain Le Quernec
269 François Ruy-Vidal
270 Barrie Tucker

AGENCY / AGENTUR / AGENCE – STUDIO:

261–264 Alain Le Quernec
265, 266 René Gauch
270 Barrie Tucker Design & Illustration

261

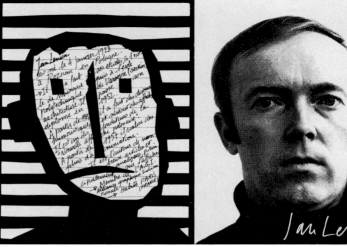

262

265

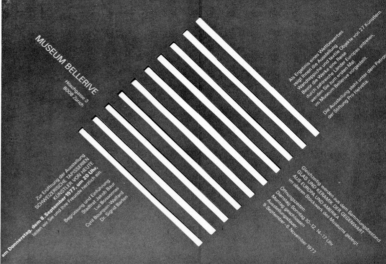

266

269

261–264 Cover (in flat colours) and three double spreads (in black and white) from the catalogue of an exhibition of the work of Jan Lenica in Quimper. (FRA)
265, 266 Cover and inside of an invitation to an exhibition of modern Swiss tapestries in a Zurich museum. White lettering on red. The perforations produce a woven effect. (SWI)
267, 268 Examples of "diplomas" awarded by the North German Radio for the correct answers in a literary and musical competition. In colour. (GER)
269 New Year's card for a publisher. Full colour. (FRA)
270 Inside of a programme for a performance of a Shakespeare play in Adelaide. Linocut illustrations printed in red-brown. (AUS)

261–264 Umschlag (in flach aufgetragenen Farben) und drei Doppelseiten (schwarzweiss) aus einem Ausstellungskatalog des polnischen Künstlers Jan Lenica. (FRA)
265, 266 Perforierte Einladungskarte (zugeklappt und offen) zur Ausstellung schweizerischer Tapisserien im Zürcher Museum Bellerive. Weisse Schrift auf Rot. (SWI)
267, 268 «Diplome» für richtige Lösungen eines literarisch-musikalischen Rätselspiels des Norddeutschen Rundfunks. Es sind Illustrationen (farbig) der gesuchten Lösungsworte. (GER)
269 Farbige Neujahrskarte eines Verlegers (Buchillustration). (FRA)
270 Innenseite eines Programmheftes für eine Aufführung von Shakespeares *Wie es Euch gefällt* in Adelaide. Linolschnitt-Illustrationen in Rotbraun. (AUS)

261–264 Couverture (en couleurs à-plat) et trois pages doubles (en noir et blanc) d'un catalogue pour une exposition de l'œuvre de Jan Lenica à Quimper. (FRA)
265, 266 Invitation (fermée et ouverte) pour une exposition de tapisseries suisses dans un musée de Zurich. Typo rouge sur blanc. Les perforations produisent l'effet d'un tissus. (SWI)
267, 268 Exemples de «diplômes» délivrés par la radiodiffusion du Nord d'Allemagne aux personnes ayant donné une réponse correcte dans un concours littéraire et musical. En polychromie. (GER)
269 Carte de Nouvel An d'une maison d'éditions. En polychromie. (FRA)
270 Vue intérieure d'un programme pour la représentation d'une pièce de Shakespeare. Linos imprimés en brun rouge. (AUS)

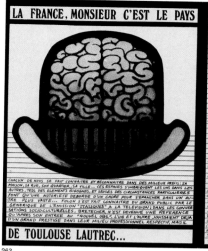

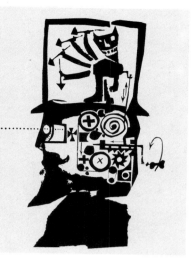

Booklets / Prospekte / Brochures

William Shakespeare's As·You·Like·It

The opening of the play has nothing of the calm and light-heartedness that, following the nineteenth-century pattern, critics still try to detect in AS YOU LIKE IT and TWELFTH NIGHT. It even seems singularly dark: a tyrant has ascended the throne, a brother persecutes his brother, love and friendship have been destroyed by ambition, the world is ruled by sheer force and money. From the duke's feast wrestlers are being carried away with broken ribs. The air is stuffy and everyone is afraid. The new prince is distrustful, suspicious, jealous of everything and everybody, unsure of his position, sensing the enemy in everyone. The only hope of salvation is escape; escape at any price as fast as one can.

This is no place; this house is but a butchery (II, 3).

The opening of the play is violent and brutal; the close — naive and idyllic, written in a few lines, deliberately devoid of motivation. Between the dark and the fairy-tale epilogue there is the Forest of Arden.

Jan Kott

Those who have faced corruption have been sickened by it; but given a forest island of temporary respite from it they have begun to reconstruct their lives and society. The natural woodland provides a morally restorative and regenerative stimulus. Here, with the astringent qualities of forest life that *"feelingly persuade me what I am"*, the Duke Senior has been able to *"translate the stubbornness of fortune 'Into so quiet and so sweet a style"*.

In like manner, Orlando and Rosalind have achieved their happiness by being able to keep their spirits high and their minds alert to the realities of the world. The play thus presents the view that human beings, given a brief respite from corruption and placed in the healthy environment of nature, can and will build a good life. In entitling his play AS YOU LIKE IT, Shakespeare seems to express his confidence that we, his audience, share his vision.

Ralph M. Sargent

The Forest of Arden mocks Arcadia and constitutes a new Arcadia. Love is the escape from cruel history to an invented forest. Shakespeare is like a Bible, he creates his own myths. The Forest of Arden is a place in which all dreams meet; it is a dream and the awakening from a dream.

Coincidentia oppositorum! The unification of all opposites!

In the Forest of Arden love is both earthly and platonically sublimated. Rosalind is Ganymede and the most girlish of girls. Constant-fickle, calm-violent, fair-dark, shy-impudent, prudent-madcap, tender-mocking, childish-grownup, cowardly-courageous, bashful-passionate. As in Leonardo, she is an almost perfect androgyny and personifies the same longing for the lost Paradise where there had as yet been no division into the male and female elements.

All this the world well knows; yet none knows well
To shun the heaven that leads men to this hell.
(Sonnet, CXXIX)

Jan Kott

Through the apparently casual flow of events in AS YOU LIKE IT may be seen some of Shakespeare's most skilled dramatic structure. In the first act he presents his sound characters as victims of a hostile world. When in the second act he brings his characters to the salubrious environment of Arden he does not divert attention to a possible clash between the good forces and the bad; in short, he eschews melodrama. Rather, he concentrates on the present situation of the characters in the forest and their formation of a new community. In bringing these characters together in "encounters" he is not bothered about improbabilities. His care is directed to bringing the right persons together at the desired time. In the progress of the play the sequence of encounters forms a virtual permutation of character confrontations, a structural feature pleasing in itself. But through this sequence, with its cumulative revelation of characters, attitudes and relationship, and conflicts, Shakespeare presents that manifold view and acceptance of diversity within pattern which makes AS YOU LIKE IT a paradigm of civilized society.

Ralph M. Sargent

AS YOU LIKE IT can be dated as of 1599 or early 1600. Shakespeare's comedy is based on the prose version of "Rosalynde, Euphues' Golden Legacie" (1590) by Thomas Lodge, which had in its turn been suggested by the pseudo-Chaucerian "Tale of Gamelyn." Shakespeare elaborates the role of Rosalind, somewhat curtails that of Orlando, and develops the character of the banished Duke from his slight role in "Rosalynde". Jacques, Touchstone, and Audrey are wholly Shakespeare's creations.

AS YOU LIKE IT has the overwhelming advantage of being written for the most part in prose instead of in blank verse, which any fool can write. And such prose! The first scene alone, with its energy of exposition, each phrase driving its meaning and feeling in up to the head at one brief, rare stroke, is worth ten acts of the ordinary Elizabethan sing-song. The popularity of Rosalind is due to three main causes. First, she only speaks blank verse for a few minutes. Second, she only wears a skirt for a few minutes. Third, she makes love to the man instead of waiting for the man to make love to her — a piece of natural history which has kept Shakespeare's heroines alive, whilst generations of properly governessed young ladies, taught to say "No" three times at least, have miserably perished.

George Bernard Shaw

The journey to the Forest of Arden was almost like Pilgrim's Progress, it was the progress to the place where you may find yourself and also find another person, and make a union with that other person. Everybody who goes to Arden is looking for themselves, and most of them find themselves or the one they love. Now I don't think this has a modern parallel because today there is a general kind of fear of abandonment of self that will lead to knowledge of somebody else . . . and today there's an ambiguity. Either you're a man and you love another man, or you're a woman and you love another woman, or you're a woman and you love a man. I mean it's fairly clear. But it was troubling in Shakespeare's time, I guess, and fascinating and enriching. We've lost interest in the marvellous paradox of quest, and joy and mirth, amusement, guilt, remorse, exquisite pleasure, all together each other and producing a kind of harmony, I don't know if we're after these kind of things at the moment, are we?

Vanessa Redgrave

271, 272 Invitation to a ball marking the centenary of a riding club in Schaffhausen; cover in cerise and brown and drawing from the inside of the folder. (SWI)
273 Catalogue for an exhibition in Nuremberg of the work of a group of artists known as *Der Kreis* (The Circle). (GER)
274 Greetings card by a French illustrator of children's books. (USA)
275 Invitation to a two-artist exhibition in Cincinnati. Printed brown. (USA)
276 Invitation to the awards presentation of the Swiss art directors club. Pink fairy floss. (SWI)
277 Illustration (full colour) from a concertina-type folder supporting a candidate for the office of mayor in the town of Americana. (BRA)
278 Mailer for *Swissair*. The pigeon brings greetings in a real capsule. (SWI)

271, 272 Einladungskarte (Vorderseite und Innenillustration) zu einem Jubiläumsball des Reitvereins Schaffhausen. Braun auf Beige mit roter 100. (SWI)
273 Katalog der Nürnberger Künstlervereinigung *Der Kreis* für eine Ausstellung in der Kunsthalle Nürnberg. (GER)
274 Glückwunschkarte einer französischen Illustratorin von Kinderbüchern. (USA)
275 Einladung zu einer Ausstellung von zwei Künstlern. Braun gedruckt. (USA)
276 Einladung zum Prämierungsfest des schweizerischen Art Directors Club. Braune Gestalt mit Zuckerwatte in Rosa. (SWI)
277 Farbige Illustration aus einem Leporelloprospekt als Werbung für einen Kandidaten für das Amt des Bürgermeisters der Stadt Americana. (BRA)
278 Direktwerbung der *Swissair* mit Brieftaube und handgefertigter Hülse. (SWI)

ARTIST / KÜNSTLER:

271, 272 Gamin Ulmer
274 Christine Chagnoux
275 Bob Cosgrove
276 Willi Rieser
277 Zélio Alves Pinto
278 Walter Linsenmaier

DESIGNER / GESTALTER:

271, 272 Gamin Ulmer
273 Gerhard Preiss
275 Bob Cosgrove

ART DIRECTOR:

275 Bob & Margie Cosgrove
276 Jörg Kissling
278 Luigi Grendene

AGENCY / AGENTUR:

271, 272 Atelier P. G. Ulmer
275 Intermedia, Inc.
276 Jörg Kissling Werbung
278 Grendene & Lanz

271

272

275

276

271, 272 Invitation à un bal à l'occasion du centenaire d'une société hippique à Schaffhouse. Couverture en cerise et brun et dessin à l'intérieur. (SWI)
273 Catalogue pour une exposition à Nuremberg présentant les œuvres d'un groupe d'artistes appelé *Der Kreis* (Le Cercle). (GER)
274 Carte de vœux d'une illustratrice française de livres d'enfant. (USA)
275 Invitation à une exposition de deux artistes à Cincinnati. Impression en brun. (USA)
276 Invitation à la présentation des lauréats du Club des directeurs artistiques de la Suisse. Brun et rose. (SWI)
277 Illustration (en couleurs) d'un dépliant en accordéon en faveur d'un candidat postulant la fonction de maire de la ville d'Americana. (BRA)
278 Publicité de *Swissair*: un pigeon voyageur porte des vœux dans une capsule vraie. (SWI)

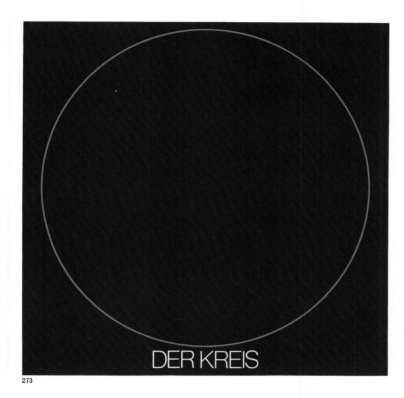

273

274

277

278

103

279

280

279 Composite female-male portrait formed by two gatefolds advertising *Spalding* skis and *Cober* boots in a sports promotion publication. (GER)
280 One side of a large tourist folder about the South Tyrol. Full colour. (AUT)
281 One side of a triangular folder (representing a sail) for the Kiel Week regatta, 1978. Full-colour illustrations. (GER)
282 Announcement of a summer festival of music and art at the resort of Sambi. Blue design. (JPN)
283 Leaflet about a book from a series of fantastic stories published by Franco Maria Ricci. Black and red on grey. (ITA)
284, 285 Complete cover of an *Esso* regional map of England, and cover illustration of another. (GBR)

279 Weibliche und männliche Gesichtshälfte auf auseinander-klappbaren Seiten, als Werbung für *Spalding*-Ski und *Cober*-Stiefel aus der Sportartikel-Werbebroschüre *Sportive*. (GER)
280 Farbige Seite aus einem grossformatigen Faltprospekt als Touristenwerbung für Südtirol. (AUT)
281 Dreieckiger (segelförmiger) Prospekt für die Kieler Woche 1978 mit farbigen Illustrationen. (GER)
282 Ankündigung eines Sommerfestivals für Musik und Kunst im japanischen Kurort Sambi. Blaue Graphik. (JPN)
283 Katalog über ein Buch aus einer Reihe phantastischer Geschichten. Schwarz und rot auf grauem Karton. (ITA)
284, 285 Vorderseite einer *Esso*-Regionalstrassenkarte von England und Umschlagillustration einer weiteren Karte. (GBR)

279 Visage masculin-féminin composé par deux pages à repli insérées dans une publication pour la promotion d'articles de sport, ici pour les skis *Spalding* et les chaussures *Cober*. (GER)
280 Panneau d'un dépliant grand format pour la promotion touristique du Haut-Adige. En polychromie. (AUT)
281 Vue d'un dépliant triangulaire (représentant une voile) pour le Festival de Kiel 1978. Illustrations couleurs. (GER)
282 Elément annonçant un festival d'été de musique et d'art organisé par la station japonaise Sambi. Design bleu. (JPN)
283 Dépliant sur un livre figurant dans une série d'histoires fantastiques publiée par Franco Maria Ricci. Noir et rouge. (ITA)
284, 285 Couverture d'une carte routière régionale de l'Angleterre et illustration de couverture d'une autre carte. (GBR)

281

2nd SAMBI FESTIVAL 1977

讃美祭
8/6-7

282

ARTIST / KÜNSTLER / ARTISTE:

279 Heinz H. Rauner
280 Karin Welponer
282 Takenobu Igarashi
283 Victor Burton
284, 285 Susanne Dolesch

DESIGNER / GESTALTER / MAQUETTISTE:

279 Helmut Mätzler
280 Dieter Graf
281 Georges Lacroix
282 Takenobu Igarashi
284, 285 Susanne Dolesch

ART DIRECTOR / DIRECTEUR ARTISTIQUE:

279 Helmut Mätzler
280 Dieter Graf
281 Georges Lacroix
282 Takenobu Igarashi
283 Franco Maria Ricci
284, 285 Susanne Dolesch

AGENCY / AGENTUR / AGENCE – STUDIO:

279 Sportive Werbeproduktion
280 Herrwerth & Partner
281 Georges Lacroix
284, 285 George Philip Printers Ltd.

283

284

285

286

Make-up Your Ad!

Ein Wettbewerb
für die Kreativsten der Kreativen.
Also für Sie!

288

289

290

You, too, can see all this and double at the
Jordan/Tamraz/Caruso
Christmas party &
10 year celebration

Wednesday, December 21, 1977 5pm to 9pm FACES 940 North Rush St.
By invitation only

291

Toutes les questions
sur la coloration
et les réponses de l'Oréal.

L'ORÉAL

287

286, 287 Illustration and complete cover of a brochure containing advice on hair dyeing, issued by L'Oréal. (BEL)
288, 289 Invitation to take part in a competition organized by newspapers and printers to encourage four-colour newspaper advertising, with detail of the artwork. (SWI)
290 Front of a card listing the members of a fashion boutique association. Flesh shades and pink. (FRA)
291 Invitation to a tenth anniversary celebration of the Jordan/ Tamraz/Caruso agency, Chicago. Green bottle. (USA)
292 One side of a full-colour folder about sneakers made by PF Industries. Also used as a poster. (USA)
293 Concertina-type Christmas card for Sherin & Matejka, Inc. Black on silver. (USA)

286, 287 Illustration und Umschlagseite einer Broschüre von L'Oréal über das Haarfärben. (BEL)
288, 289 Einladung (mit Detail) zur Teilnahme an einem Wettbewerb, veranstaltet von Zeitungen und Druckern, um den Vierfarbendruck für Zeitungsanzeigen zu fördern. (SWI)
290 Vorderseite einer Karte, auf deren Rückseite die Mitglieder des Salon Boutique aufgeführt sind. (FRA)
291 Einladung zum 10jährigen Jubiläum und Weihnachtsfeier einer Agentur. Grüne Flasche. (USA)
292 Seite eines farbigen Faltprospektes für Turn- und Tennisschuhe. Wird auch als Plakat verwendet. (USA)
293 Leporello-artige Weihnachtskarte von Sherin & Metejka, Inc. Schwarz auf Silber. (USA)

286, 287 Illustration et couverture d'une brochure de L'Oréal consacrée à la coloration des cheveux. (BEL)
288, 289 Invitation à participer à une compétition organisée par divers journaux et imprimeurs afin d'encourager la publicité couleur dans les journaux, et détail. (SWI)
290 Recto d'une carte qui présente au verso une liste des membres du Salon Boutique. (FRA)
291 Invitation pour une fête à l'occasion du 10e anniversaire d'une agence de publicité. Bouteille verte. (USA)
292 Panneau d'un dépliant polychrome pour une marque de chaussures de gymnastique et de tennis. (USA)
293 Carte de Noël en accordéon de Sherin & Matejka, Inc. Noir sur argent. (USA)

293

292

3

Magazine Covers
Magazine Illustrations
Newspaper Illustrations
Trade Magazines
House Organs
Book Covers
Annual Reports

Zeitschriften-Umschläge
Zeitschriften-Illustrationen
Zeitungs-Illustrationen
Fachzeitschriften
Hauszeitschriften
Buchumschläge
Jahresberichte

Couvertures de périodiques
Illustrations de périodiques
Illustrations de journaux
Revues professionnelles
Journaux d'entreprises
Couvertures de livres
Rapports annuels

294

295

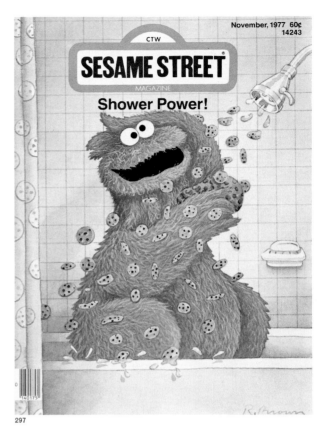

297

296

298

294–296 Covers of the magazine *TV Guide* with caricatures of personalities in the news. Full colour. (USA)
297 Cover of the children's magazine *Sesame Street*. (USA)
298 A little symbolism on the cover of the satirical magazine *Szpilki*. (POL)
299, 300 Covers of a magazine containing collections of stories. (JPN)
301, 302 Covers of the illustrated magazine *Poland,* which appears in six languages. The titles of these two covers are "Sea Holiday" and "Landscapes" (a contrasting landscape of the technical age appears on the back cover of this issue). (POL)

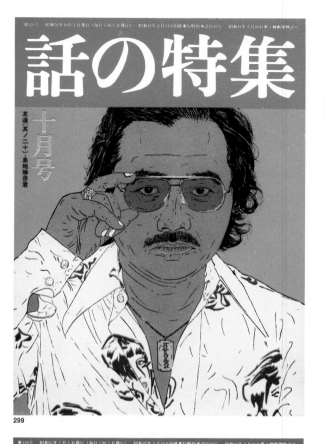

299

301

300

302

ARTIST / KÜNSTLER:

294, 295 Al Hirschfeld
296 Ronald Searle
297 Richard Brown
298 Grzegorz Stanczyk
299, 300 Tadanori Yokoo
301 Andrzej Krajewski
302 Lech Zahorski

DESIGNER / GESTALTER:

294–296 Jerry Alten
297 Richard Brown
298 Grzegorz Stanczyk
299, 300 Tadanori Yokoo

ART DIRECTOR:

294–296 Jerry Alten
297 Richard Weigand
299, 300 Tadanori Yokoo

AGENCY / AGENTUR:

297 Children's Television Workshop

PUBLISHER / VERLEGER

294–296 Triangle Publications, Inc.
297 Children's Television Workshop
298 Szpilki
299, 300 Hanashinotokushu
301, 302 Polish Interpress Agency

294–296 Mehrfarbige Umschlagseiten des *TV Guide* mit Karikaturen von dem amerikanischen TV-Publikum bekannten Persönlichkeiten. (USA)
297 Farbiger Umschlag des Heftes *Sesame Street,* das im Zusammenhang mit der TV-Kindersendung zehnmal jährlich erscheint. (USA)
298 Farbige Umschlagillustration des satirischen Magazins *Szpilki.* (POL)
299, 300 Umschlagseiten einer japanischen Zeitschrift. (JPN)
301, 302 Umschlagseiten der Zeitschrift *Polen,* die in sechs Sprachen publiziert wird. Hier sind die Themen «Ferien am Meer» und «Landschaften» (Rückseite mit kontrastierender technisierter Landschaft). (POL)

294–296 Couvertures (en couleurs) d'un programme de TV américain avec des caricatures de personnalités bien connues par les émissions télévisées. (USA)
297 Couverture de *Sesame Street,* magazine pour enfants. (USA)
298 Illustration de couverture du magazine satirique *Szpilki.* (POL)
299, 300 Couvertures d'un magazine contenant une collection d'histoires. (JPN)
301, 302 Couvertures du magazine illustré *Pologne* qui paraît en six langues. Les illustrations portent les titres «Vacances au bord de la mer» et «Paysages» (au verso de cette couverture on présente un paysage contrastant de l'ère technique). (POL)

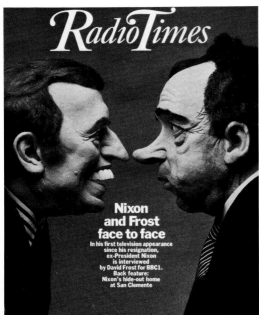

303

ARTIST / KÜNSTLER / ARTISTE:

303 Luck & Flaw
304 Roman Cieslewicz
305, 306 Mieczyslaw Wasilewski
309 Richard Hess
310 Edward Sorel

DESIGNER / GESTALTER / MAQUETTISTE:

303 David Driver
304 Roman Cieslewicz

ART DIRECTOR / DIRECTEUR ARTISTIQUE:

303 David Driver
304 Maurice Demet
305, 306 Mieczyslaw Wasilewski

PUBLISHER / VERLEGER / EDITEUR:

303 BBC Publications
304 Formation Permanente
305, 306 Problemy
307–310 Time, Inc.

304

Magazine Covers
Zeitschriftenumschläge
Couvertures de périodiques

303 Cover of the *Radio Times* announcing a television interview of ex-President Nixon by David Frost, both shown as three-dimensional puppets. (GBR)
304 Cover of a review of further education. (FRA)
305, 306 Back covers of a popular science monthly, relating to science fiction features. Black on white. (POL)
307–310 Four full-colour covers for the weekly political and news magazine *Time*. The references are to a cooking craze in the USA, to the Panama Canal, *The New York Times* and Jimmy Carter on the international stage. (USA)

303 Farbige Umschlagillustration des Radio- und TV-Programmheftes *Radio Times*, mit Bezug auf das erste Fernsehinterview mit Richard Nixon nach dessen Rücktritt. (GBR)
304 Umschlagillustration einer Monatszeitschrift über Weiterbildungsmöglichkeiten. (FRA)
305, 306 Zwei Umschlagseiten der polnischen Zeitschrift *Problemy*. Die Illustrationen (schwarzweiss) beziehen sich auf Science-Fiction-Geschichten in diesen Ausgaben. (POL)
307–310 Farbige Umschlagseiten der Wochenzeitschrift *Time* zu aktuellen nationalen und internationalen Themen. (USA)

303 Couverture d'un programme de radio et de télévision annonçant un interview de David Frost avec l'ex-président Nixon, présentés ici en marionnettes tridimensionnelles. (GBR)
304 Illustration de couverture de la revue mensuelle *Formation Permanente*. (FRA)
305, 306 Verso de deux couvertures d'un mensuel avec référence à des histoires de science fiction. Noir et blanc. (POL)
307–310 Couvertures polychromes de *Time,* magazine d'information politique. Elles se réfèrent à des sujets d'actualité sur le plan national et international. (USA)

305

306

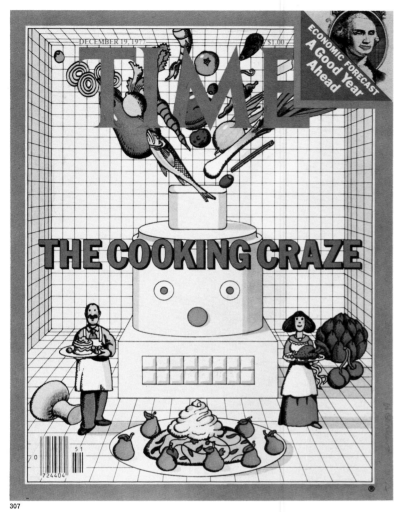

307

308

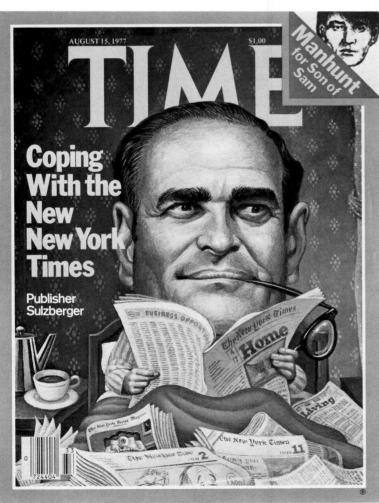

309

310

311

312

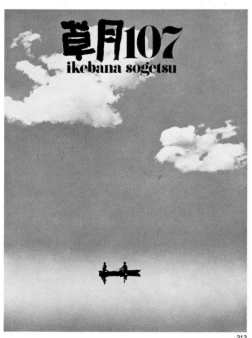

313

314

311, 312 Two covers of the satirical weekly *Nebelspalter*. One is a winter issue, the other refers to the "television newspaper" of the future. (SWI)
313 Cover of an issue of a magazine devoted to *ikebana*. Blue sky, green water. (JPN)
314 Cover of a monthly magazine for children. Yellow title, blue ground, green apple and pail. (FRA)
315, 316 Two covers for the literary monthly *The New Yorker*. Objects in Fig. 316 in pastel shades. (USA)
317, 318 Cover and artwork of an issue of *New York* containing an article on recent fighting in Vietnam. (USA)
319 "Wet paint." Cover of an issue of the satirical weekly *Nebelspalter* (literally "Mist-cleaver"). (SWI)

311, 312 Farbige Umschlagseiten der satirischen Zeitschrift *Nebelspalter*. (SWI)
313 Umschlag eines japanischen Magazins. Blauer Himmel in Weiss/Grün übergehend, mit schwarzem Boot. (JPN)
314 Farbiger Umschlag eines monatlich erscheinenden Heftes für Kinder. (FRA)
315, 316 Umschlagseiten des amerikanischen Kultur-Magazins *The New Yorker*. (USA)
317, 318 Gesamtwiedergabe des Umschlags und Illustration der Wochenzeitschrift *New York*. «Der Krieg, den wir zurückgelassen haben». (USA)
319 Umschlag des Magazins *Nebelspalter*. (SWI)

311, 312 Couvertures de l'hebdomadaire satirique *Nebelspalter*. L'une a été conçue pour un numéro d'hiver, l'autre fait allusion au «journal sur l'écran» de l'avenir. (SWI)
313 Couverture d'un numéro d'un magazine consacré à *ikebana*. Ciel bleu, eau verte. (JPN)
314 Couverture du mensuel *Pomme d'api*, magazine destiné aux enfants. Titre jaune, fond bleu, pomme et seau en vert. (FRA)
315, 316 Deux couvertures du mensuel littéraire *The New Yorker*. Fig. 316 en tons pastel. (USA)
317, 318 D'un numéro de *New York* contenant un article sur la situation politique actuelle au Viêt-nam. (USA)
319 «Peinture fraîche.» Couverture de l'hebdomadaire satirique *Nebelspalter*. (SWI)

ARTIST / KÜNSTLER:

311, 312 Barth
313 Yusaku Kamekura
314 Nicole Lafeuille
315, 316 R.O. Blechman
317, 318 Jean Lagarrigue
319 Jüsp

DESIGNER / GESTALTER:

313 Yusaku Kamekura
314 Michèle Isvy
315, 316 R.O. Blechman
317, 318 Jean-Claude Suarès

ART DIRECTOR:

311, 312, 319 Franz Mächler
313 Yusaku Kamekura
314 Mijo Beccaria
315, 316 Lee Lorenz
317, 318 Jean Lagarrigue

PUBLISHER / VERLEGER / EDITEUR:

311, 312, 319 Nebelspalter-Verlag
313 Sogetsu Shuppan Inc.
314 Bayard-Presse
315, 316 The New Yorker
Magazine, Inc.
317, 318 New York Magazine

Magazine Covers
Zeitschriftenumschläge
Couvertures de périodiques

317

315

316

318

319

320 Double spread opening a detective story in the German version of *Playboy* magazine. (GER)
321 Illustration for a humorous article in *Playboy* on incidents surrounding the making of a film. (USA)
322 Opening of a feature in the French edition of *Playboy*. Red and purple shades, yellow type. FRA)
323 Double spread in full colour opening an article in *Playboy* on international terror. In one eye, green continents on a blue globe. (USA)
324 Full-page illustration for a feature entitled «Secrets d'alcôve» in the French edition of *Playboy*. (FRA)

320 Doppelseitige Illustration zu einem Krimi aus dem deutschen *Playboy*-Magazin. (GER)
321 Illustration zu einem humoristischen Artikel über die Begleitumstände der Dreharbeiten für einen Film, im amerikanischen *Playboy*. (USA)
322 Doppelseite in Violett-, Rot- und Blautönen aus dem französischen *Playboy*. (FRA)
323 Farbige Doppelseite als Einleitung zu einem *Playboy*-Artikel über internationalen Terror. (USA)
324 Ganzseitige Illustration zu einer Geschichte im *Playboy*: «Geheimnisse der Alkoven». (FRA)

320 Première page double d'un roman policier publié dans l'édition allemande de *Playboy*. (GER)
321 Illustration d'un article humoristique de *Playboy* sur les incidents se passant en tournant un film. (USA)
322 Première page double d'un article publié dans l'édition française de *Playboy*. Tons rouges et lilas, typographie jaune. (FRA)
323 Page double (en couleurs) d'un article de *Playboy* traitant du terrorisme sur le plan international. Dans l'œil, continents verts sur un globe bleu. (USA)
324 *Playboy* français: «Secrets d'alcôve». (FRA)

321

ARTIST / KÜNSTLER:

320 Dieter Ziegenfeuter
321 Randall Enos
322 Cyril Arnstam
323 Eraldo Carugati

DESIGNER / GESTALTER:

323 Len Willis

ART DIRECTOR:

320 Rainer Wörtmann
321 Bob Post
322, 324 Régis Pagniez
323 Arthur Paul

PUBLISHER / VERLEGER:

320 Heinrich Bauer
    Verlag
321, 323 Playboy
    Enterprises, Inc.
322, 324 Publications
    Filipacchi

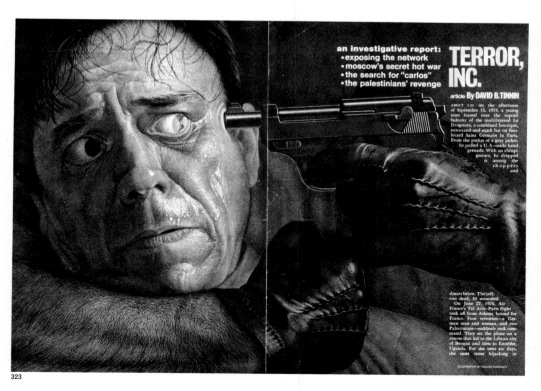

323

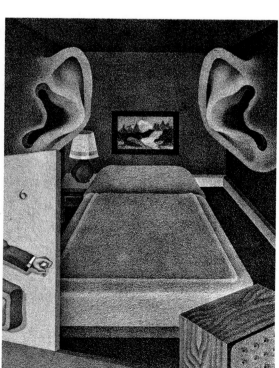

324

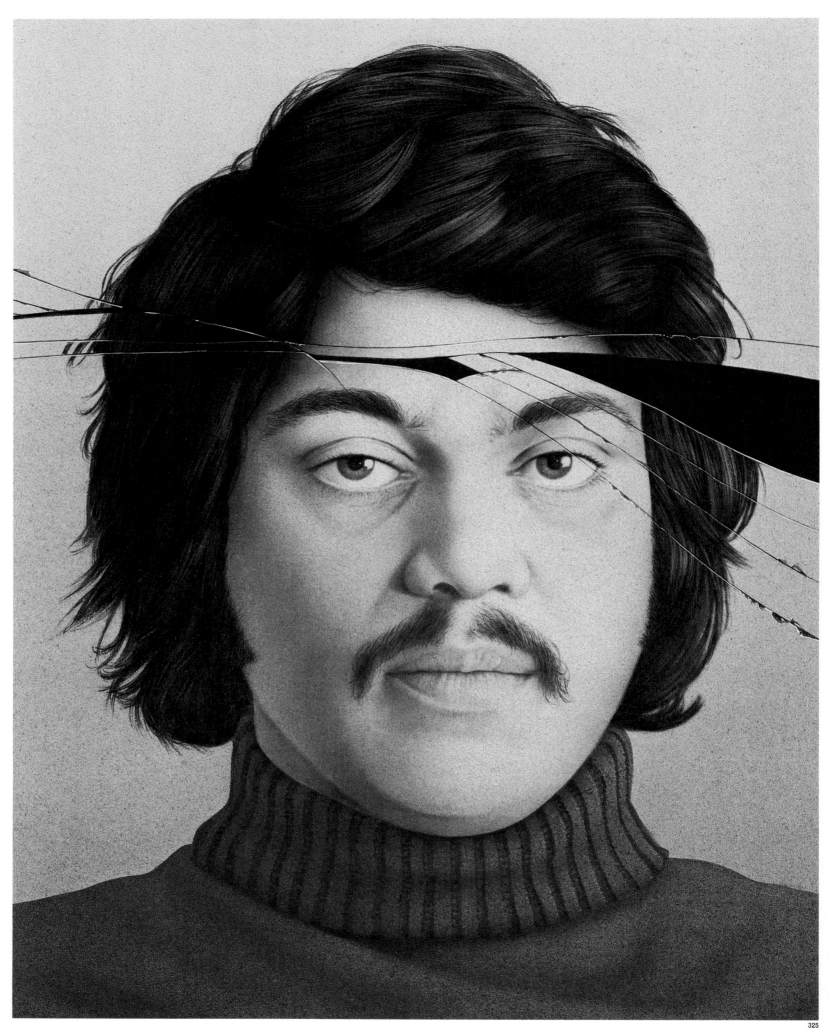

326

"I DON'T MAKE HOCUS-POCUS"

327

325 Full-page illustration (reproduced in actual size) from an article in *Playboy* on the death of Freddie Prinze. (USA)
326, 327 Illustration and opening of an article on a clairvoyant in *Playboy*. (USA)
328 Opening of a story taken from a new thriller by Graham Greene, in *Playboy*. (USA)
329 Opening of a story with a Russian background published in the German *Playboy*. (GER)

325 Ganzseitige Illustration (Originalgrösse) zu einem Artikel im *Playboy* über den Tod von Freddie Prinze. (USA)
326, 327 Illustration und Doppelseite zu einem Artikel im *Playboy* über einen Hellseher. (USA)
328 Farbige Doppelseite zu einem Spionage-Roman von Graham Greene, aus *Playboy*. (USA)
329 Einleitende Doppelseite zu einer Erzählung mit russischem Hintergrund, aus *Playboy*. (GER)

325 Illustration pleine page d'un article de *Playboy* sur la mort de Freddie Prinze. (USA)
326, 327 Illustration et première page d'un article sur un clairvoyant. De *Playboy*. (USA)
328 Page double introduisant une nouvelle faisant partie d'un nouveau roman policier de Graham Greene. Elément du magazine *Playboy*. (USA)
329 Première page double d'une nouvelle se déroulant en Russie, publiée dans *Playboy*. (GER)

ARTIST / KÜNSTLER / ARTISTE:
325 Alan Magee
326, 327 Eraldo Carugati
328 John O'Leary
329 Bengt Fosshag

DESIGNER / GESTALTER / MAQUETTISTE:
328 John O'Leary/Kerig Pope
329 Karl W. Henschel/Bengt Fosshag

ART DIRECTOR / DIRECTEUR ARTISTIQUE:
325 Arthur Paul
326, 327 Arthur Paul/Gordon Mortensen
328 Arthur Paul/Kerig Pope
329 Rainer Wörtmann

AGENCY / AGENTUR / AGENCE – STUDIO:
329 Studio Sign

PUBLISHER / VERLEGER / EDITEUR:
325–328 Playboy Enterprises, Inc.
329 Heinrich Bauer Verlag

328

329

330

ARTIST / KÜNSTLER / ARTISTE:

330 Erhard Göttlicher
331 Brad Holland
332 Dennis Magdich
333 Kathy Calderwood
334 Charles Bragg
335 Reagan Wilson

DESIGNER / GESTALTER / MAQUETTISTE:

330 Hans van Blommestein
332 Kerig Pope
334 Bob Post
335 Norm Schaefer

ART DIRECTOR / DIRECTEUR ARTISTIQUE:

330 Dick de Moei
331–335 Arthur Paul

AGENCY / AGENTUR / AGENCE – STUDIO:

330 Avenue

PUBLISHER / VERLEGER / EDITEUR:

330 De Geillustreerde pers b.v.
331–335 Playboy Enterprises, Inc.

332

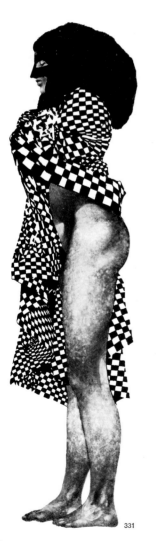

331

333

334

335

330 Opening of an article about anatomy and destiny published in *Avenue*. (NLD)
331 Illustration for a series of "ribald classics" reprinted in *Playboy*. (USA)
332 Illustration (full colour) for an article in *Playboy* on Raquel Welch. (USA)
333 Illustration for a story called "Adulterer's Luck" in *Playboy*. (USA)
334 Double-spread illustration opening an article in *Playboy* on the commodities market ("You've really got to be an animal"). (USA)
335 Illustration (full colour) for a *Playboy* preview of American football. (USA)

330 Farbige Doppelseite mit einem Artikel über Anatomie und Schicksal, aus der Zeitschrift *Avenue*. (NLD)
331 Detail einer Illustration für eine Reihe «Klassiker», aus *Playboy*. (USA)
332 Ganzseitige farbige Illustration zu einem *Playboy*-Artikel über Raquel Welch. (USA)
333 Illustration für eine Geschichte im *Playboy*, «Glück des Ehebrechers». (USA)
334 Illustration zu einem *Playboy*-Artikel über den Konsumgütermarkt. (USA)
335 Illustration zu einem *Playboy*-Artikel über amerikanischen Fussball. (USA)

330 Page double introduisant un article publié dans le magazine *Avenue* sur l'anatomie et le destin. (NLD)
331 Illustration pour une série «d'histoires grivoises» publiées dans *Playboy*. (USA)
332 Illustration (en couleurs) pour un article de *Playboy* sur Raquel Welch. (USA)
333 Illustration pour une nouvelle intitulée «La chance de l'adultère». (USA)
334 Illustration sur page double introduisant un article de *Playboy* consacré au marché d'articles de consommation. (USA)
335 Illustration (en couleurs) figurant dans un aperçu du football américain. (USA)

Magazine Illustrations

336

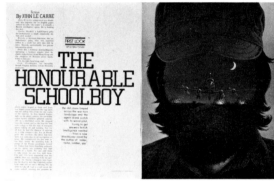

338

ARTIST / KÜNSTLER / ARTISTE:

336 Cyril Arnstam
337 Josse Goffin
338–340 Alan Magee
341, 342 Hans-Ulrich Osterwalder

DESIGNER / GESTALTER / MAQUETTISTE:

337 Joe Brooks
338–340 Kerig Pope

ART DIRECTOR / DIRECTEUR ARTISTIQUE:

336 Régis Pagniez
337 Joe Brooks
338–340 Arthur Paul
341, 342 Rainer Wörtmann

PUBLISHER / VERLEGER / EDITEUR:

336 Publications Filipacchi
337 Penthouse International Ltd.
338–340 Playboy Enterprises, Inc.
341, 342 Heinrich Bauer Verlag

336 Illustration facing the opening of an article in the French *Playboy* entitled "Are the French calves (= oafs)?". (FRA)
337 Illustration for a story in *Penthouse* about a women's restaurant. Blue shades, polychrome eye and earring. (USA)
338–340 Opening double spread and two full-page illustrations from an excerpt from a new novel about espionage published in *Playboy*. Full colour. (USA)
341, 342 Illustrations (both in full colour) from an article in the German edition of *Playboy* about "supertrips" to Kenya, the Maldives and Greenland. (GER)

336 Detail einer Illustration im französischen *Playboy* zu einem Artikel mit dem Titel «Sind die Franzosen Rindviecher?». (FRA)
337 Farbige Illustration aus *Penthouse* zu einer Geschichte mit dem Titel «Das Frauen-Restaurant». (USA)
338–340 Doppelseite als Beginn und farbige Illustrationen zu einem neuen Spionage-Roman von John Le Carré, aus *Playboy*. (USA)
341, 342 Farbige Illustrationen zu ausgefallenen Reisevorschlägen im *Playboy*. Abb. 341 bezieht sich auf eine Grönlandreise, Abb. 342 ist eine Collage aller Reisevorschläge. (GER)

336 Illustration introduisant un article intitulé «Les Français sont-ils des vaux?». Elément de l'édition française de *Playboy*. (FRA)
337 Illustration du magazine *Penthouse* pour un article consacré à un restaurant pour femmes. En polychromie. (USA)
338–340 Première page double et deux illustrations pleines pages d'un extrait d'un nouveau roman d'espionnage publié dans le magazine *Playboy*. En polychromie. (USA)
341, 342 Illustrations (en couleurs) tirées d'un article de l'édition allemande de *Playboy* sur les «voyages sensationnels» au Kenya, aux Maledives et au Groenland. (GER)

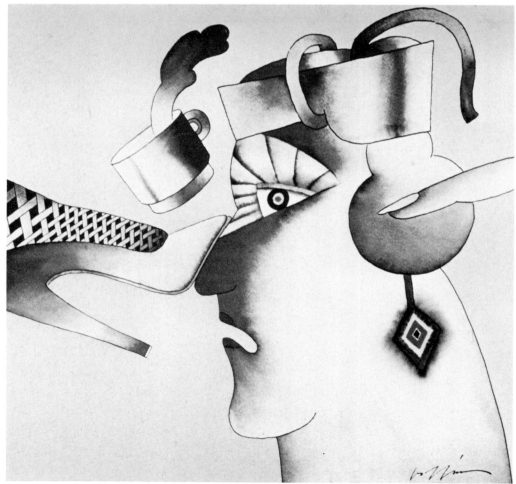

337

Magazine Illustrations
Zeitschriften-Illustrationen
Illustrations de périodiques

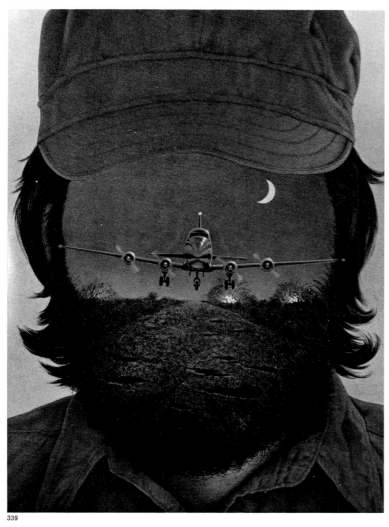

339

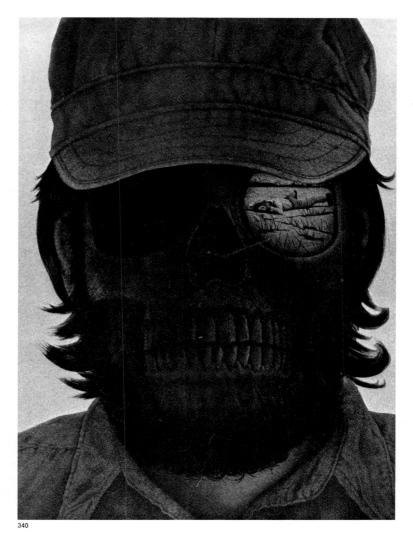

340

341

342

DIE NACKTEN UND DIE BLOSSEN

zwei ziehen aus,
sylt und seine frauen zu erobern
erzählung von
GÜNTER HERBURGER

ALS ICH ERWACHTE, fuhr der Zug in einer langgestreckten Kurve über das Meer. Am Fuße des Steindamms brachen sich kleine Schaumkronen, Wind schlug ins geöffnete Abteil, während Möwen, die sich schreiend vom Himmel herabstürzten, jeden, der sich ein wenig aus dem Fenster beugte, angreifen zu wollen schienen. Kurz vor dem Aufprall jagten sie wieder hoch und über die Wagendächer hinweg. An den Zug waren doppelstöckige, offene Loren voller Autos angehängt worden. Die lange, schwere Eisenbahnschlange, die über das Wasser glitt, glich einer Invasion. Wir eroberten die Insel der Sehnsucht. Der Schlamm des

Wattenmeers roch nach Versäumnis, das endlich eingeholt würde. Die ziehenden Wolken am blauen Himmel sahen wie Gondeln aus, in denen Verbündete saßen. Dort am Horizont lag Land in der nadelspitz salzenen Luft. Nachdem ich in Westerland ausgestiegen war, wo zwischen alten Ziegelhäusern Betonbauten standen, und in einer Bank die letzten Dollars, die ich besaß, gewechselt hatte, kaufte ich mir ein einfaches Fahrrad. Ich machte mich auf den Weg zu Charly. Und schon hatte der Wind wieder gedreht, wie immer, wenn man sich auf ein Fahrrad setzte. Er kam nicht mehr von der See, sondern

vom Festland her. Ich mußte mich auf die Pedale stellen und mit äußerster Kraft treten, um vorwärtszukommen, obwohl die Straße eben verlief. Es war beinahe schon ein Sturm, der mich festhielt, dann wieder zur Seite drückte, mir das Hemd aufriß, mit Schlägen meinen Nacken bearbeitete und manchmal Schauer von Sandkörnern über mich schüttete, als hagelte es. Ich strengte mich landeinwärts an, dem Watt, dem Schlick, einer niedrig stehenden Brühe entgegen. Kälber drängten sich um einen Wasserwagen, Vögel schossen pfeilschnell über das Gras und ließen sich wieder hochtragen. Ein Reiter,

343

Magazine Illustrations

343 Double spread opening a story ("The Naked and the Bare") about the island of Sylt in the German *Playboy*. Pink and flesh shades on a pale blue ground. (GER)
344, 345 Illustration and complete double spread opening an article in the French edition of *Playboy* on the Concorde—"the European challenge?". (FRA)
346 Double spread from a publication of the National Association of Educational Broadcasters, about a convention they had held in Las Vegas. (USA)
347 "Give me my money back, J. Edgar Hoover." Double spread with colour illustration from an article on the FBI. (BRA)
348 Double spread from an annual report of the *Weyerhaeuser* company, who present themselves as a "forest products industry". Full colour. (USA)

343 Farbige Doppelseite als Einleitung zu einer Erzählung über Sylt und seine Frauen, aus der deutschen Ausgabe des *Playboy*. (GER)
344, 345 Illustration und ganze Doppelseite für einen Artikel mit dem Titel «Concorde, die europäische Herausforderung?», der Aufschluss darüber geben will, was sich zwischen Amerikanern und Europäern auf diesem Gebiet abspielt; aus dem französischen *Playboy*. (FRA)
346 Doppelseite aus einer Publikation des nationalen Verbandes der Bildungs-Sender mit Bericht über ihre Tagung in Las Vegas. (USA)
347 Einleitende Doppelseite zu dem Artikel «Mr. J. Edgar Hoover, ich will mein Geld zurück haben». (Hoover war sehr lange Chef des FBI.) (BRA)
348 Farbige Doppelseite zu dem Thema «forstwirtschaftliche Industrie». (USA)

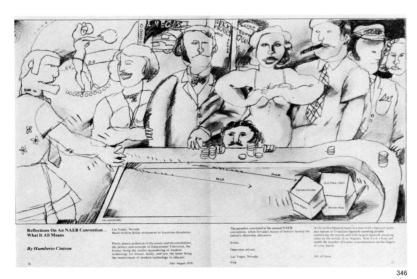

Me dá meu dinheiro de volta, J. Edgar Hoover!

Durante os 48 anos em que J. Edgar Hoover foi o chefe supremo do FBI, o cinema, a televisão e os quadrinhos ensinaram aos americanos (e, por extensão, a todos nós, os vizinhos mais pobres) que os agentes do Federal Bureau of Investigation eram corajosos, intrépidos, valentes, bonzinhos, incorruptíveis.
Aconteceu que o cinema, a televisão e os quadrinhos estavam mentindo: não era nada disso.

Texto de Sérgio Augusto

346   347

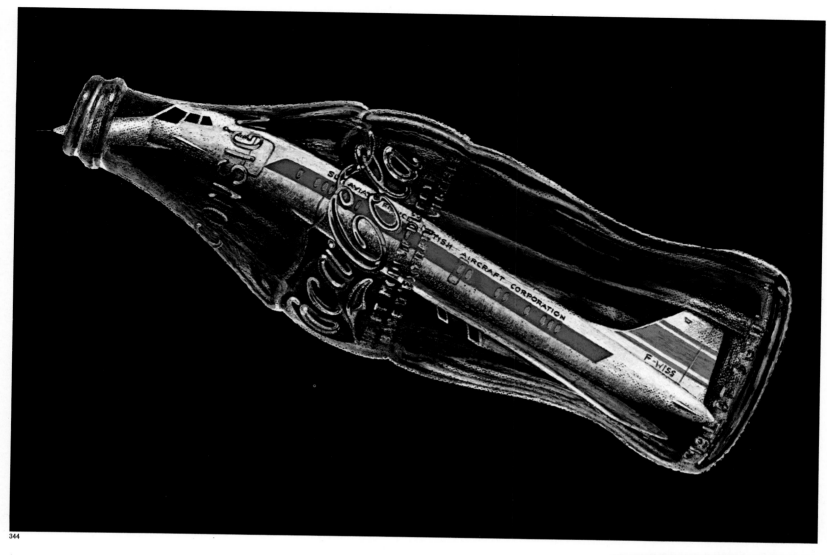

344

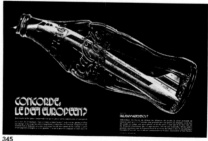

345

343 Page double introduisant un article intitulé «Les nus et les dénudés», article traitant de l'île de Sylt en Allemagne du Nord. Tons roses sur fond bleu pâle. (GER)
344, 345 Illustration et page double complète introduisant un article dans l'édition française de *Playboy* sur la Concorde. (FRA)
346 Page double de la publication d'une association nationale de stations de radiodiffusion pédagogique contenant un rapport sur une conférence à Las Vegas. (USA)
347 «Rends-moi mon argent, J. Edgar Hoover.» Page double avec illustration en couleurs figurant dans un article sur le FBI. (BRA)
348 Page double d'un rapport annuel de la société *Weyerhaeuser* qui se présente en tant que compagnie industrielle de produits forestiers. En polychromie. (USA)

348

ARTIST / KÜNSTLER / ARTISTE:

343 Erhard Göttlicher
344, 345 Cyril Arnstam
346 Salvador Bru
347 Sandra Abdalla
348 Jim Hays

DESIGNER / GESTALTER / MAQUETTISTE:

343 George Guther
346 Salvador Bru

ART DIRECTOR / DIRECTEUR ARTISTIQUE:

343 Rainer Wörtmann
344, 345 Régis Pagniez
346 Salvador Bru
347 Fernando Lion
348 John Van Dyke/Vic Warren

AGENCY / AGENTUR / AGENCE – STUDIO:

346 Bru Assoc.
348 Van Dyke Warren

PUBLISHER / VERLEGER / EDITEUR:

343 Heinrich Bauer Verlag
344, 345 Publications Filipacchi
346 National Assoc. of Educational Broadcasters
347 Status
348 Weyerhaeuser Co.

126

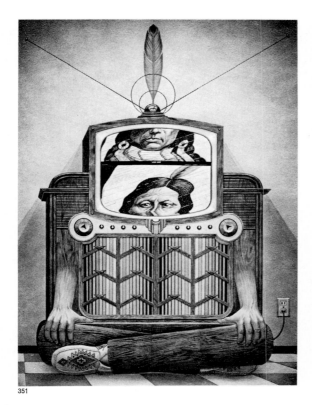

351

352

349, 350 Illustration in actual size and complete spread from an article in *Penthouse* on Vietnam veterans fighting in Rhodesia. (USA)
351 Full-page illustration in full colour from an article in *Penthouse* on the «elimination of TV». (USA)
352 Full-page colour illustration for a story in *Penthouse*. (USA)
353 Full-page illustration for a feature in *Penthouse* entitled "Polygamy". Full colour. (USA)

349, 350 Illustration und Doppelseite eines Artikels in *Penthouse* über Vietnam-Veteranen, die in Rhodesien kämpfen. (USA)
351 Farbige, ganzseitige Illustration zu einem Artikel in *Penthouse* mit dem Titel «Eliminierung des Fernsehens». (USA)
352 Farbige Illustration (Grün und Rot dominieren) zu einer Geschichte in *Penthouse* mit dem Titel «Der Leibwächter». (USA)
353 Farbige Illustration zum Thema Polygamie in *Penthouse*. (USA)

349, 350 Illustration en grandeur nature et page double d'un article du magazine *Penthouse* sur les anciens combattants du Viêt-nam qui se battent en Rhodésie. (USA)
351 Illustration pleine page (en couleurs) figurant dans un article de *Penthouse* sur «l'élimination de la télévision». (USA)
352 Illustration pleine page tirée d'un article de *Penthouse*. (USA)
353 Illustration d'un article de *Penthouse* intitulé «Polygamie». (USA)

ARTIST / KÜNSTLER / ARTISTE:
349, 350 Wilson McLean
351—353 Sean Early

DESIGNER / GESTALTER / MAQUETTISTE:
352 Susan Howe

ART DIRECTOR / DIRECTEUR ARTISTIQUE:
349—353 Joe Brooks

PUBLISHER / VERLEGER / EDITEUR:
349—351, 353 Penthouse International Ltd.
352 Penthouse Publications Ltd.

349   350

353

356

355

BRIE ET COMPAGNIE (I)

357

354, 355 From a series of *fiches-consommation* for cookery published in the French women's magazine *Elle,* here showing a cabbage from a series of vegetables and a Brie cheese from a series of dairy products. (FRA)
356 Illustration (full colour) for a series of detective stories in the women's magazine *Elle.* (FRA)
357 Illustration for an article on the television comedian John Cleese published in *The Sunday Times Magazine.* (GBR)
358 Portrait of the Marquis de Sade for an article on him published in *Prisma* magazine. In colour. (SWE)

354 Illustration für die Seite «Der Kohl» aus der Folge «Gartengemüse», die in *Elle* veröffentlicht wurde. (FRA)
355 Illustration für «Brie & Co.» aus der Folge «Die grünen Weiden» in der Zeitschrift *Elle.* Kombination von Photographie (Käse und Messer) und gemaltem Hintergrund. (FRA)
356 Farbige Illustration, Photomontage auf gemaltem Hintergrund, für eine Serie von Kriminalgeschichten in *Elle.* (FRA)
357 Farbige Illustration zu einem Artikel in *The Sunday Times Magazine* über den TV-Komiker John Cleese. (GBR)
358 Marquis de Sade: Illustration aus *Prisma.* (SWE)

354, 355 D'une série d'illustrations figurant en tête des *Fiches-consommation* du magazine féminin *Elle.* Fig. 354: «Chou vert» de la série des «Légumes du potager»; fig. 355: «Brie et compagnie» de la série «Verts pâturages». (FRA)
356 Illustration (en couleurs) pour la série des «énigmes policières», publiée dans le magazine *Elle.* (FRA)
357 Illustration figurant dans un article consacré au comédien John Cleese. Elément du *Sunday Times Magazine.* (GBR)
358 Portrait du Marquis de Sade pour illustrer un article consacré à lui dans le magazine *Prisma.* En polychromie. (SWE)

ARTIST / KÜNSTLER / ARTISTE:

354, 355 Manfred Seelow
356 François Duffort
357 Robert Grossman
358 Dan Jonsson

DESIGNER / GESTALTER / MAQUETTISTE:

356 Roland Leduc
358 Dan Jonsson

ART DIRECTOR / DIRECTEUR ARTISTIQUE:

354–356 Peter Knapp/Antoine Kieffer
357 Michael Rand
358 Dan Jonsson

AGENCY / AGENTUR / AGENCE – STUDIO:

358 Dan Jonsson AB

PUBLISHER / VERLEGER / EDITEUR:

354–356 Elle/France Editions et Publications
357 The Sunday Times
358 Prisma

Magazine Illustrations

358

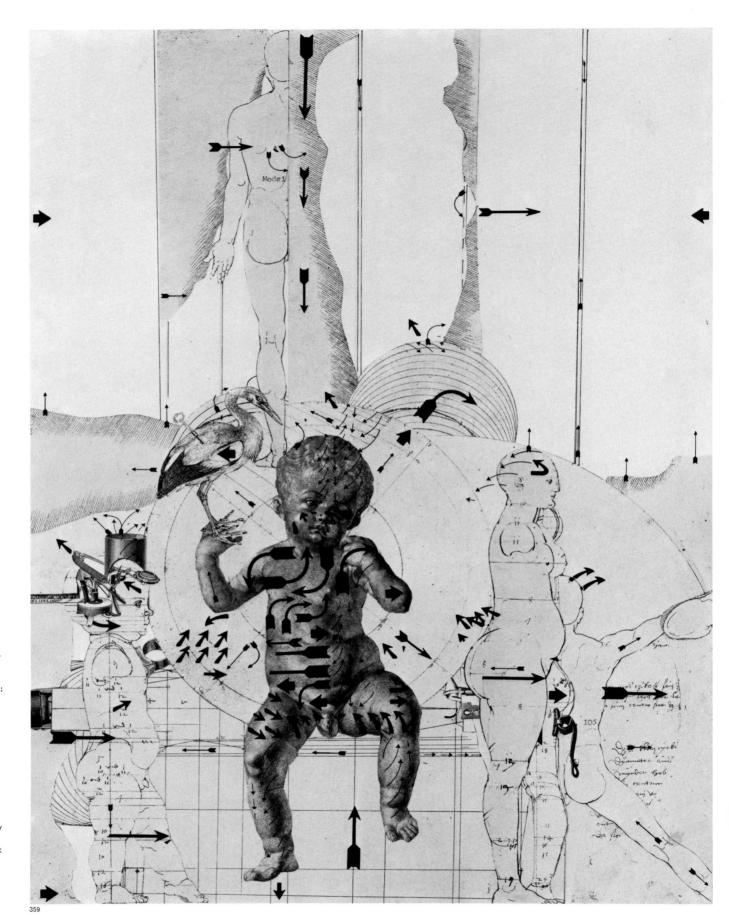

ARTIST / KÜNSTLER
359 Anita Siegel
360 Beate Brömse
361 Mark Alan Stamaty
362, 363 Tom Wilson

DESIGNER / GESTALTER:
359 Milton Glaser
362, 363 Tom Wilson

ART DIRECTOR:
359 Walter Bernard
360 Karl-Heinz
    Wendlandt
361 Tom Bentkowski
362, 363 Robert Banks

AGENCY / AGENTUR
362, 363 U.S.
    Information Agency

PUBLISHER / VERLEGER:
359, 361 New York
    Magazine
360 Van Nouhuys
362, 363 Economic
    Impact Magazine

359

Magazine Illustrations

ABENTEUER ATLANTIK

Seit Dr. Santiago Genovés im Früh-sommer verkündete, er wolle sich «möglichst noch in diesem Jahr» auf einem Floß «ganz allein» von Afrika nach Amerika treiben lassen, ist das Atlantikfieber erneut ausge-brochen. Überall denken wieder Men-schen daran, sich möglichst sonderbare und ungemütliche Arten aus diesem Gewässer zu überqueren.

Wenn Vernunft die Geste seiner Gedanken bestimmte, dann müßte der mexikanische Wis-senschaftler Genovés den Atlantik wie die Pest meiden. Denn der Mann hat zu Oscar Anfang der 70er Jahre bereits zweimal mit einem Floß bewältigt und dabei jedesmal eine Gruppe gleich-gesinnter Männer und Frauen mitgenommen. Die Fahrten trugen ihm damals zweifelhaften Schlagzeilen-Ruhm ein: «Gruppensex hoch zur See» ein und ver-schafften ihm zurückblick das äußerst unerfreuli-che Erlebnis, wie Menschen unter den Strapazen einer solchen Tour, in der Enge eines solchen Floßes, zu Bestien werden.

Doch wie als Lemminge absichtlich ins Verder-ben stürzen, so sammelt der Doktor aus Mexiko jetzt erneut Geld, um abermals – diesmal allein – eine Floßfahrt über das mörderische Gewässer zu bestehen. Genovés will unbedingt «das menschliche Verhalten unter den Bedingungen der totalen Isolation studieren» – doch wenn es Genovés wirklich nur um die Auslotung der menschlichen Psyche in Situationen extremer Belastung ginge, dann brauchte er nur den deut-schen Arzt Dr. Hannes Lindemann zu fragen, der den Atlantik insgesamt dreimal – zweimal da-von allein – überquert hat.

Lindemann paddelte 1955 im Einbaum von Eu-ropa nach St. Thomas; auf den Antillen und wie-derholte diesen Ausflug 1976 in einem Faltboot – sicher nicht, weil s so schön war. Was er dabei in 72 Tagen unsäglicher physischer und psychi-scher Strapazen erlebte, hat er detailliert und sachlich berichtet.

Schon am dritten Tag war er nahe daran schlapp-zumachen und fühlte Selbstgespräche wie: «Du, spring über Bord!» Wer kümmert sich denn schon um dich! Und zugleich dröhnten ihm die Sätze im Kopf, die er sich vor dem Abenteuer sugge-stiv, gleichsam als posthypnotische Befehle, eingehämmert hatte: «Nicht aufgeben! Kurs West! Keine Hilfe annehmen!» und siehe da, er wurde getröstet. Denn die «Spritzdecke» seines Faltbootes begann auf ihn zu sprechen und be-ruhigte ihn: «Schlaf ruhig ein bißchen! Ich paß schon auf!»

In der folgenden Zeit bekam Hannes Lindemann

360

361

362

363

359 Illustration from an article in *New York* magazine on the problems of sperm banks. Buff shades. (USA)
360 Double spread opening an article in the German edition of *Lui* on adventurous Atlantic crossings. (GER)
361 Black-and-white illustration for an article in *New York* magazine about a crossword solving competition. (USA)
362, 363 Full-page illustrations from an issue of the quarterly *Economic Impact* devoted to water: Fig. 362 (black and white) faces an article on "Our Liquid Future", Fig. 363 (full colour) one on "Water and Food". (USA)

359 Illustration zu einem Artikel aus dem Magazin *New York* über das Problem künstlicher Befruchtung. (USA)
360 Doppelseite mit farbiger Illustration zu einem Artikel über abenteuerliche Atlantiküberquerungen in *Lui*. (GER)
361 Schwarzweiss-Illustration zu einem Artikel in *New York* über einen Kreuzworträtsel-Wettbewerb. (USA)
362, 363 Schwarzweiss-Illustration zu einem Artikel von Jacques Cousteau über die Zukunft der Gewässer und farbige Illustration zu einem Artikel über das Thema «Wasser und Nahrung» aus *Economic Impact*. (USA)

359 Illustration figurant dans un article du magazine *New York* sur les problèmes de l'insémination artificielle. (USA)
360 Page introduisant un article de l'édition allemande de *Lui* sur les traversées aventureuses de l'Atlantique. (GER)
361 Illustration en noir et blanc tirée d'un article sur une compétition de mots-croisistes. (USA)
362, 363 Illustrations pleines pages d'un numéro du magazine économique trimestriel *Impact* consacré à l'eau: fig. 362 (noir-blanc), article intitulé «Notre avenir liquide»; fig. 363 (en cou-leurs), article intitulé «Eau et alimentation». (USA)

364

AS ENFERMEIRAS DO SEXO

A impotência, a ejaculação precoce e outras deficiências sexuais têm novo auxílio terapêutico: uma ajudante ensinando o amor ao paciente. E os resultados são os melhores.

Por Marilyn Elias
Tradução de Ângela Cozetti

ARTIST / KÜNSTLER / ARTISTE:

364 Vilma Gomez
365 Beate Brömse
366 Steve Pietzsch
367 Zengo Yoshida
368, 369 Wilson McLean

DESIGNER / GESTALTER / MAQUETTISTE:

367 Saul Bass

ART DIRECTOR / DIRECTEUR ARTISTIQUE:

364 Licínio de Melo
365 Wolfgang Rollmann
366, 368, 369 Joe Brooks
367 Art Goodman

364 Page opening an article in the magazine *Ele* on a new remedy for sexual disorders. Monochrome. (BRA)
365 Full-page illustration for a Christmas story about a girl who would like a doll, from *Madame* magazine. (GER)
366 Double spread opening an article in *Penthouse* on false statements made by Jimmy Carter. Full colour. (USA)
367 Illustration for a feature in the magazine *Creatividad*. Black and white. (USA)
368, 369 Illustration and complete double spread from a story in *Penthouse* about a woman who changes her personality. (USA)

364 Illustration zu einem Artikel in *Ele* über ein neues Mittel gegen sexuelle Störungen. Braun auf gelbem Papier. (BRA)
365 Illustration zu einer Weihnachtsgeschichte in der Zeitschrift *Madame*: «Ein Mädchen wünscht sich eine Puppe». (GER)
366 Doppelseitige, farbige Illustration zu einem in *Penthouse* erschienenen Artikel mit dem Titel: «Die ersten hundert Lügen Jimmy Carters». (USA)
367 Schwarzweiss-Illustration aus dem Magazin *Creatividad*. (USA)
368, 369 Illustration und Doppelseite zu einer Geschichte über die sexuelle Schizophrenie einer Frau, in *Penthouse*. (USA)

364 Page introduisant un article du magazine *Ele* consacré à un nouveau produit contre les troubles sexuels. Noir et blanc. (BRA)
365 Illustration pleine page pour un conte de Noël traitant d'une jeune fille qui aimerait avoir une poupée. (GER)
366 Page double en tête d'un article de *Penthouse* sur les fausses déclarations de Jimmy Carter. En polychromie. (USA)
367 Illustration pour un article publié dans le magazine *Creatividad*. Noir et blanc. (USA)
368, 369 Illustration et page double complète d'une histoire d'une femme qui a changé sa personnalité. Elément de *Penthouse*. (USA)

365

CARTERGATE V
THE FIRST HUNDRED LIES OF JIMMY CARTER

When he was running for office, our president told us that he would never, never tell a lie. On the contrary, it is extremely difficult for him to tell the truth.

BY CRAIG S. KARPEL

Jimmy Carter is a liar. The president of the United States is a habitual, compulsive teller of untruths who, throughout his campaign and administration, has woven a tangled web of false and misleading statements.

366

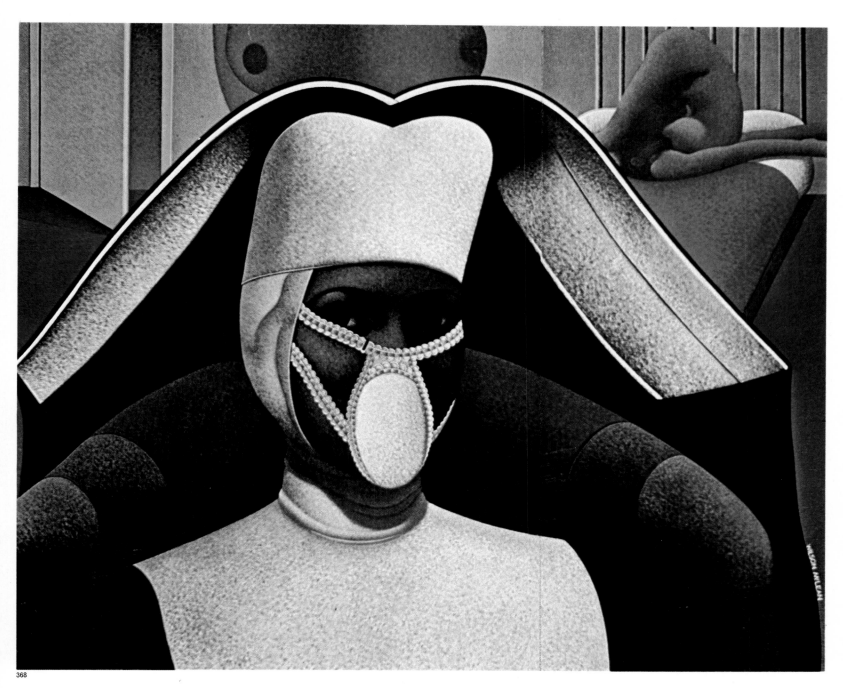

368

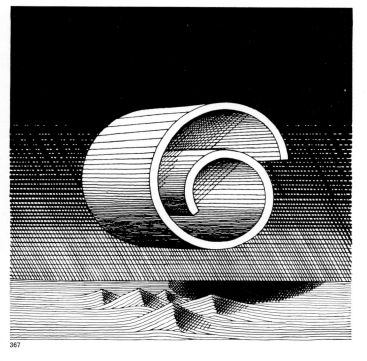

367

AGENCY / AGENTUR / AGENCE – STUDIO:
367 Saul Bass & Assoc.

PUBLISHER / VERLEGER / EDITEUR:
364 Bloch Editores
365 Dr. Heilmaier-Verlag
366, 368–369 Penthouse International Ltd.
367 Creatividad

369

Magazine Illustrations
Zeitschriften-Illustrationen
Illustrations de périodiques

370

370, 371 Illustration in actual size and complete double spread opening an article on the love life of Lord Byron published in *Penthouse* magazine. (GBR)
372 Double spread (full colour) opening an article in *Penthouse* on the Federal Reserve Bank. (USA)
373 Double spread (full colour) opening an article in *Penthouse* on the life of Eva Peron. (GBR)

370, 371 Illustration und Doppelseite zu den «geheimen Memoiren» von Lord Byron, aus *Penthouse*. (GBR)
372 Doppelseite mit farbiger Illustration zu einem sogenannten «Insider»-Bericht über die staatlichen Bankreserven, aus *Penthouse*. (USA)
373 Doppelseite mit farbiger Illustration zu einem *Penthouse*-Artikel über Eva Peron, «Die Macht hinter dem Glanz». (GBR)

371

ARTIST / KÜNSTLER / ARTISTE:
370, 371, 373 James Marsh
372 Fred Otnes

DESIGNER / GESTALTER / MAQUETTISTE:
370, 371, 373 Alison Daines

ART DIRECTOR / DIRECTEUR ARTISTIQUE:
370, 371, 373 David K. Jones
372 Joe Brooks

DON'T BANK ON IT

BY LEE BERTON

372

373

370, 371 Illustration en grandeur nature et page double complète introduisant un article sur la vie amoureuse de Lord Byron, publié dans le magazine *Penthouse*. (GBR)
372 Page double (en couleurs) en tête d'un article de *Penthouse* sur la Federal Reserve Bank. (USA)
373 Page double (en couleurs) de *Penthouse* introduisant un article sur la vie de Eva Peron. (GBR)

AGENCY / AGENTUR / AGENCE – STUDIO:
370, 371, 373 Andrew Archer Associates

PUBLISHER / VERLEGER / EDITEUR:
370, 371, 373 Penthouse Publications Ltd.
372 Penthouse International Ltd.

Magazine Illustrations

374 Illustration (full colour) for fish soup recipes in *The News*. (USA)
375 Illustration (black and white) for an article on football in *Pardon*. (GER)
376, 378, 379 Two colour illustrations and one complete page from a feature in the magazine *Mieux Etre* about vegetables with an aphrodisiac effect. (FRA)
377 Double-spread illustration from a magazine of Sankei Publishing Ltd. (JPN)
380 Page (with colour vignettes) from a regular feature on gardens in the women's magazine *Femina*. (SWE)

374 «Es ist ein Fisch in meiner Suppe». Illustration zu Kochrezepten. (USA)
375 Schwarzweiss-Illustration zu einem Artikel über «National-Stress Fussball» aus der satirischen Zeitschrift *Pardon*. (GER)
376, 378, 379 Farbige Illustrationen und ganze Seite zu einem Artikel über aphrodisische Gemüsesorten: «Die Küche der Liebe» aus *Mieux Etre*. (FRA)
377 Doppelseitige Illustration aus einer japanischen Zeitschrift. (JPN)
380 Seite aus der «Garten-Rubrik» einer Frauenzeitschrift. (SWE)

374 Illustration (en couleurs) accompagnant des recettes pour préparer des soupes au poisson. Série publiée dans le magazine *The News*. (USA)
375 Illustration noir-blanc tirée d'un article consacré au football. (GER)
376, 378, 379 Illustrations couleur et page double d'un article du magazine *Mieux Etre* intitulé «La cuisine de l'amour». (FRA)
377 Illustration sur page double d'un magazine japonais. (JPN)
380 Page avec des vignettes couleur figurant dans un article sur le jardin. (SWE)

374

37

375

376

La cuisine de l'amour

Les aphrodisiaques naturels ont leur légende
et leur place aujourd'hui parmi nos aliments.
Mais les connaissez-vous?

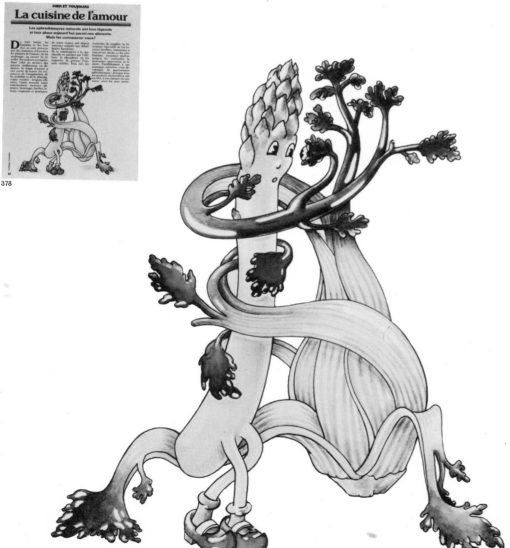

378

379

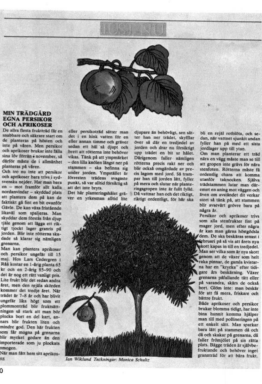

**MIN TRÄDGÅRD
EGNA PERSIKOR
OCH APRIKOSER**

Jan Wiklund Teckningar: Monica Schulz

380

PUBLISHER / VERLEGER / EDITEUR:

374 The News
375 Pardon Verlagsgesellschaft mbH
376, 378, 379 Mieux Etre
377 Sankei Publishing Ltd.
380 Femina

Magazine Illustrations

381

ARTIST / KÜNSTLER / ARTISTE:

381 Anita Siegel
382 Valeri Pavlow
383, 386 Oskar Weiss
384 Jean-Claude Suarès
385 Barbara Redmond
387 Cathy Hull

DESIGNER / GESTALTER / MAQUETTISTE:

382 Valeri Pavlow
383, 386 Oskar Weiss
385 Barbara Redmond

ART DIRECTOR / DIRECTEUR ARTISTIQUE:

381 David Scheiderman
382 Vasil Sotirov
383, 386 Markus M. Ronner
384 Pam Vassil
385 Barbara Redmond/Jim Martin
387 Jerry Demoney

Newspaper Illustrations
Zeitungs-Illustrationen
Illustrations de journaux

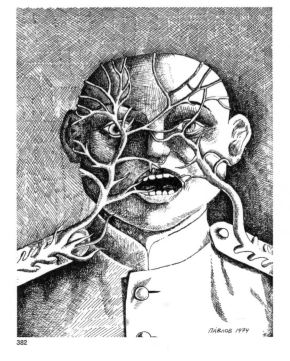

382

383

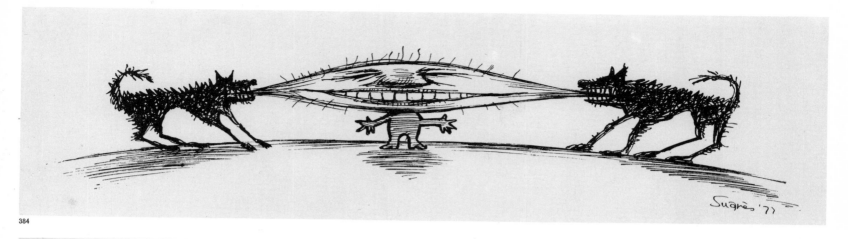

384

Taste/la charcuterie
THE MINNEAPOLIS STAR 12/14/77

385

381 Black-and-white editorial illustration from *The New York Times*. Actual size. (USA)
382 Lithographic illustration for a radio magazine. (BUL)
383, 386 Drawings for a satirical feature in a supplement of the weekly *Die Weltwoche*. (SWI)
384 Black-and-white illustration for an article appearing on the Op-Ed page of *The New York Times*. (USA)
385 Full-page illustration in full colour opening a section on food in *The Minneapolis Star*. (USA)
387 Black-and-white illustration for bouillabaisse recipes published in the *Daily News*. (USA)

381 Schwarzweiss-Illustration (Originalgrösse) zu einem Artikel in der *New York Times*. (USA)
382 Schwarzweiss-Illustration für ein Radio-Magazin. (BUL)
383, 386 Illustrationen aus der Serie «Satirisches» im *Weltwoche-«Magazyn»*. (SWI)
384 Schwarzweiss-Illustration einer Seite der *New York Times*, die unabhängigen Meinungen gewidmet ist. (USA)
385 Ganzseitige, einleitende Illustration für den Kochrezeptsektor der Zeitung *Minneapolis Star*, farbig. (USA)
387 «Bouillabaisse» – einleitende Illustration in Schwarzweiss für die Rezeptseite einer Zeitung. (USA)

381 Illustration en noir et blanc accompagnant un article publié dans le *New York Times*. (USA)
382 Illustration noir-blanc pour un magazine. (BUL)
383, 386 Illustrations d'une série satirique (jeu de mots sur satire et animal) du *Weltwoche Magazyn*. (SWI)
384 Illustration noir-blanc de la page Op-Ed (face à l'éditorial) du *New York Times*. (USA)
385 Illustration pleine page introduisant la section des recettes du journal *Minneapolis Star*. En polychromie. (USA)
387 Illustration noir-blanc accompagnant des recettes de «bouillabaisses» d'un quotidien. (USA)

AGENCY / AGENTUR / AGENCE – STUDIO:
385 Redmond Design

PUBLISHER / VERLEGER / EDITEUR:
381, 384 The New York Times
382 Bulgarkso Radio
383, 386 Weltwoche-Verlag AG
385 The Minneapolis Star
387 Daily News

386

387

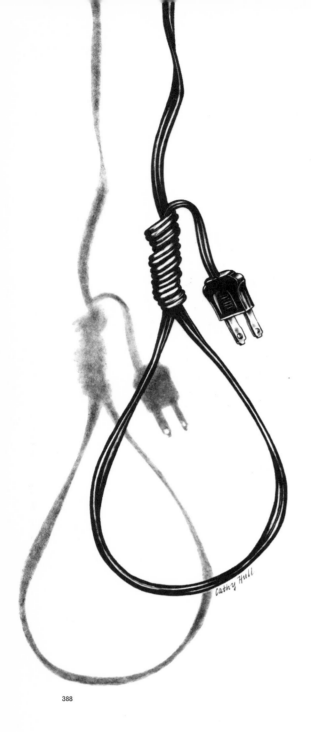

388

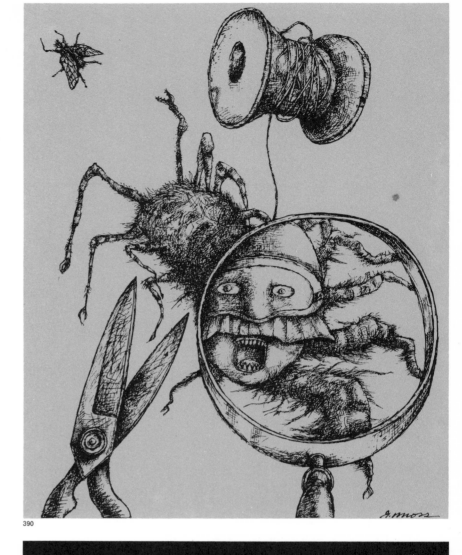

390

392

389

Newspaper Illustrations
Zeitungs-Illustrationen
Illustrations de journaux

391

393

ARTIST / KÜNSTLER / ARTISTE:

388, 389 Cathy Hull
390, 391 Geoffrey Moss
392 Jean-Claude Suarès
393 Lars Melander

DESIGNER / GESTALTER / MAQUETTISTE:

393 Lars Melander

ART DIRECTOR / DIRECTEUR ARTISTIQUE:

388, 389 Bob Elsner
392 Pam Vassil

PUBLISHER / VERLEGER / EDITEUR:

388, 389, 392 The New York Times
390, 391 Hawthorn Books, Inc.

388, 389 Illustration and complete page of *The New York Times* with an article on our dangerous dependency on electricity. Black and white. (USA)
390, 391 Two satirical drawings (black and white) from the *Washington Post*. (USA)
392 Black-and-white illustration from the Op-Ed page of *The New York Times*. (USA)
393 Newspaper page used as self-promotion by the artist. Black and white. (SWE)

388, 389 Detail der Illustration und ganze Seite aus der *New York Times* mit einem Artikel über das Energieproblem: «Das gute Leben hat eine Grenze erreicht». (USA)
390, 391 Zwei satirische Zeichnungen (schwarzweiss) aus der *Washington Post*. (USA)
392 Illustration der Seite für redaktionell unabhängige Artikel aus der *New York Times*. (USA)
393 Zeitungsseite (schwarzweiss) als Eigenwerbung für einen Designer. (SWE)

388, 389 Illustration et page complète du *New York Times* présentant un article sur les problèmes de la production d'énergie. Noir et blanc. (USA)
390, 391 Deux dessins satiriques en noir et blanc du *Washington Post*. (USA)
392 Illustration noir-blanc de la page Op-Ed du *New York Times*. (USA)
393 Page d'un journal utilisée en tant qu'élément autopromotionnel d'un artiste. (SWE)

394

395

Newspaper Illustrations
Zeitungs-Illustrationen
Illustrations de journaux

396

397

398

399

400

ARTIST / KÜNSTLER / ARTISTE:

399–401 Eugene Mihaesco
402 Cathy Hull
403 Miran
404 Robert Pryor

DESIGNER / GESTALTER / MAQUETTISTE:
404 Steve Heller

ART DIRECTOR / DIRECTEUR ARTISTIQUE:

402 Nicki Kalish
403 Oswaldo Miranda
404 Steve Heller

PUBLISHER / VERLEGER / EDITEUR:

399–402, 404 The New York Times
403 Diário do Paraná

401

402

403

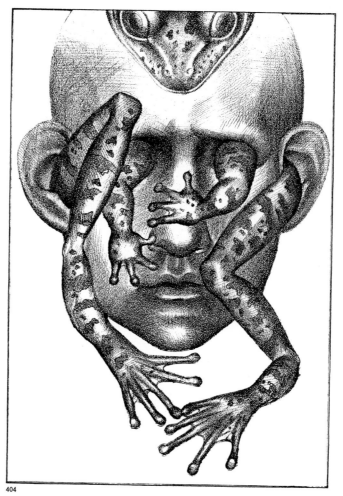

404

ARTIST / KÜNSTLER / ARTISTE:
405–407 Hans Arnold
408 Alain Le Saux
409 Jacqueline Chwast
410 Tim Lewis

DESIGNER / GESTALTER / MAQUETTISTE:
408 Jean-Pierre Holley
409, 410 Carol March

ART DIRECTOR / DIRECTEUR ARTISTIQUE:
408 Mike Brock
409, 410 Tom Bentkowski

PUBLISHER / VERLEGER / EDITEUR:
405–407 Hemmets-Journal
408 Playboy Publications, Inc.
409, 410 New York Magazine

405

406

405–407 Illustrations (all in full colour) from the magazine *Hemmets-Journal*. Fig. 405 in blue shades, Fig. 406 with blue stones and cliffs, polychrome face. (SWE)
408 Double spread opening an article in *Oui* magazine on lie detectors. Brown face on mustard ground, green tubes. (USA)
409 Black-and-white illustration for a review of a film about nuns. From *New York* magazine. (USA)
410 Illustration for an article in *New York* magazine on aspects of cosmetic surgery. (USA)

405–407 Farbige Illustrationen aus der Zeitschrift *Hemmets-Journal*. Abb. 405 in Blautönen, Abb. 406 mit blauen Steinen und Felsen und buntem Gesicht. (SWE)
408 «Die ganze Wahrheit und nichts als die Wahrheit über Lügendetektoren – so wahr uns Gott helfe.» Farbige Illustration zu einem Artikel aus dem Magazin *Oui*. (USA)
409 Illustration zu einer Filmkritik über *Nasty Habits* (Schlechte Gewohnheiten), aus der Zeitschrift *New York*. (USA)
410 Illustration zu einem Artikel über die Kosten kosmetischer Operationen, aus *New York*. (USA)

405–407 Illustrations (toutes en couleurs) du magazine *Hemmets-Journal*. Fig. 405 en tons bleus, fig. 406 avec des pierres et falaises bleues; visage polychrome. (SWE)
408 Page double introduisant un article du magazine *Oui* sur les détecteurs de mensonges. Brun sur fond moutarde, tubes verts. (USA)
409 Illustration noir-blanc figurant dans le compte rendu d'un film sur des religieuses avec des allusions à l'affaire Watergate. Elément du magazine *New York*. (USA)
410 Illustration accompagnant un article dans le magazine *New York* présentant différents aspects d'opérations cosmétiques. (USA)

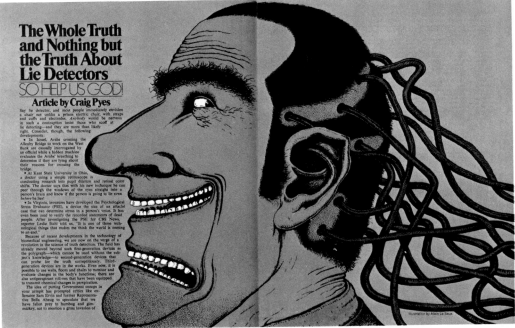

408

407

Magazine Illustrations

409

410

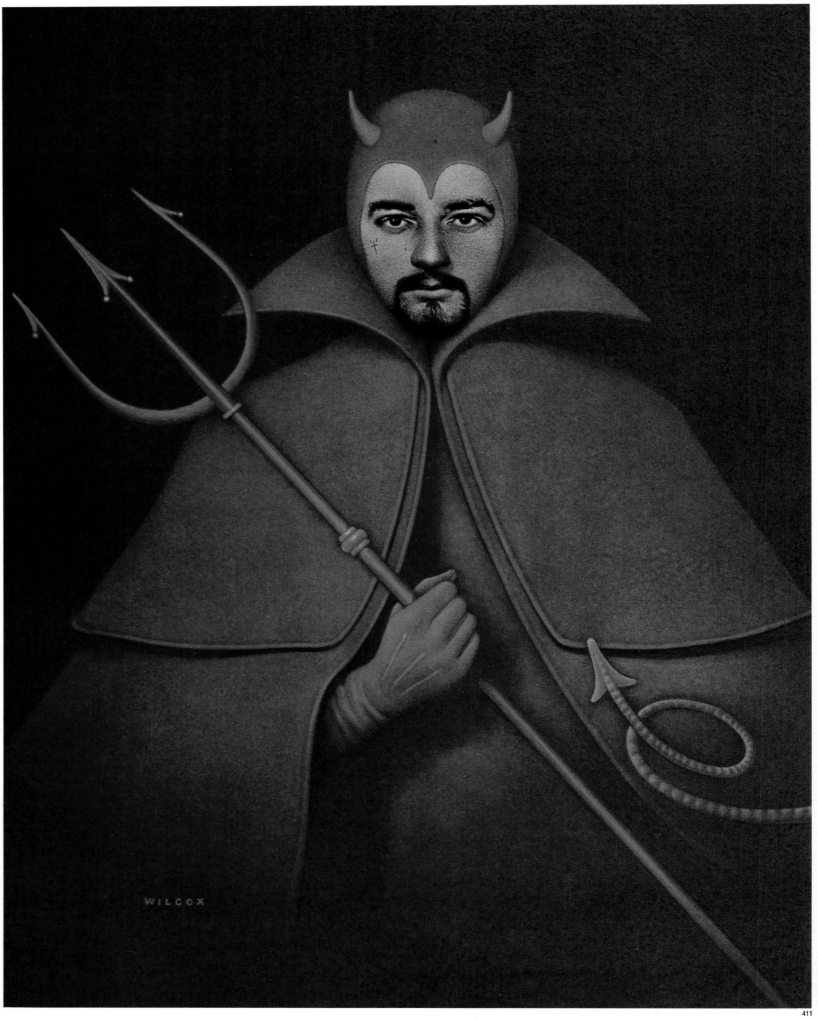

WILCOX

411

412

411, 412 Illustration in actual size and complete double spread opening an article in *Oui* on a murder trial that got a good deal of publicity in America. (USA)
413 Double spread opening an article about FBI snooping in *Oui* magazine. Eagle in brown, gold and pink. (USA)
414 Double spread opening an article on film actor Bud Cort in *Oui* magazine. Pastel shades of blue, green and lilac. (USA)

411, 412 Illustration und ganze Doppelseite eines Artikels aus *Oui* über Tom Creech, dem man u.a. mehr als 30 Morde vorwirft. (USA)
413 Farbige Doppelseite aus *Oui* zu einem Artikel über Informationen und Aktenmaterial des FBI. (USA)
414 Farbige Doppelseite zu einem Artikel über den amerikanischen Schauspieler Bud Cort, der ein ungewöhnliches Leben und eine ungewöhnliche Karriere hinter sich hat. «Er glitt über das Kuckucksnest» und «schlüpfte aus der Schlinge». Aus *Oui*. (USA)

411, 412 Illustration en grandeur nature et page double complète en tête d'un article publié dans le magazine *Oui* sur la condamnation d'un assassin. (USA)
413 Page double introduisant un article du magazine *Oui* sur le furetage du FBI. Aigle en brun, or et rose. (USA)
414 Page double du magazine *Oui* introduisant un article consacré à Bud Cort, acteur de cinéma. Tons pastel. (USA)

413

414

ARTIST / KÜNSTLER / ARTISTE:
411, 412 Dave Wilcox
413 Alex Gnidziejko
414 Don Punchatz

DESIGNER / GESTALTER / MAQUETTISTE:
411–413 Don Menell
414 Mike Brock

ART DIRECTOR / DIRECTEUR ARTISTIQUE:
411–414 Don Menell

PUBLISHER / VERLEGER / EDITEUR:
411–414 Playboy Publications, Inc.

415

416

415 Full-page colour illustration for an article on America's changing racist problems, published in the magazine *Oui*. (USA)
416 Full-page illustration from an article in *Oui* on Kissinger as President. Pink skin, green brickwork. (USA)
417, 418 Complete spread and illustration for an excerpt from the novel *Fear and Loathing in Las Vegas* translated into German in the magazine *Sounds*. Black and white. (GER)
419, 420 Illustration and corresponding page from *Pardon* magazine, with verses entitled "A Hangman Thinks". (GER)
421 Full-page rendering of a bra on a blue ground from the magazine *The News*. (USA)

415 Farbige Illustration zu einer Diskussion in *Oui* über die gegenwärtigen Formen des Rassismus in den USA mit prominenten Teilnehmern schwarzer Hautfarbe. (USA)
416 Farbige Illustration zu der Geschichte eines Verlegers und seiner Idee zu einem Buch mit dem Titel «Präsident Kissinger», aus dem Magazin *Oui*. (USA)
417, 418 Komplette Doppelseite und Illustration aus dem Magazin *Sounds* mit einem Auszug aus dem Buch *Angst und Schrecken in Las Vegas*. (GER)
419, 420 Illustration und ganze Seite aus *Pardon* mit Gedicht «Ein Henker denkt». «... Ne letzte Zigarette, ein letzter Schoppen Wein, ein letzter Blick von Mensch zu Mensch...». (GER)
421 Ganzseitige farbige Illustration aus *The News* zum Thema BH-Hochkonjunktur. (USA)

415 Illustration pleine page (en couleurs) accompagnant une discussion avec des personnes noires sur les problèmes raciaux aux Etats-Unis. Article publié dans le magazine *Oui*. (USA)
416 Illustration pleine page figurant dans un article présentant Kissinger comme président. Peau rose, briques vertes. Elément du magazine *Oui*. (USA)
417, 418 Page double et illustration de l'extrait d'un roman (La crainte et le dégoût à Las Vegas) publié dans le magazine *Sounds*. Noir et blanc. (GER)
419, 420 Illustration et page correspondante du magazine *Pardon* présentant un poème intitulé «Un bourreau pense». (GER)
421 Illustration pleine page d'un soutien-gorge sur fond bleu, du magazine *The News*. (USA)

417

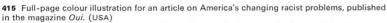

418

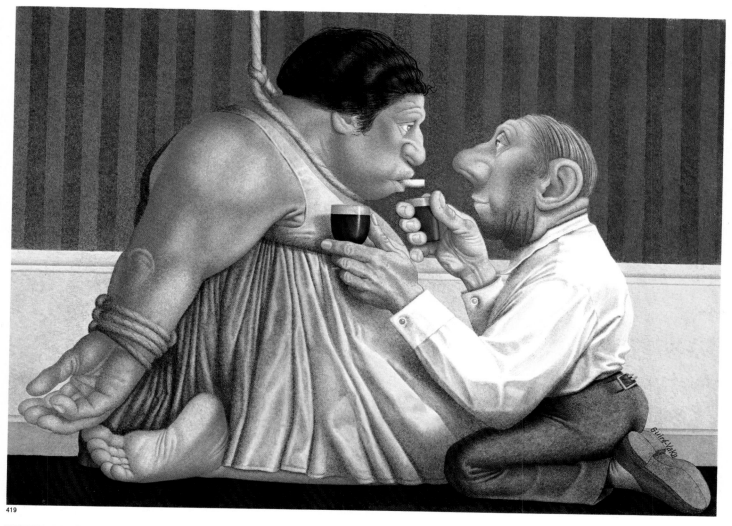

419

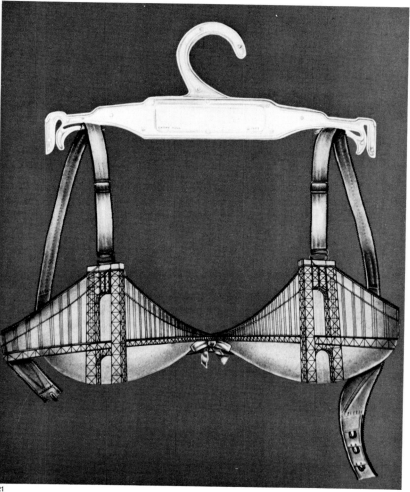

421

Ein Henker denkt

420

Magazine Illustrations

422 Double spread from the children's magazine *Sesame Street* presenting a puzzle. (USA)
423 Double spread opening an article ("In search of lost youth") in the magazine *Revista de Domingo*. Shades of yellowish green. (BRA)
424, 425 Complete spread and detail from an article in *Working Woman* on salary secrecy. (USA)
426 Full-page illustration for an article on financially unequal matches in *Seventeen*. (USA)
427, 428 Two pages as self-contained statements from *Politicks* magazine. Black and white. (USA)
429 Full-page colour illustration from an astrology feature in *Avenue* magazine. (NLD)
430 Illustration for a book club's magazine reviewing a book on a multinational company. (BRA)

422 Farbige Doppelseite mit einer Aufgabe aus dem Kinder-Magazin *Sesame Street.* (USA)
423 Doppelseite aus dem Magazin *Revista de Domingo.* Thema: Verlorene Jugend. (BRA)
424, 425 Doppelseite aus einer Frauenzeitschrift über Geheimhaltung des Lohnes. (USA)
426 Illustration in *Seventeen* zum Thema «Aschenputtel»-Verbindungen. (USA)
427, 428 Illustrationen zu sozialen Missständen aus *Politicks.* Hier die Haltung der Ärzte gegenüber Nichtversicherten und Misshandlung eines Invaliden durch jugendliche Banden. (USA)
429 Farbige Illustration zum Thema Astrologie aus der Zeitschrift *Avenue.* (NLD)
430 Illustration zu einer Buchbesprechung. Thema: Die Macht einer Multinationalen. (BRA)

422 Page double de *Sesame Street,* magazine pour enfants, présentant un puzzle. (USA)
423 D'un article intitulé «A la recherche de la jeunesse perdue». Tons jaune verdâtre. (BRA)
424, 425 Article sur la «cachotterie» quant au salaire, publié dans un magazine féminin. (USA)
426 D'un article sur les relations de deux personnes se trouvant dans une situation financière tout à fait différente. Illustration *Seventeen* du magazine *Seventeen.* (USA)
427, 428 Pages consacrées à des conditions sociales lamentables. Du magazine *Politicks.* (USA)
429 Illustration pleine page (en couleurs) d'une série astrologique du magazine *Avenue.* (NLD)
430 Illustration tirée d'un compte rendu d'un livre sur une compagnie multinationale. (BRA)

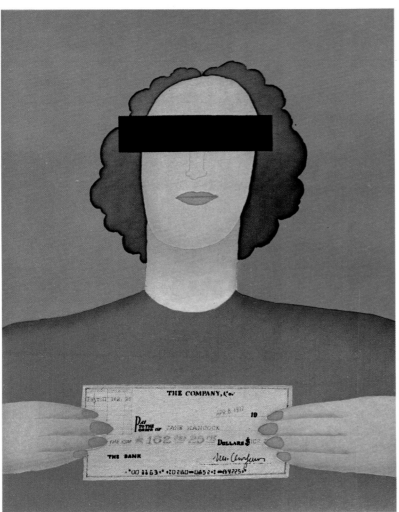

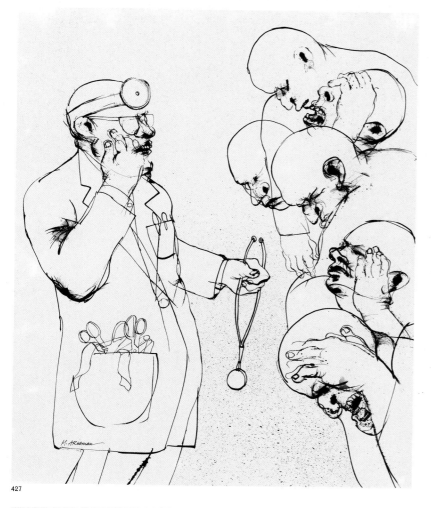

427

429

A crippled man on Broadway was spray-painted by a gang of youths

428

430

ARTIST / KÜNSTLER / ARTISTE:
422 James Endicott
423 Vilma Gomez
424–426 Guy Billout
427, 428 Marshall Arisman
429 Karin Blume
430 Alfredo Aquino

DESIGNER / GESTALTER / MAQUETTISTE:
422 Richard Weigand/James Endicott

ART DIRECTOR / DIRECTEUR ARTISTIQUE:
422 Richard Weigand
423 Vilma Gomez
424–426 Paul Hardy
427, 428 Mary Morgan
429 Dick de Moei
430 Alfredo Aquino

AGENCY / AGENTUR / AGENCE – STUDIO:
422 Children's Television Workshop
429 Avenue

PUBLISHER / VERLEGER / EDITEUR:
422 Children's Television Workshop
423 Revista de Domingo
424–426 Working Woman
427, 428 Politicks Magazine
429 De Geillustreerde pers b.v.
430 Círculo do Livro

Magazine Illustrations

431

432

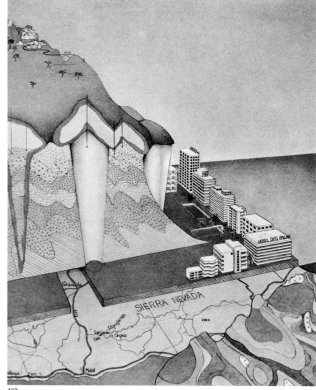

433

ARTIST / KÜNSTLER:

431, 432 François Pierre Bleau
433 Candida Amsden
434 Robert Grossman
435 Eraldo Carugati
436—438 Dietrich Lange

DESIGNER / GESTALTER:

433 Terry Segal

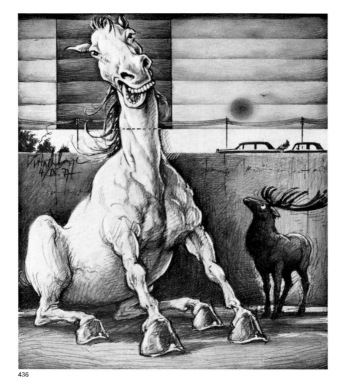

436

437

ART DIRECTOR / DIRECTEUR ARTISTIQUE:

431, 432 Michel St-Denis
434, 435 Neil Shakery

PUBLISHER / VERLEGER / EDITEUR:

431, 432 Nous Magazine
433 Observer Magazine
434, 435 Ziff-Davis Publishing
436–438 Gruner & Jahr AG & Co

434

435

438

431, 432 Illustration (full colour) and spread from an article in *Nous* magazine asking "who killed the wonder woman?". (CAN)
433 Full-page colour illustration for a travel article about the mountains of Spain in the *Observer* magazine. (GBR)
434 A study on the air passenger's out-of-phase feeling from *Psychology Today*. Full colour. (USA)
435 Full-page colour illustration for a feature on King Kong published in *Psychology Today*. (USA)
436–438 Black-and-white illustrations for a regular feature in *Stern* dealing with abuses of the German language. (GER)

431, 432 Farbige Illustration und Doppelseite zu einem Artikel aus der Zeitschrift *Nous* mit dem Titel «Wer hat die Wunderfrau getötet?». (CAN)
433 Farbige Illustration zu einem Reisebericht über die Berge Spaniens aus der Zeitschrift *Observer*. (GBR)
434, 435 Farbige Illustrationen aus der Zeitschrift *Psychology Today*. Der Titel des Artikels zu Abb. 435: «Ein faszinierender König namens Kong». (USA)
436–438 Illustrationen aus der Reihe *Deutsch für Besserwisser* im *Stern,* hier der Amtsschimmel «... unter Ausserachtlassung», ein «eisernes Hochzeitspaar» und «gehobene Tätigkeiten». (GER)

431, 432 Illustration (en couleurs) et page double d'un article dans lequel une lectrice du magazine *Nous* raconte un bout de sa vie de femme. (CAN)
433 Illustration pleine page d'un article touristique consacré aux montagnes de l'Espagne. Du magazine *Observer*. (GBR)
434 Etude publiée dans un magazine psychologique. (USA)
435 Illustration pleine page en couleurs d'un article consacré à King Kong. Du magazine *Psychology Today*. (USA)
436–438 Illustrations d'une longue série du magazine *Stern* consacrée aux abus de la langue allemande. Tous les dessins sont en noir et blanc. (GER)

**Magazine Illustrations
Zeitschriften-Illustrationen
Illustrations de périodiques**

439 Double spread opening an article in the parents' magazine *Wij en Onze Kinderen* on how to deal with buzzing and biting insects. Full colour. (NLD)
440 Illustration for an article in *New York* on abrupt boundaries within the capital. (USA)
441 Full-colour illustration in *Pardon*: the motorcycle as a public nuisance. (GER)
442–446 From a series of eleven full-colour illustrations for a story by Patrick Quentin published in instalments in the weekly *Ahoj na Sobotu*. (CSR)

439 Doppelseite aus einem Magazin für Eltern mit farbiger Illustration zu einem Artikel über die Ängste von Kindern vor brummenden und stechenden Insekten. (NLD)
440 Farbige Illustration aus *New York* zu den krassen Grenzen im Stadtzentrum New Yorks. (USA)
441 Farbige Illustration zu einem Artikel in *Pardon* über Motorräder. (GER)
442–446 Farbige Illustration zu einer Kriminalgeschichte des Amerikaners Patrick Quentin, die in einer tschechischen Wochenzeitschrift in Fortsetzungen veröffentlicht wurde. (CSR)

439 Page double introduisant un article sur les insectes qui bourdonnent et piquent et qui font peur aux enfants. Elément d'un magazine destiné aux parents. En polychromie. (NLD)
440 Illustration accompagnant un article sur les grosses différences au centre de New York. (USA)
441 Illustration couleur du magazine *Pardon*: les motos, une calamité publique. (GER)
442–446 D'une série de onze illustrations couleur conçues pour une nouvelle de Patrick Quentin qui est publiée en feuilletons dans l'hebdomadaire *Ahoj na Sobotu*. (CSR)

439

440

441

ARTIST / KÜNSTLER / ARTISTE:

439 Braldt Bralds
440 Guy Billout
441 Hans Arnold
442–446 Jiří Šalamoun

ART DIRECTOR / DIRECTEUR ARTISTIQUE:

439 Lineke Huizenga
440 Tom Bentkowski/Carol March
442–446 Ladislav Hojny

PUBLISHER / VERLEGER / EDITEUR:

439 Spaarnestad B.V.
440 New York Magazine
441 Pardon Verlagsgesellschaft mbH
442–446 Melantrich/Ahoy Na Sobotu

Magazine Illustrations
Zeitschriften-Illustrationen
Illustrations de périodiques

442

443

444

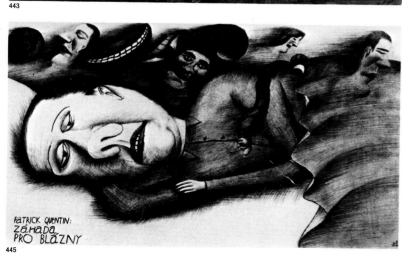

445

446

447

447 Illustration of the "ten thousand dollar pyramid" from a series about what people will do to make money, in *National Lampoon*. (USA)
448 Double spread from the graphic design magazine *Idea*, with illustrations of American games in which people can make money. (JPN)
449–451 Three double spreads, all in full colour, from the young people's magazine *Bananas*. The subjects are unsolved mysteries, re-creating extinct species and the girl singer Linda Ronstadt respectively. (USA)

447 Illustration aus einer Reihe der humoristischen Zeitschrift *National Lampoon*: was die Leute alles auf sich nehmen, um zu Geld zu kommen. (USA)
448 Doppelseite aus dem Graphik-Magazin *Idea* mit Illustrationen von amerikanischen Spielen, bei denen Geld zu gewinnen ist. (JPN)
449–451 Farbige Doppelseiten aus der Zeitschrift für junge Leute *Bananas*. Die Themen sind «mysteriöse, ungeklärte Begebenheiten», «die künstliche Herstellung von Lebewesen» (Science Fiction) und die Folk- und Pop-Sängerin Linda Ronstadt. (USA)

449

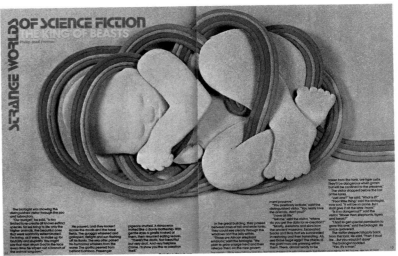

450

448

447 Illustration de la «pyramide de dix mille dollars» figurant dans une série qui discute ce que les gens sont prêts à faire pour gagner de l'argent. Elément de *National Lampoon*. (USA)
448 Page double tirée d'un magazine d'art graphique japonais. Les illustrations présentent des jeux américains pour gagner de l'argent. (JPN)
449–451 Trois pages doubles, toutes en couleurs, figurant dans le magazine *Bananas*, magazine pour la jeune génération. On y traite les sujets suivants: des incidents mystérieux non éclaircis, comment recréer des espèces disparues et la chanteuse Linda Ronstadt. (USA)

451

ARTIST / KÜNSTLER / ARTISTE:

447, 448 Sue Coe
449 Richard Sparks
450 Eileen Herman
451 William Murphy

DESIGNER / GESTALTER / MAQUETTISTE:

447 Peter Kleinman
449, 450 Bob Feldgus
451 Bob Feldgus/William Murphy

ART DIRECTOR / DIREKTEUR ARTISTIQUE:

447 Peter Kleinman
449–451 Bob Feldgus

PUBLISHER / VERLEGER / EDITEUR:

447 21st Century Communications, Inc.
448 Seibundo-Shinkosha Publishing Co., Ltd.
449–451 Scholastic Mags. Inc.

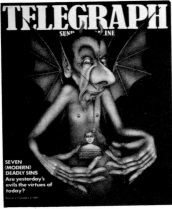

452

ARTIST / KÜNSTLER / ARTISTE:

452, 453 Wayne Anderson
454, 456 James Marsh
455 Frank Bozzo

DESIGNER / GESTALTER / MAQUETTISTE:

455 Tom VinkLainas

ART DIRECTOR / DIRECTEUR ARTISTIQUE:

452, 453 Geoff Axbey
454, 456 Roger Watt
455 Tom VinkLainas

AGENCY / AGENTUR / AGENCE – STUDIO:

455 Frank Bozzo

PUBLISHER / VERLEGER / EDITEUR:

452, 453 Telegraph Sunday Magazine
454, 456 Paul Raymond Publishing
455 Classic Magazine

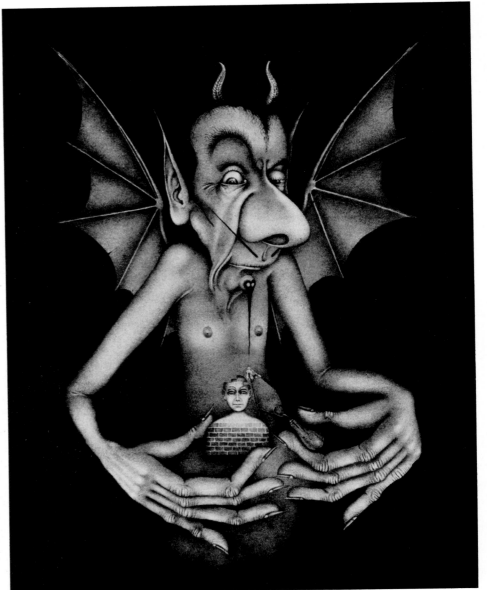

453

452, 453 Complete cover of an issue of the *Sunday Tele-graph Magazine* containing an article on the Seven Deadly Sins of modern times, with detail of the artwork (figure chiefly in greenish shades). (GBR)
454 Double spread opening a story in *Men Only* about a sadistic film director. Blue girl, tawny lion with olive face. (GBR)
455 Double-spread illustration of a feature on horse-jumping in *Classic* magazine. (USA)
456 Full-colour illustration running over one page and a half for an article in *Men Only* on sexual practices among males in Australia. (GBR)

452, 453 Umschlag einer Ausgabe des *Sunday Telegraph Magazine* mit Bezug auf einen Artikel über die sieben Tod-sünden moderner Zeiten, mit Detail der Illustration (vorwie-gend in grünlichen Tönen). (GBR)
454 Doppelseite mit Beginn einer Geschichte in *Men Only* über einen sadistischen Filmproduzenten. Blaues Mädchen, gelbbrauner Löwe mit olivefarbenem Gesicht. (GBR)
455 Doppelseitige Illustration aus dem Magazin *Classic* zu einem Artikel über das Springreiten. (USA)
456 Illustration zu einem Artikel in *Men Only* über sexuelle Praktiken junger Männer in Australien. Grau- und Braun-töne, Henne weiss in rotem Kleid. (GBR)

452, 453 Couverture d'un numéro du *Sunday Telegraph Magazine*, se référant à un article sur les sept péchés mor-tels des temps modernes, et détail de la composition (pré-dominance de tons verdâtres). (GBR)
454 Page double introduisant un article traitant d'un cinéaste sadique. Fille bleue, lion à tête olive. Elément du magazine *Men Only*. (GBR)
455 Page double illustrant un article consacré au hippisme. Elément du magazine *Classic*. (USA)
456 Illustration en couleur (sur une page et demie) conçue pour un article sur les pratiques sexuels des hommes en Australie. Du magazine *Men Only*. (GBR)

454

455

456

457

Magazine Illustrations
Zeitschriften-Illustrationen
Illustrations de périodiques

458

459

457–459 Three illustrations from a satirical feature in the *Sunday Times Magazine* in which roles were allocated to each of the nine nations of the European Economic Community as a United States of Europe—here the Italians as soldiers, the Dutch as hostages and the Irish as population controllers. All were portrayed by means of three-dimensional figures. (GBR)
460 Drawing illustrating the compulsory bouncer in an article in *Psychology Today* about psychological aspects of tennis. Black and white. (USA)

457–459 Seiten aus dem *Sunday Times Magazine* zu einem humoristischen Artikel, worin jede der neun Nationen der Europäischen Wirtschaftsgemeinschaft eine Rolle zugeteilt bekommt, innerhalb der «Vereinigten Staaten von Europa». Hier die Italiener als Soldaten, die Holländer als Geiseln, die Iren als Geburtenüberwacher. Alle sind in lebhaften Szenen als dreidimensionale Puppen porträtiert. (GBR)
460 Schwarzweiss-Illustration aus *Psychology Today* zu einer Abhandlung über die psychologischen Aspekte des Tennisspielens. (USA)

457–459 Illustrations d'un article satirique du *Sunday Times Magazine* où les neuf nations composant la Communauté économique européenne se voient attribuer des rôles amusants dans cet embryon d'Etats-Unis d'Europe: les Italiens sont les soldats, les Néerlandais les otages et les Irlandais les contrôleurs de la démographie. Chaque nation est illustrée par des figurines tridimensionnelles. (GBR)
460 Dessin illustrant un article publié dans le magazine *Psychology Today* sur les aspects psychologiques du tennis. Noir et blanc. (USA)

ARTIST / KÜNSTLER / ARTISTE:
460 Robert Grossman

DESIGNER / GESTALTER / MAQUETTISTE:
457–459 Gilurie Misstear

ART DIRECTOR / DIRECTEUR ARTISTIQUE:
457–459 Edwin Taylor
460 Neil Shakery

PUBLISHER / VERLEGER / EDITEUR:
457–459 The Sunday Times
460 Ziff-Davis Publishing

460

461

461, 462 Full-page illustration and corresponding double spread from a story published in the women's magazine *Freundin*. (GER)
463, 464 Complete spread and colour illustration for a story in *Freundin*. (GER)
465, 466 Spread and colour illustration from *Freundin*. The story is by Dorothy Sayers. (GER)
467 Full-page illustration for a story in *Freundin*. Purple dress and hat, brown floor. (GER)
468 Full-page illustration for a story in *Freundin*. Shades of light brown and yellow. (GER)

461, 462 Ganzseitige Illustration und Doppelseite einer Geschichte in *Freundin*. (GER)
463, 464 Doppelseite und Illustration zu einer Geschichte von M. Spark in *Freundin*. (GER)
465, 466 Doppelseite und Illustration (farbig) zu einer Geschichte in *Freundin*. (GER)
467 Ganzseitige Illustration (Brauntöne, violettes Kleid und Hut) zu einer Kurzgeschichte in *Freundin*. (GER)
468 Ganzseitige Illustration zu einer Geschichte in *Freundin*. Helle Brauntöne, Gelb. (GER)

461, 462 Illustration pleine page pour une nouvelle d'Alan Sillitoe publiée dans le magazine féminin *Freundin*. En polychromie. (GER)
463, 464 Illustration couleur pour une nouvelle de Muriel Spark, paru dans *Freundin*. (GER)
465, 466 Page double et illustration couleur de *Freundin* pour une histoire de D. Sayers. (GER)
467 Illustration pleine page pour une nouvelle publiée dans *Freundin*. Polychromie. (GER)
468 Illustration pleine page de *Freundin*. Brun pâle et jaune. (GER)

463

ARTIST / KÜNSTLER / ARTISTE:

461, 462 Arnhild Johne
463, 464 Katrin Lindley
465–467 Bengt Fosshag
468 Heseler & Heseler

ART DIRECTOR / DIRECTEUR ARTISTIQUE:

461–468 Eberhard Henschel

PUBLISHER / VERLEGER / EDITEUR:

461–468 Burda Verlag GmbH

Magazine Illustrations
Zeitschriften-Illustrationen
Illustrations de périodiques

462

465

464

467

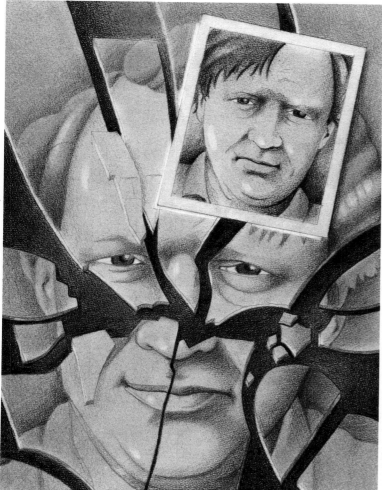

466

468

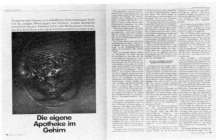

469

470

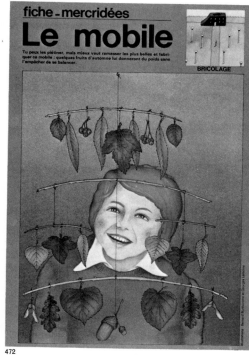

fiche-mercridées
Le mobile

Tu peux les piétiner, mais mieux vaut ramasser les plus belles et fabri-
quer ce mobile : quelques fruits d'automne lui donneront du poids sans
l'empêcher de se balancer.

BRICOLAGE

471

472

473

ARTIST / KÜNSTLER / ARTISTE:

469, 470 Hans-Ulrich Osterwalder
471 Richard Hess
472 Bernard Bonhomme/Georges Lemoine
473 Rozier-Gaudriault

DESIGNER / GESTALTER / MAQUETTISTE:

469, 470 Hans-Ulrich Osterwalder

ART DIRECTOR / DIRECTEUR ARTISTIQUE:

469, 470 Dietmar Maier
471 Emma Landau
472 Denys Prache
473 Antoine Kieffer

PUBLISHER / VERLEGER / EDITEUR:

469, 470 Theobald-Verlag
471 American Heritage Press
472 Bayard-Presse
473 Elle/France Editions et Publications

469, 470 Double spread opening an article on the chemistry of
pain control in the brain, and detail of the illustration. From the
magazine *Warum!* (GER)
471 Illustration from an article in *American Heritage* on Roger D.
Amboy, who never quite became American President. (USA)
472 Page from the young people's magazine *Okapi,* with instructions for making an autumn mobile. Full colour. (FRA)
473 Full-page illustration of a runner bean from a series of
fiches-consommation for the kitchen published in the women's
magazine *Elle.* (FRA)

469, 470 Doppelseite und Detail der Schwarzweiss-Illustration
aus der Zeitschrift für Psychologie und Lebenstechnik *Warum!*,
unter der Rubrik Schmerzforschung. (GER)
471 Illustration zu einem Artikel aus *American Heritage* über
Roger Darcy Amboy, der nie Präsident der USA wurde. (USA)
472 Farbige Seite aus dem französischen Jugend-Magazin *Okapi,*
mit Anleitung zur Herstellung eines Mobiles. (FRA)
473 Farbige Illustration einer grünen Bohne aus einer Serie über
verschiedene Gemüsesorten in der Zeitschrift *Elle.* Grün- und
Gelbtöne, Kleidung der Kinder rot und blau. (FRA)

469, 470 Page double initiale d'un article sur le contrôle de la
douleur dans le cerveau même et détail de l'illustration noir-
blanc. Elément du magazine *Warum!* (GER)
471 Illustration introduisant un article sur Roger Darcy
Amboy qui a failli être élu président des Etats-Unis. (USA)
472 Page du magazine *Okapi,* publication destiné à la jeune
génération: instructions pour faire un mobile. (FRA)
473 Illustration pleine page du «Haricot vert», dans la série
«Le printemps dans votre assiette». Elle figurait en tête des
Fiches-consommation de la revue *Elle.* (FRA)

474–476 Three double spreads from an article in *Skeptic* magazine on the assassination of Martin Luther King. Black and coloured inks and wash, integrated with the artist's handwritten captions. (USA)

477, 478 Illustration (brown face, yellowish planes) and complete double spread from a critical article in *Skeptic* magazine on the supersonic *Concorde*. (USA)

479 Colour spread opening an article in *Skeptic* on aliens who illegally enter the United States. (USA)

474–476 Drei Doppelseiten aus der Zeitschrift *Skeptic* mit einem Artikel über die Ermordung von Martin Luther King. Aquarellierte Tuschzeichnung, integrierte handschriftliche Legenden des Künstlers. (USA)

477, 478 Farbige Illustration und Doppelseite aus *Skeptic* mit einem kritischen Artikel über die *Concorde*. (USA)

479 Farbige Doppelseite aus *Skeptic* zum Problem illegaler Einwanderungen in den USA: «Was wurde aus dem Land der unbegrenzten Möglichkeiten?». (USA)

474–476 Trois pages doubles figurant dans un article du magazine *Skeptic* sur l'assassinat de Martin Luther King. Dessin au lavis avec légendes ecrites par l'artiste. (USA)

477, 478 Illustration (visage brun, avions jaunâtres) et page double tirées d'un article critique sur la *Concorde*. Elément du magazine *Skeptic*. (USA)

479 Page double initiale (en couleurs) du magazine *Skeptic*. L'article discute le problème des étrangers immigrés illégalement aux Etats-Unis. (USA)

The Assassination of Martin Luther King Jr.

KING WAS A MAN OF GOD, NONVIOLENCE, AND CIVIL RIGHTS. HE WAS ALSO A MAN WITH MANY ENEMIES.

BY RON RIDENOUR

Martin Luther King, Jr. whose leadership of the civil rights movement had won him the 1964 Nobel Peace Prize, died in Memphis on April 4, 1968 at the age of 39. He was the victim of an assassin, who had aimed a rifle at King's head from the bathroom window of a rooming house about 200 feet away from the motel balcony where King was standing. King died an hour later on a hospital operating table.

To many it was not surprising that the "father of the sit-ins" would be killed by an assassin, but the shock set off a week of demonstrations and riots in 125 cities, the worst of them in Washington, DC; Baltimore; Kansas City, Missouri; and Chicago. Altogether, 46 people were killed (42 of them blacks); 2,600 people were injured; 21,270 were arrested (mostly for looting); as much as $70 million was lost in property damage (largely from fires); 55,000 troops were activated.

Martin Luther King was the 14th American and the third black man to win the Nobel Peace Prize. He earned it the hard way. He was arrested 16 times for his civil rights activities; he was stabbed in the chest; his home was bombed three times and he got almost daily death threats for a dozen years.

King's career as a reformer

14

474

475   476

477

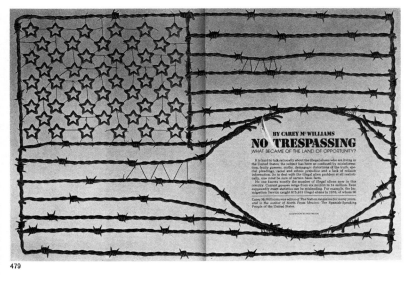

479

ARTIST / KÜNSTLER / ARTISTE:

474—476 Alan E. Cober
477, 478 Ed Soyka
479 Fred Nelson

DESIGNER / GESTALTER / MAQUETTISTE:

474—479 Gordon Mortensen

ART DIRECTOR / DIRECTEUR ARTISTIQUE:

474—479 Gordon Mortensen

PUBLISHER / VERLEGER / EDITEUR:

474—479 Skeptic Magazine, Inc.

478

Magazine Illustrations
Zeitschriften-Illustrationen
Illustrations de périodiques

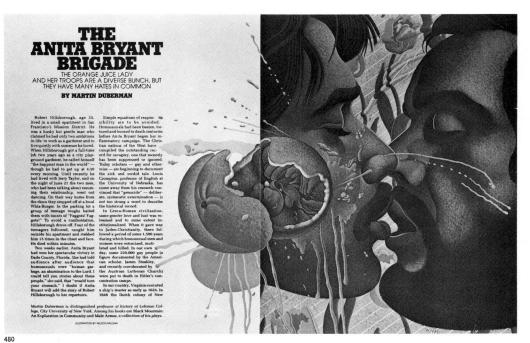

480 Double spread with colour illustration opening an article in *Skeptic* magazine on haters of homosexuality. (USA)
481 Colourful spread opening an article in *Skeptic* magazine on US-Cuban relations. (USA)
482 Full-colour illustration for an article in *Skeptic* on the opposition to the rights of homosexuals. (USA)
483 Full-page colour illustration for an article in *Skeptic* magazine on Cuba as a Communist base. (USA)
484 Illustration (full page, full colour) for an article on the American pet mania in *Skeptic* magazine. (USA)
485 Colour illustration for an article on children's perception of forms published in the magazine *Psychologie*. (FRA)
486 Full-page illustration in full colour for an article in *Privé* about Fernand Legros and his picture sales. (FRA)

480 Doppelseite mit farbiger Illustration zu einem Artikel aus dem Magazin *Skeptic* über eine Anti-Homosexuellen-Kampagne. (USA)
481 Farbige Doppelseite aus *Skeptic* mit einem Artikel über die Beziehungen USA–Kuba. (USA)
482 Farbige Illustration zu einem Artikel aus *Skeptic* über die Anti-Homosexuellen-Kampagne in den USA. (USA)
483 Farbige Illustration zu einem Artikel aus *Skeptic* über Kuba als kommunistischer Stützpunkt. (USA)
484 Farbige Illustration zu einem Artikel über das Problem der ständig wachsenden Zahl von Haustieren in den USA, aus *Skeptic*. (USA)
485 Farbige Illustration aus der Zeitschrift *Psychologie* zu einem Artikel über die Formenwahrnehmung von Kindern. (FRA)
486 Farbige Illustration zu einem Artikel in *Privé* über Fernand Legros, dem Verkäufe gefälschter Bilder unterstellt werden. (FRA)

480 Page double avec illustration en couleurs d'un article de *Skeptic* consacré à une campagne lancée contre les homosexuels. (USA)
481 Page double initiale (en couleurs vives) d'un article sur les relations entre les Etats-Unis et le Cuba. De *Skeptic*. (USA)
482 Illustration couleur accompagnant un article du magazine *Skeptic* sur l'opposition aux droits des homosexuels. (USA)
483 Illustration pleine page (en couleurs) d'un article présentant le Cuba en tant que base communiste. Du magazine *Skeptic*. (USA)
484 Illustration couleur (pleine page) d'un article sur la manie des Américains de tenir des animaux domestiques. (USA)
485 Illustration couleur d'un article discutant la perception des formes chez les enfants. Elément du magazine *Psychologie*. (FRA)
486 Illustration pleine page (en couleurs) d'un article dans *Privé* consacré à Fernand Legros, marchand de tableaux. (FRA)

ARTIST / KÜNSTLER / ARTISTE:

480 Wilson McLean
481 Doug Johnson
482 Sue Coe
483 Eraldo Carugati
484 Ed Soyka
485 Frédéric Courtadon
486 Sato Yamamoto

DESIGNER / GESTALTER / MAQUETTISTE:

480–484 Gordon Mortensen

ART DIRECTOR / DIRECTEUR ARTISTIQUE:

480–484 Gordon Mortensen
485 Daniel Sinay
486 Gérard Vilocel

PUBLISHER / VERLEGER / EDITEUR:

480–484 Skeptic Magazine, Inc.
485 Psychologie
486 Editions de France

Magazine Illustrations
Zeitschriften-Illustrationen
Illustrations de périodiques

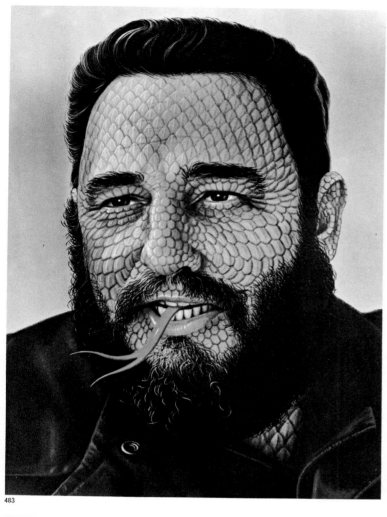

483

484

485

486

488

490

487

ARTIST / KÜNSTLER / ARTISTE:

487, 488 Edward Sorel
489 Beate Brömse
490, 491 Les Mason
492 Haruo Miyauchi
493 John O'Leary
494 Dave Willardson

DESIGNER / GESTALTER / MAQUETTISTE:

492—494 Roger Black

ART DIRECTOR / DIRECTEUR ARTISTIQUE:

487, 488 Joe Brooks
489 Heinrich Streichsbier
492—494 Roger Black

AGENCY / AGENTUR / AGENCE – STUDIO:

490, 491 Les Mason Graphic Design

PUBLISHER / VERLEGER / EDITEUR:

487, 488 Penthouse International Ltd.
489 Kauka-Verlag
490, 491 Lawrence Publishing Co. Pty Ltd
492—494 Straight Arrow Publishers

487, 488 Complete spread and illustration (full colour) from a feature in *Penthouse* about a reunion of the Watergate gang. (USA)
489 Colour spread with a psychological quiz ("Are you afraid of the future?") in the magazine *Mädchen*. (GER)
490, 491 Double spread and illustration from an article on French cuisine in *The Epicurean*. Black and white. (AUS)
492, 494 Full-page colour illustrations from *Rolling Stone*, for articles on sound systems and on sex and stereo. (USA)
493 Illustration (full page, full colour) for a story in *Rolling Stone* about a boy who turned into a snake. (USA)

487, 488 Farbige Illustration und Doppelseite zu einem Artikel in *Penthouse* über ein Treffen der «Watergate»-Beteiligten. (USA)
489 Farbige Doppelseite zu einem psychologischen Test im Magazin *Mädchen*. (GER)
490, 491 Doppelseite und Detail der Illustration zu einem Artikel über die französische Küche, aus *The Epicurean*. (AUS)
492, 494 Farbige Illustrationen aus dem Magazin *Rolling Stone* zu Artikeln über Ton-Systeme und über Sex und Stereo. (USA)
493 Ganzseitige, farbige Illustration zu einer Kurzgeschichte aus dem Magazin *Rolling Stone* über einen Jungen, der sich in eine Schlange verwandelte. (USA)

487, 488 Page double et illustration en couleur d'un article de *Penthouse* sur une réunion du gang Watergate. (USA)
489 Page double en couleur présentant un quiz psychologique («Avez-vous peur de l'avenir?»). Du magazine *Mädchen*. (GER)
490, 491 Page double et illustration accompagnant un article sur la cuisine française dans le magazine *Epicurean*. Noir-blanc. (AUS)
492, 494 Illustrations pleines pages (en couleurs) tirées du magazine *Rolling Stone*. Elles accompagnent des articles sur les systèmes sonores et sur le sexe et la stéréophonie. (USA)
493 Illustration (pleine page en couleurs) figurant dans une histoire de *Rolling Stone* sur un garçon transformé en serpent. (USA)

489

491

492

493

494

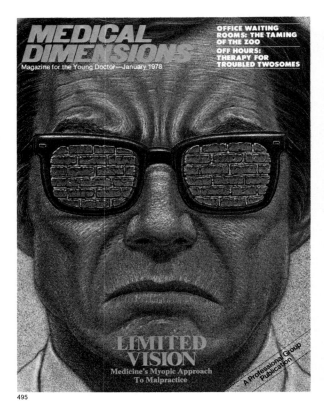

495

496

495 Cover of *Medical Dimensions,* a magazine for young doctors. Brown face with red bricks symbolizing blocked vision. (USA)
496 Cover illustration of a *Roussel* publication dealing with a new treatment for the gums. Full colour. (FRA)
497 Cover of the literary and philosophic review *Errata.* White head, blue lock and key, yellow ground. (FRA)
498 Illustration for an article on "What makes the candidate run?" published in *Psychology Today.* The black-and-white drawing shows candidates from past presidential elections in the United States. (USA)
499 Cover of an issue of *New Scientist* containing a study of animal behaviour. Pastel shades. (GBR)

495 Umschlag der Fachzeitschrift für junge Ärzte, *Medical Dimensions.* Symbolisiert ist die Kurzsichtigkeit der Medizin. Gesicht in Brauntönen mit roten Ziegelsteinen. (USA)
496 Farbiger Umschlag einer *Roussel*-Publikation über neue Behandlungsmethoden für das Zahnfleisch. (FRA)
497 Farbige Umschlag-Illustration (Kopf in Schwarzweiss) der Zeitschrift für Literatur und Philosophie *Errata.* (FRA)
498 Illustration zu einem Artikel über die Motivation der Präsidentschaftskandidaten in den USA, aus *Psychology Today.* (USA)
499 Umschlag der Zeitschrift *New Scientist* mit Bezug auf eine Studie über das Verhalten von Tieren. (GBR)

495 Couverture de *Medical Dimensions,* un magazine destiné aux jeunes médecins. Les briques rouges devraient symboliser la vue bloquée de la médecine. (USA)
496 Illustration de couverture d'une publication *Roussel* consacrée à un nouveau traitement de la gencive. En polychromie. (FRA)
497 Couverture de *Errata,* revue littéraire et philosophique. Tête blanche, serrure et clef bleues sur fond jaune. (FRA)
498 Illustration accompagnant un article sur la motivation des candidats à la présidence des Etats-Unis. Le dessin noir-blanc présente nombre de candidats d'élections présidentielles. (USA)
499 Couverture d'un numéro du magazine *New Scientist* contenant un article sur le comportement des animaux. (GBR)

497

Trade Magazines
Fachzeitschriften
Revues professionelles

498

How animal behaviour became a science

499

ARTIST / KÜNSTLER / ARTISTE:

495 Ed Soyka
496 Pierre Peyrolle
497 Devis Grebu
498 Robert Pryor
499 Brian Grimwood

DESIGNER / GESTALTER / MAQUETTISTE:

495 Cathy Cacchione
496 Pierre Peyrolle
498 Noel Werrett
499 Brian Grimwood

ART DIRECTOR / DIRECTEUR ARTISTIQUE:

495 John C. Jay
498 Neil Shakery
499 Tom Reynolds

AGENCY / AGENTUR / AGENCE – STUDIO:

495 MBA Communications, Inc.
496 Orange Création

PUBLISHER / VERLEGER / EDITEUR:

495 Medical Dimensions
496 Laboratoires Roussel
497 Errata
498 Ziff-Davis Publishing
499 Newscientist

500

ARTIST / KÜNSTLER / ARTISTE:

500–504 Lanny Sommese
505, 506 Rudolph de Harak
507, 508 Etienne Delessert

DESIGNER / GESTALTER / MAQUETTISTE:

500–504 Lanny Sommese
507 Béat Brusch
508 Etienne Delessert

ART DIRECTOR / DIRECTEUR ARTISTIQUE:

500–504 Lanny Sommese
507, 508 Martin Berthommier

AGENCY / AGENTUR / AGENCE – STUDIO:

500–504 Lanny Sommese Design
507, 508 Carabosse

PUBLISHER / VERLEGER / EDITEUR:

500–504 Eastern Communication Assoc.
505, 506 Family Planning Perspectives
507, 508 Bayard Presse

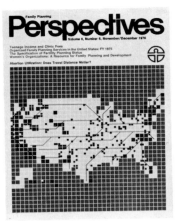
505 a

500, 501 Black-and-white illustration and complete back and front cover of the journal of the Eastern Communication Association. (USA)
502–504 Three further complete covers of *Communication Quarterly*. Fig. 502 in ochre on black, Fig. 503 in black on green, Fig. 504 in black and white. (USA)
505, 505a, 506 Complete cover of *Family Planning Perspectives* and details of the cover design for this and for another issue. (USA)
507 Cover of a special dossier on dreams issued by the young people's magazine *Record*. Brightly coloured inset in black head. (FRA)
508 Portrait of Vorster (full colour) opening a section of a *Record* dossier. (FRA)

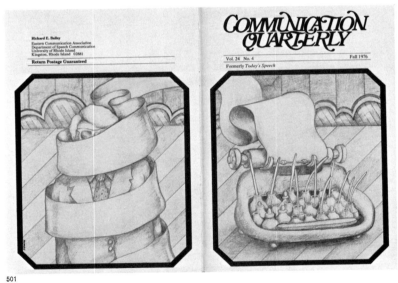
501

502

503

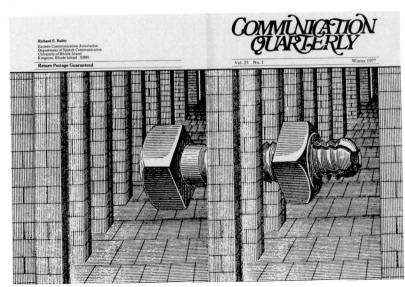
504

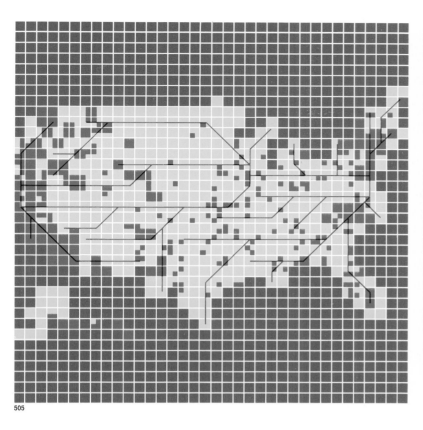

505

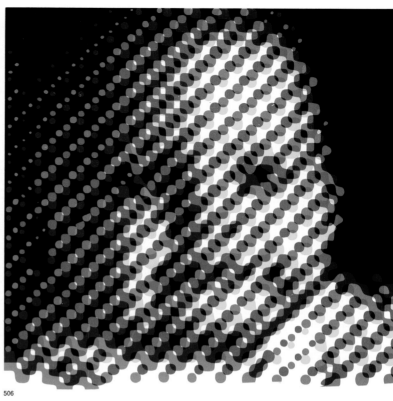

506

507

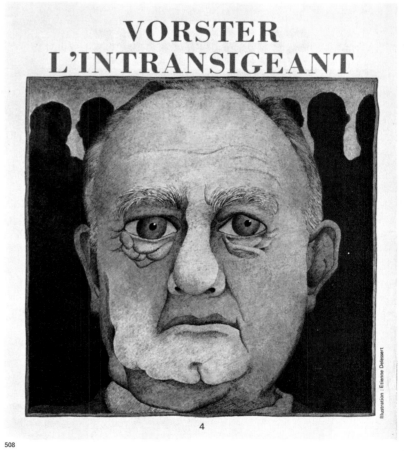

508

500–504 Detail einer Illustration und ganze Umschlagseiten der von Eastern Communication Assoc. herausgegebenen Publikation zum Thema Kommunikation *(Communication Quarterly)*. Abb. 500, 501 in Schwarzweiss, Abb. 502–504 einfarbiger Druck auf farbigem Papier. (USA)
505, 505a, 506 Kompletter Umschlag einer Zeitschrift über Familienplanung und Details der Umschlagillustrationen für diese und eine weitere Ausgabe. (USA)
507 Farbige Umschlagseite der Jugend-Zeitschrift *Record* zum Thema «Träume». Bunte Farben im Kreis und Umrandung des Kopfes, das Kopfinnere ist schwarz. (FRA)
508 Farbige Illustration zu einem Artikel über den südafrikanischen Premier Vorster mit dem Titel «Vorster, der Starrsinnige», aus der Zeitschrift *Record*. (FRA)

500, 501 Illustration noir-blanc et recto et verso de la couverture d'une revue trimestrielle. (USA)
502–504 Trois autres couvertures de *Communication Quarterly*. Fig. 502 en ocre sur fond noir, fig. 503 en noir sur fond vert, fig. 504 en noir et blanc. (USA)
505, 505a, 506 Couverture d'un magazine consacré au planning familial et détails des illustrations de couverture de ce numéro et d'un autre. (USA)
507 Couverture du dossier spécial de *Record*, magazine destiné à la jeune génération; celui-ci est consacré aux rêves. Tête noire avec des couleurs vives. (FRA)
508 Illustration (en couleurs) accompagnant un article présentant un portrait de Vorster, premier ministre d'Afrique du Sud. Du magazine *Record*. (FRA)

Australia 85 cents. Canada $1.00. Germany DM 3.50.
New Zealand 85 cents. U.S.A. (by air) $2.25. Malaysia $2.00
ISSN 0028-6664

10 November 1977 Vol 76 No 1077 Weekly 35p

new**scientist**

**Accidents at home—
the grim toll**

509

511

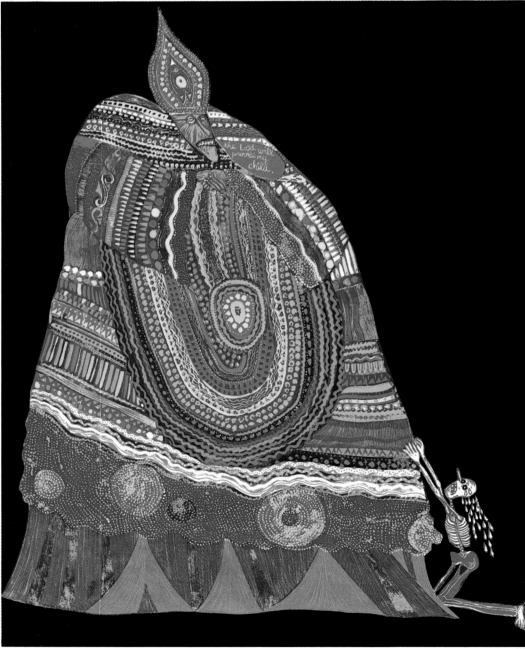

510

512

ARTIST / KÜNSTLER / ARTISTE:

509 Louis-Pierre Bougie
510 Randall Enos
511 Robin Harris
512 Jack & Pam Lefkowitz
513 David M. Seager
514, 516 Richard Brown
515 Heinz Klinkon
517 Stanislaw Fernandes
518 Armando Testa

DESIGNER / GESTALTER / MAQUETTISTE:

512 Jack & Pam Lefkowitz
513 David M. Seager
514, 516 Richard Brown
517 John Vogler/Stanislaw Fernandes
518 Franco del Rosso

ART DIRECTOR / DIRECTEUR ARTISTIQUE:

509 Gilles Brault
510 Andrew Kner
511 Tom Reynolds
512 Jack Lefkowitz
513 Bernard B. Sanders
514, 516 Gene Freidman
515 Phil Jordan
517 John Vogler
518 Armando Testa

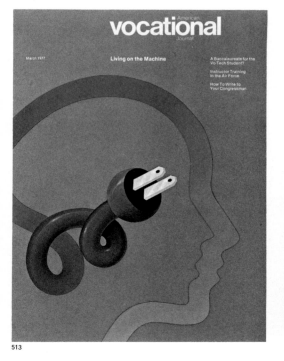
513

515

517

514

516

518

AGENCY / AGENTUR / AGENCE – STUDIO:

512 Jack Lefkowitz Inc.
513 Sanders & Noe, Inc.
514, 516 Scholastic Magazines, Inc.
515 Beveridge & Associates, Inc.
517 Stanislaw Fernandes Design
518 Studio Armando Testa

PUBLISHER / VERLEGER / EDITEUR:

509 Société d'édition de la revue FORCES
510 RC Publications
511 Newscientist
512 Industrial Launderer
513 American Vocational Journal
514, 516 Scholastic Magazines, Inc.
515 The Construction Specifications
517 McGraw-Hill Publication
518 Editrice l'Ufficio Moderno

Trade Magazines

509 Complete cover of the review *Forces* published by the province of Quebec. Figures in bright colours. (CAN)
510 From a number of illustrations in which artists were to visualize things they wanted to get off their chests. Here: "The Lord will provide, my child", shown in *Print* magazine. (USA)
511 Cover of an issue of the *New Scientist*. Full colour. (GBR)
512 Cover of *Industrial Launderer*. The issue suggests what to do with worn-out uniforms. Yellow door, blue uniforms. (USA)
513 Cover of an issue of *American Vocational Journal* carrying an article on machines used to duplicate the mind. (USA)
514, 516 Two full-colour covers of *Scholastic Science World* referring to an inquiry as to whether animals dream. (USA)
515 Colour page in *The Construction Specifier* facing an article on glass-reinforced concrete. (USA)
517 Cover of an issue of *Business Week* containing a feature on doing business with Africa. (USA)
518 Cover of the business magazine *L'Ufficio moderno*. (ITA)

509 Kompletter Umschlag der von der Provinz Quebec herausgegebenen Schrift *Forces*. Leuchtende Farben. (CAN)
510 Aus einer Reihe von Illustrationen, in denen die Künstler ausdrücken, was Ihnen «Bauchschmerzen» bereitet. Hier eine in *Print* publizierte Illustration: «Der Herr wird sich deiner annehmen, mein Kind». (USA)
511 Umschlag einer Ausgabe des *New Scientist*. (GBR)
512 Umschlag der Wäschereizeitschrift *Industrial Launderer*. Blaue Uniformen, gelbe Tür, grüne Wände. (USA)
513 Umschlag des *American Vocational Journal* (Ausbildungs-Zeitschrift) mit Bezug auf einen Artikel über Maschinen, die das menschliche Gehirn ersetzen. (USA)
514, 516 Farbige Umschlagseiten der Schülerzeitschrift *Scholastic Science World* zu einer Umfrage, ob Tiere träumen. (USA)
515 Illustration zum Thema «glasverstärkter Beton». (USA)
517 Umschlag des Wirtschaftsmagazins *Business Week*. (USA)
518 Umschlag der Zeitschrift *L'Ufficio Moderno*. (ITA)

509 Couverture complète de la revue *Forces* publiée par la province du Québec. En couleurs vives. (CAN)
510 D'une série d'illustrations par lesquelles les artistes visualisent ce qui leur donne du tintouin. Voici une illustration de *Print*: «Dieu prendra soin de toi, mon enfant». (USA)
511 Couverture d'un numéro du *New Scientist*. (GBR)
512 Couverture de *Industrial Launderer*. Ce numéro donne des propositions quant aux vieilles uniformes. En polychromie. (USA)
513 Couverture du *American Vocational Journal* (Ausbildungs-Zeitschrift) avec référence aux machines qui remplacent le cerveau humain. (USA)
514, 516 Couvertures d'une revue scolaire contenant une enquête sur la question: les animaux, rêvent-ils? (USA)
515 Page couleur en tête d'un article sur un genre de béton renforcé de verre. (USA)
517 Couverture d'une revue économique se référant à un article sur les relations économiques avec l'Afrique. (USA)
518 Couverture du magazine *L'Ufficio Moderno*. (ITA)

519

520

521

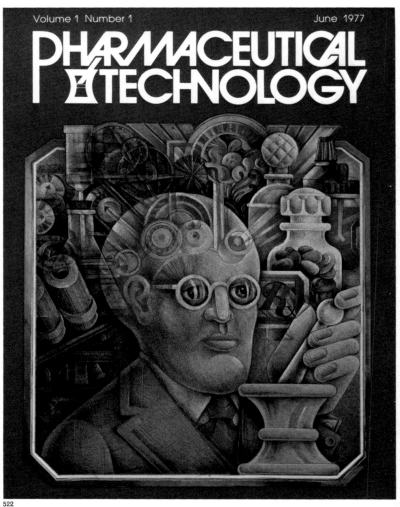

522

523

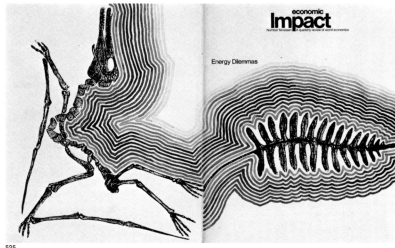

525

ARTIST / KÜNSTLER / ARTISTE:

519 Ed Soyka
520 Robert Giusti
521 Jan Sawka
522 Abe Gurvin
523 Heather Cooper
524 Grzegorz Stanczyk
525 Phil Jordan

DESIGNER / GESTALTER / MAQUETTISTE:

519 Peter Palazzo
520 Neil Shakery
521 Andrew Kner
522 Abe Gurvin
523 Heather Cooper
525 Phil Jordan

519 Cover of an issue of the business magazine *Forbes* with an article on accountants. (USA)
520 Full-page illustration on the subject of anorexia from *Psychology Today*. Full colour. (USA)
521 Cover of the graphic design magazine *Print*. Bright colours. (USA)
522 Polychrome cover for the first issue of *Pharmaceutical Technology*. (USA)
523 Full-page illustration in full colour from *Psychology Today*. (USA)
524 Cover of the magazine of visual art and design *Projekt*. Blue chair, ochre wall. (POL)
525 Complete cover of *Economic Impact*. Black, yellow, orange, red, violet and blue shades. (USA)

519 Umschlag des Wirtschaftsmagazins *Forbes*, zu einem Artikel über Buchhalter. (USA)
520 Illustration aus *Psychology Today* zum Problem der Anorexie bei jungen Mädchen. (USA)
521 Umschlagseite der Graphik-Fachzeitschrift *Print*. Leuchtende Farben. (USA)
522 Farbiger Umschlag der ersten Ausgabe von *Pharmaceutical Technology*. (USA)
523 Farbige Illustration für die Zeitschrift *Psychology Today*. (USA)
524 Farbiger Umschlag der polnischen Zeitschrift für visuelle Kunst und Graphik *Projekt*. (POL)
525 Farbige Umschlagseiten des Wirtschaftsmagazins *Economic Impact*. (USA)

519 Couverture d'un magazine économique, contenant un article sur les comptables. (USA)
520 Illustration pleine page se référant à l'anorexie. Article de *Psychology Today*. (USA)
521 Couverture de *Print*, magazine d'arts graphiques. Illustration en couleurs vives. (USA)
522 Couverture en couleurs du premier numéro du magazine *Pharmaceutical Technology*. (USA)
523 Illustration pleine page (en couleurs) figurant dans un article de *Psychology Today*. (USA)
524 Couverture de *Projekt*, magazine d'arts visuels. Chaise bleue, parois ocre. (POL)
525 Couverture (recto et verso) d'un magazine économique. En polychromie. (USA)

ART DIRECTOR / DIRECTEUR ARTISTIQUE:

519 Peter Palazzo
520, 523 Neil Shakery
521 Andrew Kner
522 Clay Camburn
524 Hubert Hilscher
525 Joseph D. Hockersmith

AGENCY / AGENTUR / AGENCE – STUDIO:

522 Abe Gurvin
523 Burns, Cooper, Hynes Ltd.
525 U.S. Information Agency

PUBLISHER / VERLEGER / EDITEUR:

519 Forbes Inc.
520, 523 Ziff-Davis Publishing
521 RC Publications
522 Pharmaceutical Technology
524 Krajowa Agencja Wydawnicza
525 U.S. Information Agency

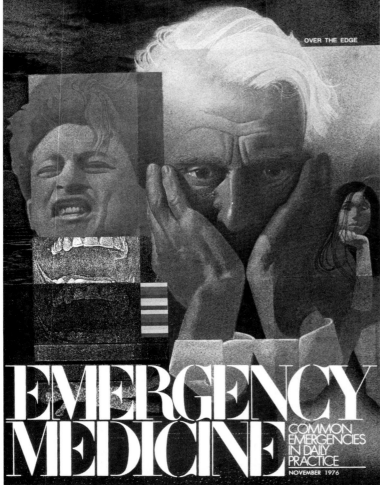

526

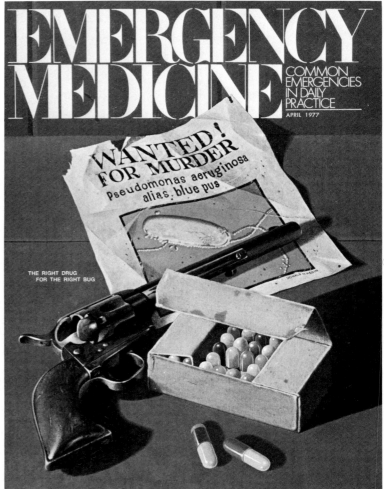

527

526, 527 Two full-colour covers for *Emergency Medicine.* One refers to "the right drug for the right bug" (see Fig. 530), the other to psychiatric problems. (USA)
528, 532 Full-page illustration (pink and red foot on yellow and blue) facing an article in *Emergency Medicine* on peripheral vascular disease (complete spread in Fig. 532). (USA)
529, 533, 534 Two black-and-white drawings and complete spread from a feature in *Emergency Medicine* on "Heart under Siege". (USA)
530 Double spread opening a feature in *Emergency Medicine* on selecting the right drug. (USA)
531 Page in *Emergency Medicine* opening an article on kernicterus in the newborn. Black and white except for yellow baby. (USA)

526, 527 Zwei farbige Umschlagseiten von *Emergency Medicine.* Eine bezieht sich auf «das richtige Medikament für die richtigen Bakterien» (siehe Abb. 530), die andere auf psychiatrische Probleme. (USA)
528, 532 Ganzseitige Illustration (Fuss in Rosa und Rot auf Gelb und Blau) und komplette Doppelseite für einen Artikel über Venenentzündungen, aus *Emergency Medicine.* (USA)
529, 533, 534 Zwei Schwarzweiss-Zeichnungen und Doppelseite von einem Artikel über den Herzinfarkt, aus *Emergency Medicine.* (USA)
530 Doppelseite aus *Emergency Medicine* über die Wahl der richtigen Medikamente. (USA)
531 Illustration aus *Emergency Medicine* zum Problem der Gelbsucht bei Säuglingen. (USA)

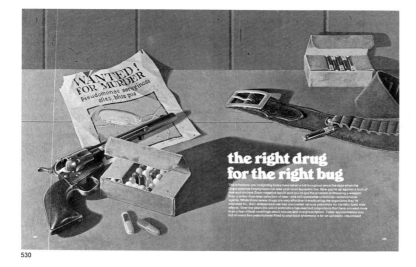

530

Trade Magazines
Fachzeitschriften
Revues professionelles

531

528

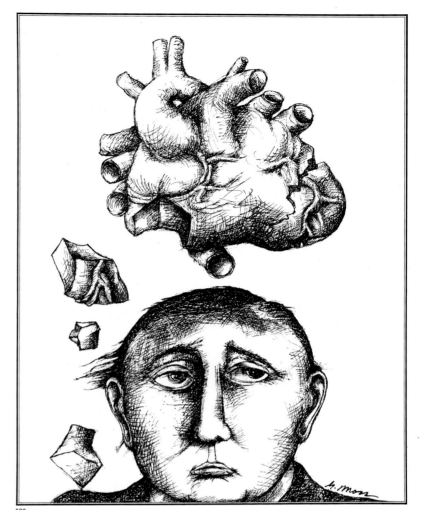

529

526, 527 Couvertures (en couleurs) de *Emergency Medicine*. Fig. 526: à chaque bactérie le médicament approprié; Fig. 527: référence aux problèmes psychiatriques. (USA)
528, 532 Illustration pleine page (pied rose et rouge sur jaune et bleu) et page double complète en tête d'un article de *Emergency Medicine* sur les inflammations de veines. (USA)
529, 533, 534 Dessins en noir et blanc et page double complète figurant dans un article de *Emergency Medicine* sur l'infarctus du myocarde. (USA)
530 Page double en tête d'un article sur le choix du médicament approprié. (USA)
531 Page de *Emergency Medicine* introduisant un article sur le problème de la jaunisse chez les bébés. Noir et blanc, bébé jaune. (USA)

ARTIST / KÜNSTLER / ARTISTE:

526, 530 Don Hedin
527 Dick Krepel
528, 532 Randy Enos
529, 533, 534 Geoffrey Moss
531 Don Weller

DESIGNER / GESTALTER / MAQUETTISTE:

526–528, 530, 532 Tom Lennon
529, 531, 533, 534 Diane Greene

ART DIRECTOR / DIRECTEUR ARTISTIQUE:

526–528, 530, 532 Ira Silberlicht/
    Tom Lennon
529, 531, 533, 534 Tom Lennon

PUBLISHER / VERLEGER / EDITEUR:

526–534 Fischer Medical Publications

532

533

534

36

The Human Zoo. Language in all its compartments, taken separately or collectively, is subject to perpetual change. How many, for instance, know that the adjunct to feminine beauty known commonly today as **falsies** existed a full century ago, but under the name of **palpitators?** Or that the phone, when it was being developed by Bell, was known as the **harmonic telegraph,** while the original telephone "hello," prior to 1880, was "ahoy"? Similarly, names have taken on new and varied meanings. Some time back, a well-known comedian repeatedly used a phrase that swept

37

the country: "Monkeys are the **cwaziest** people!" Though not quite accurate scientifically, he nonetheless had something there. Monkeys, and animals in general, are not people, but people are most assuredly animals. And the names used to describe them significantly bear (no pun intended!) this out. A toastmaster at a recent dinner referred to a guest speaker as "that jovial porcine fellow"—a marvelously polite way of saying "fat slob." No doubt about it, certain folk take on the particular characteristics of animals, and herein are several random graphic examples.

THIS ARTICLE WAS SET IN ITC KABEL AND ITC AVANT GARDE GOTHIC CONDENSED

ILLUSTRATIONS BY HEDDA JOHNSON

535

535 Double spread with a glossary of animal names applied to humans. From *U&lc,* magazine of the International Typeface Corporation. Black and white. (USA)
536 Issue of *Secretariat News,* a UN magazine, marking the 30th anniversary of the Charta. (USA)
537 Double spread in full colour about Alaska in the *Exxon* magazine *The Lamp.* (USA)
538 Full-colour cover of the *Geigy* magazine *The Family in Distress,* here referring to stresses in the single-parent family. (USA)
539 Cover of *Sallyport,* magazine of the alumni of Rice University. Black and brown. (USA)
540, 541 Cover (black, white and red) and full-colour double spread from an issue of *The Lamp,* the *Exxon* house organ. The cover is a Senoufo tapestry. The spread refers to research. (USA)

535 Doppelseite mit Tiernamen, die auch als Bezeichnung für Menschen gebraucht werden. Aus der Zeitschrift einer internationalen Typographen-Vereinigung, *U&lc.* (USA)
536 Umschlag der *Secretariat News* der UN zum 30jährigen Bestehen der UN-Charta. (USA)
537 Farbige Doppelseite über Alaska aus der *Exxon*-Hauszeitschrift *The Lamp.* (USA)
538 Farbiger Umschlag einer *Geigy*-Publikation, *The Family in Distress,* hier zum Problem von Familien mit nur einem Elternteil. (USA)
539 Umschlag von *Sallyport,* Magazin der Rice University. Schwarz auf Braun. (USA)
540, 541 Umschlag (Kunsthandwerk des Senoufo-Stammes) und farbige Doppelseite zum Thema Forschung, aus der *Exxon*-Hauszeitschrift *The Lamp.* (USA)

535 Page double avec une liste de noms d'animaux qu'on utilise aussi pour les êtres humains. Elément du magazine *U&lc* de l'International Typeface Corporation. Noir et blanc. (USA)
536 D'un magazine de l'ONU publié à l'occasion du 30e anniversaire de la Charte. (USA)
537 Page double consacrée à Alaska. Du magazine *The Lamp* de la société *Exxon.* (USA)
538 Couverture polychrome du magazine *The Family in Distress,* une publication de *Geigy.* Elle se réfère aux problèmes surgissant lorsqu'il n'y a qu'un des parents. (USA)
539 Couverture de *Sallyport,* magazine des anciens étudiants de la Rice University. (USA)
540, 541 Couverture (noir, blanc et rouge) représentant une tapisserie des Senoufo et page double (en couleurs) se référant à la recherche. De *The Lamp,* journal d'entreprise d'*Exxon.* (USA)

ARTIST / KÜNSTLER / ARTISTE:

535 Hedda Johnson
536 Georg Kintzel
537 Robert Giusti
538 Robert Heindel
539 Melissa Grimes
541 ab Nordbok

DESIGNER / GESTALTER / MAQUETTISTE:

536 Georg Kintzel
537 John J. Conley
538 John DeCesare
539 Jerry Herring
540, 541 Harry O. Diamond

ART DIRECTOR / DIRECTEUR ARTISTIQUE:

535 Herb Lubalin
536 Georg Kintzel
537 John J. Conley
538 John DeCesare
539 Jerry Herring
540, 541 Harry O. Diamond

AGENCY / AGENTUR / AGENCE – STUDIO:

539 Herring Design

536

537

184

TheFamilyInDistress

In This issue: Vol. 2., No. 3.

Stresses in the Single-Parent Family   Text prepared for Geigy Pharmaceuticals by Excerpta Medica

Ralph B. Little, M.D.

538

The Lamp

540

SALLYPORT

Association of Rice Alumni · November 1977 · Volume 33, Number 2

The Interview Game

539

PUBLISHER / VERLEGER / EDITEUR:

535 International Typeface Corporation
536 United Nations Headquarters
537, 540, 541 Exxon Corporation
538 Geigy Pharmaceuticals
539 Rice University

House Organs / Hauszeitschriften
Journaux d'entreprise

541

185

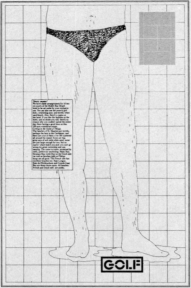

542

543

542 Inside of a large folder about a cruise organized by Itel Corporation for employees to mark its tenth anniversary. In colour. (USA)
543 Cover of a catalogue of ephemera published by the Metropolitan Museum of Art. (USA)
544 Cover of *Tempo*, the house organ of Touche Ross & Co. Green title, Punch in reds and greens. (USA)
545 Page opening a feature in *The Grantsmanship Center News*. Black and red. (USA)
546 Polychrome cover of *Westways*, magazine of the Automobile Club of Southern California. (USA)
547 Cover of *The Grantsmanship Center News*, organ of an educational institution. The subject is the same as in Fig. 545—corporate giving. Full colour. (USA)
548 Cover of *Currency*, house organ of the Reserve Bank of Australia. (AUS)

542 Ankündigung und Illustration eines Firmenausflugs (Itel Corp.) auf die Antillen-Insel St. Maarten, mit Beschreibung und Darstellung der Unterhaltungsmöglichkeiten. (USA)
543 Umschlag eines Katalogs kurzlebiger Kunst des Metropolitan Museum of Art, New York. (USA)
544 Farbiger Umschlag von *Tempo*, Hauszeitschrift von Touche Ross & Co. (USA)
545 Seite aus *Grantsmanship Center News* mit Illustration zu einem Artikel über die Frage von Firmenspenden für gemeinnützige Zwecke. Schwarz und rot. (USA)
546 Farbiger Umschlag von *Westways*, Publikation des Automobil-Clubs von Südkalifornien. (USA)
547 Farbiger Umschlag der *Grantsmanship Center News*, einer gemeinnützigen Publikation, die sich hier mit Firmen-Philanthropie befasst. Siehe auch Abb. 545. (USA)
548 Umschlag von *Currency*, Hauszeitschrift einer australischen Bank. (AUS)

542 Intérieur d'un dépliant grand format sur une croisière que l'Itel Corporation organise pour ses employés à l'occasion des dix ans d'existence de cette compagnie. En couleurs. (USA)
543 Couverture d'un catalogue d'art éphémère publié par le Metropolitan Museum of Art. (USA)
544 Couverture de *Tempo*, journal d'entreprise de Touche Ross & Co. Titre vert, Guignol en divers tons rouges et verts. (USA)
545 Page en tête d'un article publié dans le magazine *The Grantsmanship Center News*. (USA)
546 Couverture couleur de *Westways*, magazine du Club automobile du Sud de la Californie. (USA)
547 Couverture du magazine *The Grantsmanship Center News* publié par une institution d'éducation. Elle se réfère aux œuvres philanthropiques des entreprises (voir aussi fig. 545). (USA)
548 Couverture de *Currency*, journal d'entreprise d'une banque australienne. (AUS)

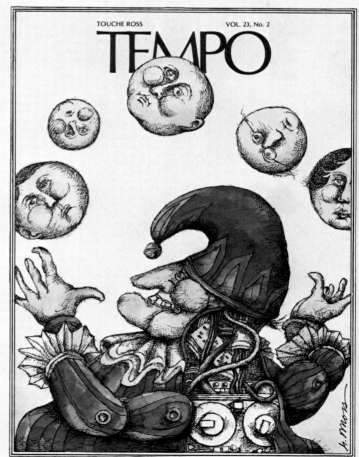

544

545

546

547

548

549

549 Pen drawing (full page) in *Tempo,* house organ of Touche Ross & Co. (USA)
550 Cover of *Messenger,* house organ of the Martin Luther Hospital Medical Center, Anaheim, California. Theme of the issue: pain. Black and white. (USA)
551, 552 Two drawings used as illustrations in *Clinch,* house organ of the printers D. Hennes-Druck. Black and white. (GER)
553 Detail of a full-page illustration in *Push Pin Graphic,* house organ of the Push Pin Studios. Theme of the issue: "Food and Violence". (USA)

ARTIST / KÜNSTLER / ARTISTE:

549 Geoffrey Moss
550 Carl Seltzer
551, 552 Wolfgang Bellingradt
553 Richard Mantel

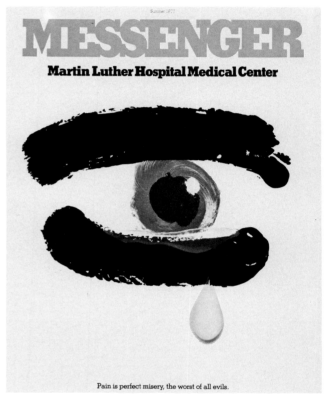

Pain is perfect misery, the worst of all evils.

550

DESIGNER / GESTALTER:

549 Tom Burns
551, 552 Wolfgang Bellingradt
553 Richard Mantel

ART DIRECTOR:

549 Tom Burns
550 Advertising Designers
551, 552 Dieter Hennes
553 Seymour Chwast

AGENCY / AGENTUR / AGENCE:

549 Tom Burns Associates
550 Advertising Designers, Inc.
553 Push Pin Studios, Inc.

PUBLISHER / VERLEGER / EDITEUR:

549 Touche Ross & Cc.
550 Pacific Health Resources
551, 552 DHD-D. Hennes Druck
553 The Push Pin Graphic, Inc.

House Organs
Hauszeitschriften
Journaux d'entreprise

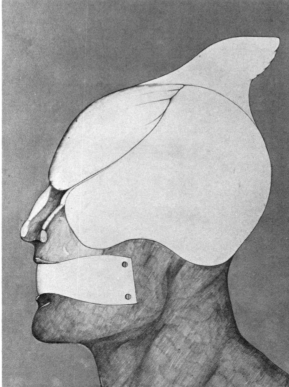

551

552

549 Federzeichnung (ganze Seite) aus *Tempo*, Hauszeitschrift von Touche Ross & Co., zum Problem der Speicherung persönlicher Daten. (USA)
550 Umschlag von *Messenger*, Hauszeitschrift eines Spitals, mit einem Zitat aus John Miltons *Paradise Lost* über den Schmerz. (USA)
551, 552 Zeichnungen, die in *Clinch*, Hauszeitschrift von D. Hennes-Druck, abgebildet wurden. Schwarzweiss. (GER)
553 Ganzseitige Illustration aus der *Push-Pin*-Hauszeitschrift. (USA)

549 Dessin à la plume (pleine page) d'un journal d'entreprise. (USA)
550 Couverture de *Messenger*, journal d'un hôpital, avec une citation du *Paradis perdu* de John Milton sur la douleur. (USA)
551, 552 Deux dessins figurant dans *Clinch*, journal d'entreprise d'une imprimerie. En noir et blanc. (GER)
553 Détail d'une illustration pleine page de *Push Pin Graphic*, journal d'entreprise des Push Pin Studios. Sujet: «Le vivre et la violence». (USA)

553

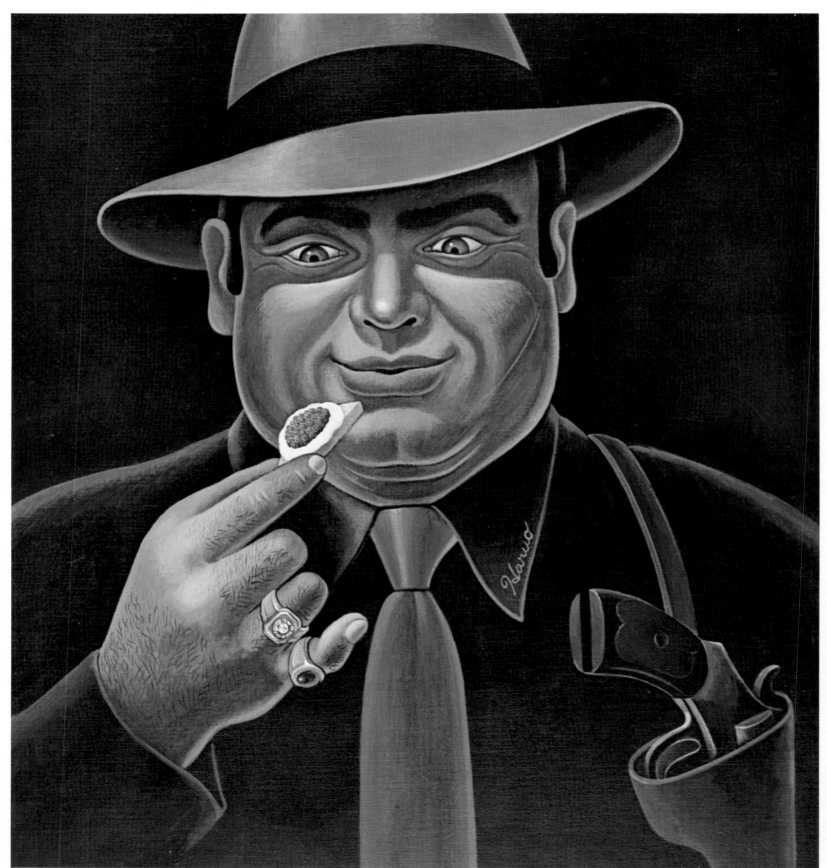

554

556

ARTIST / KÜNSTLER / ARTISTE:

554, 555 Haruo Miyauchi
556 Eduard Prüssen
557 Hedda Johnson
558 John Collier
559 Fred Marshall/Michael Hostovich

DESIGNER / GESTALTER / MAQUETTISTE:

556 Eduard Prüssen

ART DIRECTOR / DIRECTEUR ARTISTIQUE:

554, 555, 558–560 Seymour Chwast
557 Herb Lubalin

AGENCY / AGENTUR / AGENCE – STUDIO:

554, 555 558–560 Push Pin Studios, Inc.

PUBLISHER / VERLEGER / EDITEUR:

554, 555, 558–560 The Push Pin Graphic, Inc.
556 Donkey-Press
557 International Typeface Corporation

House Organs
Hauszeitschriften
Journaux d'entreprise

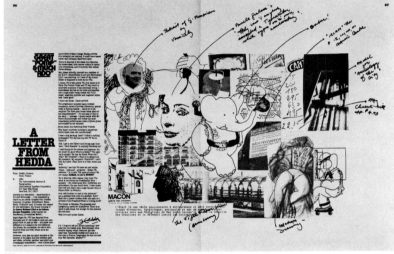

557

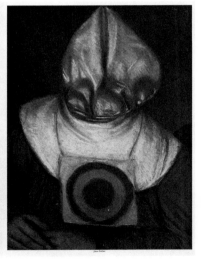

558

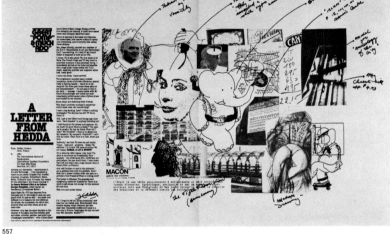

559

555

560

561

562

563

561–563, 566, 567 Four covers of *Scope*, house organ of Japan Upjohn Ltd., and detail of the artwork for one of them in actual size. Figs. 561 and 566/567 are January issues, Fig. 562 is a Christmas and Fig. 563 a Spring issue. A simplified version of each design appears on the back cover. (JPN)
564, 565 Cover of *The Five Minute Hour*, a *Geigy* publication for the psychiatric profession, and double spread from the same issue. The subjects are: opposition between doctors and lawyers (Fig. 564); how our buildings affect our characters; and a graphic interpretation of the proverb "sticks and stones will break my bones, but names will never hurt me" (Fig. 565). Brown print, black drawings on pale brown stock. (USA)

561–563, 566, 567 Vier Umschlagseiten von *Scope*, Hauszeitschrift von Japan Upjohn Ltd., und Detail der Illustration einer dieser Seiten in Originalgrösse. Abb. 561 und 566/567 sind Januar-Ausgaben, Abb. 562 ist eine Weihnachts- und Abb. 563 eine Frühjahrsausgabe. (JPN)
564, 565 Umschlag der *Geigy*-Publikation *The Five Minute Hour* (die Fünf-Minuten-Stunde) für Psychiater. Die Themen sind: Differenzen zwischen Anwälten und Ärzten (Abb. 564) Auswirkung der Architektur auf den menschlichen Charakter und eine graphische Interpretation des englischen Sprichwortes «Stöcke und Steine brechen mir die Knochen, aber Schimpfworte schaden mir nicht» (Abb. 565). (USA)

561–563, 566, 567 Couvertures de *Scope*, journal d'entreprise de Japan Upjohn Ltd. et détail de la composition en grandeur nature. Fig. 561 et 566/567 numéros de janvier, fig. 562 numéro de Noël et fig. 563 numéro de printemps. Une version simplifiée de chaque composition se trouve au verso. (JPN)
564, 565 Couverture de *The Five Minute Hour*, un publication *Geigy* destinée aux psychiatres, et page double du même numéro. Les sujets se réfèrent à l'opposition entre les médecins et les avocats (fig. 564), à l'architecture moderne et ses effets sur le charactère humain ainsi qu'à l'interprétation graphique du proverbe «les coups de bâton me cassent les os, mais les injures me heurtent pas» (fig. 565). (USA)

House Organs
Hauszeitschriften
Journaux d'entreprise

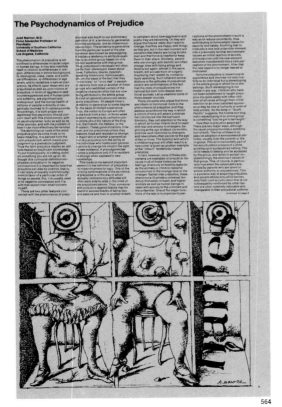

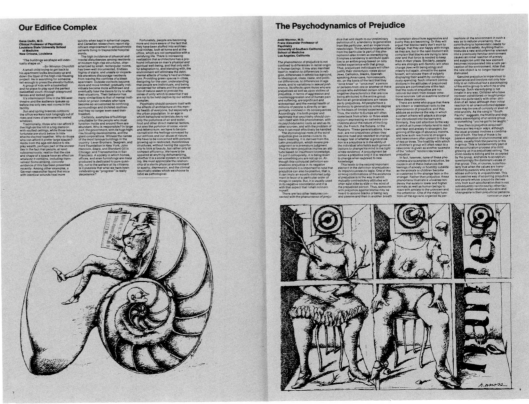

564

565

566

ARTIST / KÜNSTLER / ARTISTE:

561–563, 566, 567 Yoji Kuri
564, 565 Geoffrey Moss

DESIGNER / GESTALTER / MAQUETTISTE:

561–563, 566, 567 Yoji Kuri
564, 565 Bob Paganucci

ART DIRECTOR / DIRECTEUR ARTISTIQUE:

564, 565 Bob Paganucci

PUBLISHER / VERLEGER / EDITEUR:

561–563, 566, 567 Kodansha Ltd.
564, 565 Ciba-Geigy, Corp.

567

568

569

ARTIST / KÜNSTLER / ARTISTE:

568, 569 Mark Hess
570 Tadanori Yokoo
571 Ferenc Pintér
572 Klaus Endrikat
573 Candida Amsden
574 Ian Pollock

DESIGNER / GESTALTER / MAQUETTISTE:

570 Tadanori Yokoo
573 David Pelham
574 Ian Pollock

ART DIRECTOR / DIRECTEUR ARTISTIQUE:

568, 569 Lidia Ferrara
570 Tadanori Yokoo
571 Bruno Binosi
573 David Pelham
574 Philip Dunn

PUBLISHER / VERLEGER / EDITEUR:

568, 569 Alfred A. Knopf
570 Kodansha Ltd.
571 Arnoldo Mondadori
572 Fischer Taschenbuch Verlag
573 Penguin Books Ltd.
574 Pierrot Publishing Ltd.

571

572

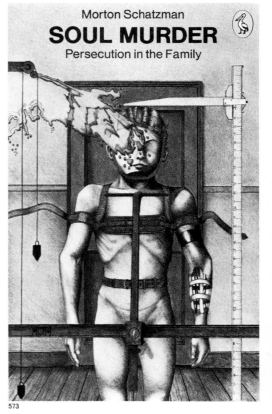

573

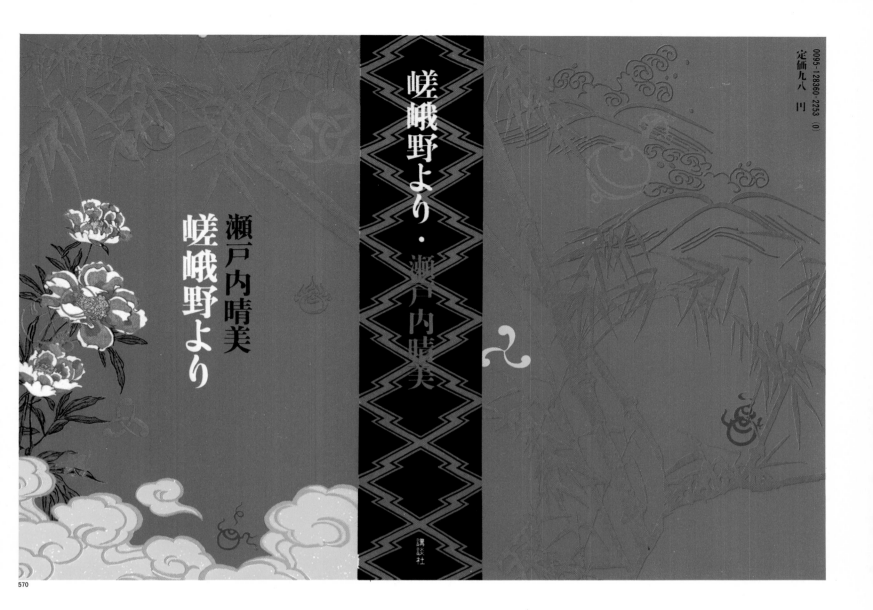

570

BEWARE OF THE CAT

DRAWINGS BY IAN POLLOCK

574

568, 569 Complete jacket and detail of the artwork for a novel about pioneering days in eighteenth-century Canada. (USA)
570 Complete jacket of a book from Kodansha Publishing Ltd. (JPN)
571 Hard cover of a book about five mysteries solved by the famous detective Ellery Queen. Red and black drawing applied to sand cover. (ITA)
572 Cover in full colour for a book (The Hounds of Hell) forming part of a *Fischer* paperback series of ghost stories. (GER)
573 Cover of a *Pelican* book about schizophrenia and family background. (GBR)
574 Cover (red title) for a book of cat drawings. (GBR)

568, 569 Schutzumschlag und Detail der Illustration für einen Roman über die Pioniertage im Kanada des achtzehnten Jahrhunderts. (USA)
570 Kompletter Schutzumschlag eines Buches des Verlags Kodansha Publishing Ltd. (JPN)
571 Fester Umschlag eines Buches über fünf Fälle, die von dem berühmten Detektiv Ellery Queen gelöst werden. Aufgeklebte Zeichnung, sandfarbene Unterlage. (ITA)
572 Umschlag für ein *Fischer*-Taschenbuch aus einer Reihe von Gespenstergeschichten. (GER)
573 Farbiger Umschlag eines Taschenbuches über Schizophrenie und ihren möglichen Ursprung in der Kindheit und Erziehung. Aus einer Reihe «Psychologie und Psychiatrie». (GBR)
574 Umschlag (roter Titel) für ein Buch mit Katzenzeichnungen. (GBR)

568, 569 Jaquette et détail pour un roman traitant des pionniers canadiens du 18e siècle. (USA)
570 Jaquette d'un livre publié par Kodansha Publishing Ltd. (JPN)
571 Couverture d'un livre contenant cinq cas mistérieux que le détective renommé Ellery Queen a su résoudre. Dessin en rouge et noir sur fond sable. (ITA)
572 Couverture (en couleurs) d'un livre de poche faisant partie d'une série de contes de revenants des éditions *Fischer*. (GER)
573 Couverture d'un livre de poche consacré à la schizophrénie et son origine éventuel dans la famille et l'éducation. De la série «Psychologie et psychiatrie». (GBR)
574 Couverture d'un livre contenant des dessins de chats. Titre rouge. (GBR)

Book Covers
Buchumschläge
Couvertures de livres

575

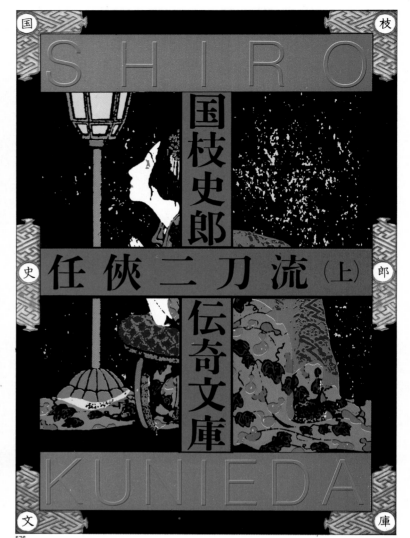

576

575, 576 Two covers in actual size from a series by the same author, from *Kodansha*. (JPN)
577, 578 Complete cover of *The Antioch Review* and detail of the artwork. The issue has a feature on the religious persecution of Jews in the Soviet Union. (USA)
579 Cover in beige and green shades for a paperback on theological matters. (GBR)
580 Dust jacket of a book (The First Glory) forming part of the author's collected works. Black and white. (POL)
581, 581a, 582 Complete cover and artwork of two examples of books from a series of detective stories published in Italian. (ITA)

575, 576 Umschläge in Originalgrösse für Bücher des gleichen Autors, von *Kodansha*. (JPN)
577, 578 Umschlag und Detail der Illustration aus einem Heft über die religiöse Verfolgung von Juden in der Sowjetunion. (USA)
579 Umschlag in grünlichbeigen Tönen für ein Taschenbuch über theologische Fragen. (GBR)
580 Schutzumschlag (schwarzweiss) eines Buches, «Der erste Ruhm», das zu einer Reihe der gesammelten Werke des Autors gehört. (POL)
581, 581a, 582 Kompletter Umschlag und Illustrationen für zwei Bücher aus einer Reihe von Kriminalgeschichten, die ins Italienische übersetzt wurden. (ITA)

ART DIRECTOR / DIRECTEUR ARTISTIQUE:

575, 576 Tadanori Yokoo
577, 578 David Battle
579 Nicolas Rous
581, 582 John Alcorn

AGENCY / AGENTUR / AGENCE – STUDIO:

577, 578 David Battle Design
579 Nicolas Rous
581, 582 Studio Ink

PUBLISHER / VERLEGER / EDITEUR:

575, 576 Kodansha Ltd.
577, 578 Antioch Review
579 A.R. Mowbray & Co Ltd.
580 Wydawnictwo Literackie
581, 582 Rizzoli S.p.A.

577

578

575, 576 Couvertures (en grandeur nature) d'une série du même auteur. Livres publiés par les éditions *Kodansha*. (JPN)

577, 578 Couverture complète et détail de la composition d'un magazine contenant un article sur la persécution religieuse des juifs en Union soviétique. (USA)

579 Couverture (tons beiges et verts) d'un livre de poche traitant de questions théologiques. (GBR)

580 Jaquette noir-blanc d'un ouvrage (la première gloire) qui fait partie des œuvres complets de l'auteur. (POL)

581, 581a, 582 Couverture complète et illustrations de couvertures de deux livres de poche figurant dans une série de romans policiers publiés par les éditions *Rizzoli*. (ITA)

ARTIST / KÜNSTLER / ARTISTE:

575 Tomiya Oda
576 Kikuzo Ito
577, 578 David Battle
579 Nicolas Rous
580 Beate Barszczewskawojda
581, 582 Giovanni Mulazzani

DESIGNER / GESTALTER / MAQUETTISTE:

575, 576 Tadanori Yokoo
577, 578 David Battle
579 Nicolas Rous
580 Beate Barszczewskawojda
581, 582 Giovanni Mulazzani

581a

579

580

581

582

583

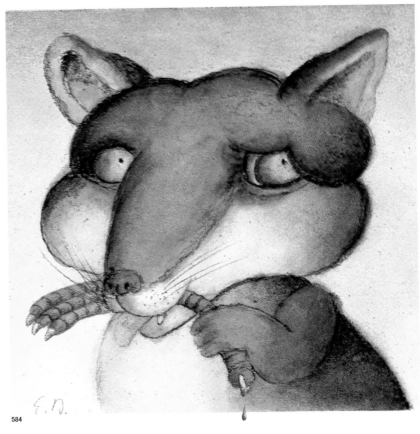

584

583 Cover of a book about time from an educational series. Pepper in full colour. (ITA)
584, 587 Detail of the artwork in actual size and complete cover of a classic from a paperback series. (FRA)
585, 586 Artwork (black and white) and dust jacket with spine for a Dutch version of the adventures of Till Eulenspiegel. (NLD)
588 Cover illustration in actual size for a new illustrated edition of the adventures of Baron Münchhausen. (SWI)

583 Umschlag eines Buches über die Zeit aus einer Reihe von Lehrbüchern. (ITA)
584, 587 Detail der Umschlagillustration in Originalgrösse und kompletter Umschlag für einen Klassiker aus einer Taschenbuchreihe. (FRA)
585, 586 Umschlagillustration (schwarzweiss) in Originalgrösse und Schutzumschlag mit Rücken für die holländische Version der Geschichte Till Eulenspiegels. (NLD)
588 Umschlagillustration in Originalgrösse für eine neu illustrierte Ausgabe der Abenteuer des Freiherrn von Münchhausen. (SWI)

583 Couverture d'un livre sur le temps publié dans une série pédagogique. Poivrons en couleurs. (ITA)
584, 587 Détail de la composition (en grandeur nature) et couverture complète d'un roman classique paru dans une série de poche des Editions *Gallimard*. (FRA)
585, 586 Composition (noir et blanc) et jaquette avec dos pour la version néerlandaise des aventures de Till Eulenspiegel. (NLD)
588 Illustration de couverture (en grandeur nature) d'une nouvelle édition illustrée des aventures du Baron Münchhausen. (SWI)

585

586

587

ARTIST / KÜNSTLER:

583 Giuseppe Rampazzo
584, 587 Etienne Delessert
585, 586 Kurt Löb
588 Binette Schroeder

DESIGNER / GESTALTER:

583 Giuseppe Rampazzo
585, 586 Joost van
de Woestijne
588 Binette Schroeder

ART DIRECTOR:

583 Giuseppe Rampazzo
584, 587 G. Duimard
588 Binette Schroeder

AGENCY / AGENTUR:

583 Giuseppe Rampazzo
584, 587 Carabosse

PUBLISHER / VERLEGER:

583 La Linea Editrice
584, 587 Ed. Gallimard
585, 586 Meulenhoff
Nederland bv
588 Nord-Süd Verlag

DIE WUNDERBAREN REISEN
UND ABENTEUER DES
FREIHERRN VON MÜNCHHAUSEN

ILLUSTRIERT VON BINETTE SCHROEDER
NORD-SÜD VERLAG

588

Book Covers
Buchumschläge
Couvertures de livres

589

Book Covers
Buchumschläge
Couvertures de livres

591

592

590

ARTIST / KÜNSTLER / ARTISTE:

589, 590 Wayne Anderson
593, 595 Renate Herter/Christian Gellner
594, 596 David Macaulay
597 Oskar Weiss

DESIGNER / GESTALTER / MAQUETTISTE:

589, 590 Wayne Anderson
591 Gun Larson
592 Carlos Rolando
593, 595 Renate Herter/Christian Gellner
594, 596 David Macaulay

593

W.F. Haug   Der hilflose Antifaschismus

Kleine Bibliothek   Pahl-Rugenstein

595

UNDERGROUND

DAVID MACAULAY

596

589, 590 Cover and artwork for an anthology of nonsense. (USA)
591 Typographic dust jacket for a religious book (Four Eyes to Live). Red and orange lettering on brown stock. (SWE)
592 Cover of a paperback edition of the famous book on the Watergate scandal. Lettering blue and black. (SPA)
593, 595 Artwork (brown, purple and white) and complete cover of a paperback on Antifascism. (GER)
594, 596 Artwork (black and tan) and complete dust jacket of a large book about the underground facilities of modern cities. (USA)
597 Colourful jacket of a book of tales from the Cordilleras. (SWI)

589, 590 Kompletter Umschlag und Detail der Illustration einer Gedichtsammlung «gereimter Ungereimtheiten». (USA)
591 Typographischer Schutzumschlag für ein religiöses Buch. (SWE)
592 Umschlag einer Taschenbuchausgabe des berühmten Buches über den Watergate-Skandal. Blaue und schwarze Buchstaben. (SPA)
593, 595 Illustration (braun, violett und weiss) und kompletter Taschenbuchumschlag: «Der hilflose Antifaschismus». (GER)
594, 596 Illustration und kompletter Schutzumschlag eines Buches über die unterirdischen Einrichtungen moderner Städte. (USA)
597 Farbenfroher Schutzumschlag eines Jugendbuches. (SWI)

594

Indianermärchen aus den Kordilleren

oskar weiss

597

ART DIRECTOR / DIRECTEUR ARTISTIQUE:

589, 590 Patrick Mortimer
592 Roberto Dosil
593, 595 Hajo Leib
594, 596 Walter Lorraine
597 Oswald Dubacher

AGENCE / AGENTUR / AGENCE – STUDIO:

592 Carlos Rolando & Asociados

PUBLISHER / VERLEGER / EDITEUR:

589, 590 Futura Publications Ltd.
591 Askild & Kärnekull
592 Euros
593, 595 Pahl-Rugenstein Verlag
594, 596 Houghton Mifflin Company
597 Ex-Libris

589, 590 Couverture d'une anthologie d'absurdités. (USA)
591 Conception typographique de la jaquette d'un livre religieux. Typo rouge et orange sur papier brun. (SWE)
592 Couverture de l'édition de poche du fameux livre sur le scandale de Watergate. Typographie en bleu et noir. (SPA)
593, 595 Composition (brun, violet et blanc) et couverture complète d'un livre de poche sur l'Antifascisme. (GER)
594, 596 Composition (noir et brun) et jaquette d'une grande publication sur les installations souterraines des villes modernes. (USA)
597 Jaquette (couleurs vives) d'un livre pour la jeunesse. (SWI)

598

599

600

601

602

603

598 Cover (full colour) of a paperback school story. (USA)
599, 600 Covers of two paperback novels from the same series. (GBR)
601 Dust jacket in full colour for an account of the writer's adventurous life and times. (USA)
602 Dust jacket of a novel with an experimental double but juxtaposed story. Illustration black on cream. (GBR)
603 Cover of a paperback about Italy. Full colour with red title and green ground. (SWE)
604, 605 Artwork and dust jacket with spine of a German edition of Dante's *Divine Comedy.* (GER)
606 Cover of a paperback collection of children's tales from Ireland. Full-colour illustration. (GER)

598 Farbiger Umschlag eines Jugend-Taschenbuches. (USA)
599, 600 Umschläge von Taschenbuchromanen. (GBR)
601 Farbiger Schutzumschlag eines Buches über das abenteuerliche Leben der Autorin. (USA)
602 Schutzumschlag («Zwei Monde») für ein Buch mit zwei sich ergänzenden Erzählungen auf gegenüberliegenden Seiten. (GBR)
603 Umschlag eines Taschenbuches über Italien. (SWE)
604, 605 Illustration und Schutzumschlag (mit Rücken) einer deutschen Ausgabe von Dantes *Göttlicher Komödie.* (GER)
606 Taschenbuchumschlag für eine Reihe von Kindergeschichten aus Irland. Farbige Illustration. (GER)

598 Couverture couleur d'un livre pour la jeunesse. (USA)
599, 600 Deux romans publiés dans une série de poche. (GBR)
601 Jaquette (en couleurs) d'un livre rapportant la vie aventureuse de l'auteur. (USA)
602 Jaquette d'un roman avec deux histoires juxtaposées et complémentaires. Illustration noire sur beige. (GBR)
603 Couverture d'un livre de poche consacré à l'Italie. Illustration couleur sur fond vert, titre rouge. (SWE)
604, 605 Composition et jaquette avec dos de la *Divine Comédie* de Dante en traduction allemande. (GER)
606 Couverture d'un livre de poche publié dans une série d'histoires irlandaises pour enfants. En couleurs. (GER)

605

604

ARTIST / KÜNSTLER / ARTISTE:

598 Mark Schuler
599, 600 Marc Boxer
601 Eduard Sorel
602 Salim Patell
603 Stellan Kristenson
604, 605 Michael Mathias Prechtl
606 Jan Buchholz/Reni Hinsch

DESIGNER / GESTALTER / MAQUETTISTE:

699, 600 Mike Dempsey
602 Barry Jackson/Salim Patell
603 Stellan Kristenson
604, 605 Hans Peter Willberg
606 Jan Buchholz/Reni Hinsch

ART DIRECTOR / DIRECTEUR ARTISTIQUE:

598 Skip Sorvino
599, 600 Mike Dempsey
601 Lidia Ferrara
602 Clive Allison
603 Stellan Kristenson
604, 605 Hans Peter Willberg
606 Jan Buchholz/Reni Hinsch

Book Covers
Buchumschläge
Couvertures de livres

606

AGENCY / AGENTUR / AGENCE – STUDIO:

598 Scholastic Magazines, Inc.

PUBLISHER / VERLEGER / EDITEUR:

598 Scholastic Book Services
599, 600 Fontana Paperbacks
601 Alfred A. Knopf
602 Allison & Busby
603 Generalstabens Litografiska Anstalts Förlag
604, 605 Büchergilde Gutenberg
606 Fischer Taschenbuch Verlag

607

607, 610 Artwork and dust jacket for a book on human behaviour. (GBR)
608 Cover of a detective story. (USA)
609 Cover of a book about students in the seventies. (USA)
611 Complete cover of a book from a series. Black and white. (JPN)
612 Complete jacket of a book on economics. (USA)
613 Cover of a book about robots. The coloured endpapers appear through the die-cut holes of the eyes. Head in silver on black. (USA)
614 Cover of a book of "memoirs of a mouse" for young readers. (FRA)
615 Jacket of a book on a famous female figure. (USA)

607, 610 Detail der Illustration und kompletter Schutzumschlag für ein Buch über menschliche Verhaltensweisen. (GBR)
608 Umschlag für einen Kriminalroman (Tod durch ein Vermächtnis). (USA)
609 Umschlag eines Buches über Studenten in den siebziger Jahren. (USA)
611 Kompletter Umschlag eines Buches aus einer Serie. Schwarzweiss. (JPN)
612 Kompletter Schutzumschlag eines Buches über Volkswirtschaft. (USA)
613 Umschlag eines Buches über Roboter. Kopf in Silber und Schwarz. Durch ausgestanzte Augenhöhlen werden Farben sichtbar. (USA)
614 Umschlag eines Jugend-Buches über die «Memoiren einer Maus». (FRA)
615 Schutzumschlag eines Buches über eine berühmte Frauengestalt. (USA)

607, 610 Détail de l'illustration et jaquette complète d'une publication discutant le comportement humain. (GBR)
608 Couverture d'un roman policier (Mort par testament). (USA)
609 Couverture d'un livre consacré aux étudiants des années 70. (USA)
611 Couverture noir-blanc d'un livre publié dans une série. (JPN)
612 Jaquette (recto et verso) d'une publication sur l'économie. (JPN)
613 Couverture d'un livre consacré aux robots. La feuille de garde est visible à travers les yeux découpés à l'emporte-pièce. (USA)
614 Couverture d'un livre destiné à la jeune génération. (FRA)
615 Jaquette d'un livre consacré à une femme de renom. (USA)

608

609

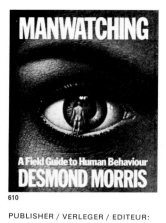

610

613

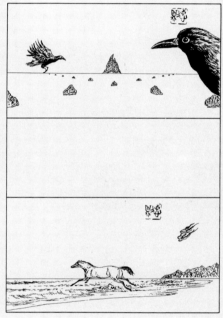

611

614

612

615

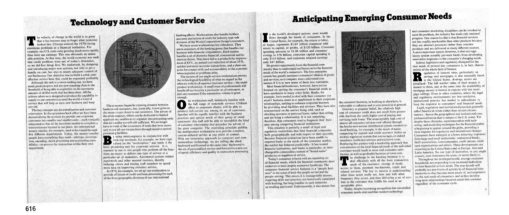

616

Annual Reports
Jahresberichte
Rapports annuels

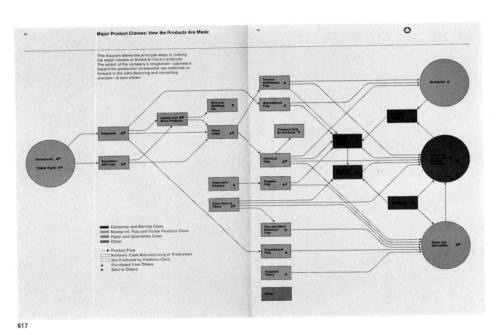

617

618

619

620

ARTIST / KÜNSTLER / ARTISTE:

627 Georg Kintzel

DESIGNER / GESTALTER / MAQUETTISTE:

617 Joe Hutchcroft
618 Alfred Briggs
619 Emmett Morava
620 Claire de Nador
621, 622, 624, 626 Peter Skalar
623 Janez Suhadolc/Davor Viličić
625 Peter Skalar/Janez Suhadolc
627 Georg Kintzel

616 Double spread from the 1976 *Citicorp* annual report. (USA)
617 Double spread from an annual report of the Kimberly-Clark Corporation: product chart, blue, orange and grey. (USA)
618 Double spread from an annual report of the Alza Corporation: products development programme, muted colours. (USA)
619 Cover of a report of the Fluor Corp. Brick-red chart. (USA)
620 Polychrome cover of the 1977 report of Plantronics, Inc. (USA)
621–626 Five annual reports and one planning report (Fig. 622) of a banking enterprise, Lubljanska Banka. Fig. 621 blue and pinks on silver, Fig. 622 yellows and reds on beige, Fig. 623 pale green and white on dark green, Fig. 624 green on grey-brown, Fig. 625 black on grey, Fig. 626 blue and red on white. (YUG)
627 Graphics on the UN "Demographic Yearbook". Mauve/black. Special topic: mortality. (GER)

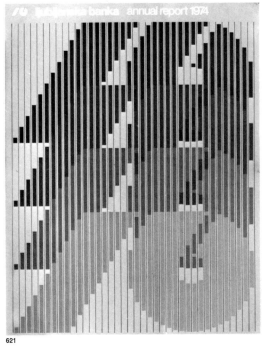

621

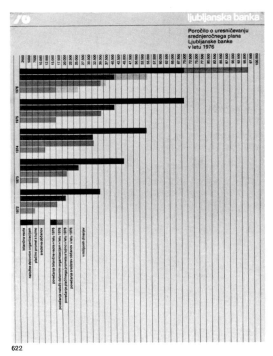

622

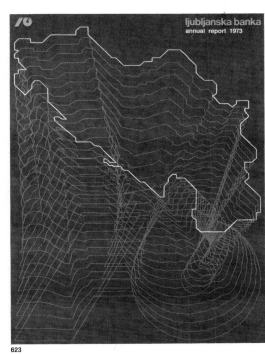

623

624

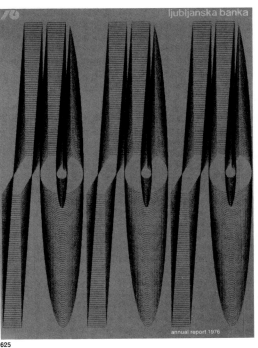

625

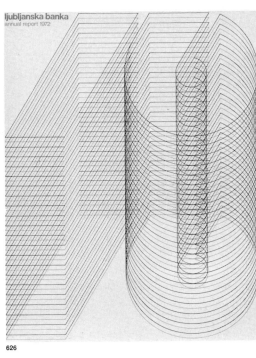

626

ART DIRECTOR / DIRECTEUR ARTISTIQUE:

617 W. Wayne Webb
618, 620 Robert Miles Runyan/Dick Rice
619 James Cross
627 Georg Kintzel

AGENCY / AGENTUR / AGENCE – STUDIO:

617 RVI Corporation
618, 620 Runyan + Rice
619 James Cross Design Office, Inc.

627

616 Doppelseite aus dem Jahresbericht 1976 von *Citicorp*. (USA)
617 Doppelseite aus einem Jahresbericht eines Papierfabrikanten. Produkt-Diagramme blau, orange und grau. (USA)
618 Doppelseite aus einem Jahresbericht der Alza Corporation mit Produktentwicklungsprogramm. Gedämpfte Farben. (USA)
619 Umschlag eines Berichtes der Fluor Corporation. (USA)
620 Umschlag des 1977-Berichtes der Plantronics Inc. (USA)
621–626 Fünf Jahresberichte und ein Planungsbericht (Abb. 622) der Bank Lubljanska Banka. Abb. 621 blau/rosa auf Silber, Abb. 622 in Gelb- und Rottönen auf Beige, Abb. 623 hellgrün/weiss auf Dunkelgrün, Abb. 624 in Grün- und Brauntönen, Abb. 625 schwarz auf Grau, Abb. 626 blau/rot auf Weiss. (YUG)
627 Graphik für das demographische Jahrbuch der UN. Spezielles Thema: Sterblichkeit. Mauve/dunkles Aubergine. (GER)

616 Page double du rapport annuel 1976 de *Citicorp*. (USA)
617 Page double du rapport annuel d'une papeterie: diagramme en bleu, orange et gris. (USA)
618 Page double du rapport annuel de l'Alza Corporation avec le programme de développement de produits. (USA)
619 Couverture du rapport de la Fluor Corp. Rouge brique. (USA)
620 Couverture du rapport '77 de *Plantronics*. Polychrome. (USA)
621–626 Rapports annuels et rapport de planning économique (fig. 622) de la Banque *Lubljanska*. Fig. 621: bleu et rose sur argent; fig. 622: tons jaunes et rouges sur beige; fig. 623: vert et blanc sur vert foncé; fig. 624: tons verts et bruns; fig. 625: noir sur gris; fig. 626: bleu et rouge sur blanc. (YUG)
627 Graphique de l'annuaire démographique de l'ONU. Sujet: la mortalité. Mauve et noir. (GER)

628

628 Black-and-white illustration from an annual report of the Great Northern Nekoosa Corporation, a paper company. It shows a quality control laboratory. (USA)
629 Page from an annual report of the Hammermill Paper Company. It illustrates the coast-to-coast character of the company's markets. Red, white and blue land, yellow sky. (USA)
630 Cover of an *Exxon* annual report. It shows a drilling platform. (USA)

628 Schwarzweiss-Illustration aus einem Jahresbericht des Papierherstellers Great Northern Nekoosa Corporation. Gezeigt wird die Qualitätskontrolle im Labor. (USA)
629 Seite aus dem Jahresbericht des Papierherstellers Hammermill Paper Company. Hier ist die Reichweite des Marktes dieser Firma von Küste zu Küste illustriert. Land rot, weiss und blau, gelber Himmel. (USA)
630 Umschlag eines Jahresberichtes von *Exxon*, mit Bohrinsel. (USA)

628 Illustration noir-blanc du rapport annuel d'une papeterie. On y montre le contrôle de qualité dans le laboratoire. (USA)
629 Page du rapport annuel d'une papeterie. La page devrait illustrer l'expansion du marché de cette compagnie de côte à côte. Pays en rouge, blanc et bleu, ciel jaune. (USA)
630 Couverture du rapport annuel d'*Exxon*. On y montre une plate-forme de forage. (USA)

ARTIST / KÜNSTLER / ARTISTE:

629 Claude Sanders
630 Fred Otnes

DESIGNER / GESTALTER / MAQUETTISTE:

628 Norman Perman
629 Richard Danne
630 Harry O. Diamond

ART DIRECTOR / DIRECTEUR ARTISTIQUE:

629 Danne & Blackburn
630 Harry O. Diamond

AGENCY / AGENTUR / AGENCE – STUDIO:

629 McGhie Associates, Inc.

Annual Reports

National Scope: All our principal product categories are distributed coast-to-coast. This gives Hammermill valuable exposure to markets of varying character and size and also imparts a good geographic balance to our business.

629

631

632

633

ARTIST / KÜNSTLER / ARTISTE:

631 Robert Giusti
633, 634 Anna Pugh
635 Shiro Tatsumi

DESIGNER / GESTALTER / MAQUETTISTE:

631–635 Henry Steiner

ART DIRECTOR / DIRECTEUR ARTISTIQUE:

631–635 Henry Steiner

AGENCY / AGENTUR / AGENCE – STUDIO:

631–635 Graphic Communication Ltd.

631–635 Three full-page illustrations (Fig. 631 in actual size), back cover and one complete double spread from the 1976 annual report of The Hongkong and Shanghai Banking Corporation, which contained an essay on the environment. Fig. 631 symbolizes deforestation as one of the early ecological misdeeds of industry (here for iron smelting). Fig. 632 is a collage of the man-made environment. Fig. 634 shows cows in an English meadow, while Fig. 635 is a picture of hospital and office blocks in Tokyo. (HKG)

631–635 Drei ganzseitige Illustrationen (Abb. 631 in Originalgrösse), Rückseite des Umschlags und eine Doppelseite aus dem Jahresbericht 1976 der Hongkong and Shanghai Banking Corporation, mit einem Artikel über Umweltfragen. Abb. 631 symbolisiert die Abholzung der Wälder als eine der ersten ökologischen Missetaten der Industrie (hier für einen Schmelzofen). Abb. 632: Rückseite des Umschlags, Abb. 634 zeigt schwarzbunte Kühe auf einer Wiese, während Abb. 635 das Bild von Spital- und Büroblocks in Tokio wiedergibt. (HKG)

631–635 Illustrations pleines pages (fig. 631 en grandeur nature), verso de la couverture et page double complète du rapport annuel de la Hongkong and Shanghai Banking Corporation, contenant un article sur des questions écologiques. Fig. 631 symbolise le déboisement, erreur écologique du passé à mettre au passif de l'industrie (ici: bois pour la fonte du fer); fig. 632 présente un collage: l'environnement créé par l'homme; fig. 634: vaches anglaises; fig. 635: hôpitaux et bureaux à Tokyo. (HKG)

634

635

4

Calendars

Trade Marks and Symbols

Letterheads

Packaging

Gramophone Record Covers

Film & TV Advertising

Kalender

Schutzmarken

Briefköpfe

Packungen

Schallplatten-Umschläge

Film- & Fernsehwerbung

Calendriers

Marques et emblèmes

En-têtes

Emballages

Pochettes de disques

Publicité télévisée

DECEMBER 1976

SUNDAY	MONDAY	TUESDAY	WEDNESDAY	THURSDAY	FRIDAY	SATURDAY
			1	2	3	4
5	6	7	8	9	10	11
12	13	14	15	16	17	18
19	20	21	22	23	24	25
26	27	28	29	30	31	

636

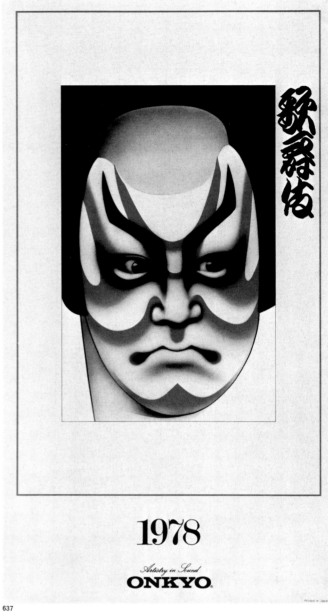

1978

Artistry in Sound
ONKYO

637

1525
Stimulated by printing presses, the wider dissemination of books, and the Renaissance spirit itself, Western Europe showed a great preoccupation with writing and instructional copy books in the first part of the 16th century.

One of the subjects studied in these books was the classical Roman lapidary capitals. Not only was there an appreciation of these letters but there were even attempts made to reduce them to a science.

In his "Divina Proportione" of 1509, Leonardo Da Vinci demonstrated the construction of the Roman capitals with geometrical elements.

And in 1525, Albrecht Dürer wrote an essay entitled "Of The Just Shaping Of Letters" as part of a treatise on applied geometry.

In this essay, Dürer constructed each letter by inscribing it in a square of specific size, building the characters from elements of the square and arcs of circles. The constructions were well formed and not distorted to conform to some predetermined system. Complete instructions and alternate designs for each letter were given in the accompanying text.

Dürer, known for his woodcuts and paintings, had made an important contribution to lettering craftsmanship with a single essay.

2 Sunday	3 Monday	4 Tuesday	5 Wednesday	6 Thursday	7 Friday	8 Saturday
					Independence Day	
9 Sunday	10 Monday	11 Tuesday	12 Wednesday	13 Thursday	14 Friday	15 Saturday

July

639

ART DIRECTOR / DIRECTEUR ARTISTIQUE:

636 Carol Carson
637 Yozo Yasuda
638 Rosenthal AG/Abt. Verkaufsförderung
639 Bill Bonnell
640–643 H.G. Mietzner

640

					1	2	3
	4	5	6	7	8	9	10
	11	12	13	14	15	16	17
	18	19	20	21	22	23	24
	25	26	27	28	29	30	31

Dezember
December
Décembre
Diciembre

K+E

Calendars/Kalender/Calendriers

ARTIST / KÜNSTLER / ARTISTE:

636 Guy Billout
637 Jyushiro Morita
638 Anton Stankowski
640–643 Otto Rieger

DESIGNER / GESTALTER / MAQUETTISTE:

636 Martha Clark
637 Central Associates Inc.
638 Gerd Wricke
639 Bill Bonnell
640–643 Otto Rieger

636 Sheet of a wall calendar for *Scholastic Magazines.* (USA)
637 Cover sheet of a wall calendar for *Onkyo* sound equipment. The full-colour motifs for the months are drawn from Japanese *kabuki*. (JPN)
638 Calendar-object from the *Rosenthal* series "Art and Technology", symbolizing the twelve months by means of over a thousand ceramic elements that belong to the company's technical production range. (GER)
639 Opening of a spirally bound typographic calendar issued by Frederic Ryder Co., Chicago. Here a Dürer letter. (USA)
640–643 Complete cover and motifs for February, May and June from the calendar of a printing-ink manufacturer. (GER)

636 Blatt eines Wandkalenders der *Scholastic Magazines.* (USA)
637 Deckblatt eines Wandkalenders mit «Kabuki»-Motiv. «Kabuki» ist eine Form des Theaters, welche die Atmosphäre in Japan und seine 700jährige Geschichte wiederspiegelt. (JPN)
638 Kalender-Objekt aus der *Rosenthal*-Reihe «Kunst und Technik». In einer Auflage von nur 700 Stück wurde das Objekt, numeriert und signiert, an Führungskräfte der Wirtschaft verteilt. Verwendet wurden über 1000 keramische Einzelteile. (GER)
639 Blatt aus einem Kalender (Spiralbindung) mit dem Thema «Das typographische Jahr». (USA)
640–643 Deckblatt und Illustration für die Monate Februar, Mai und Juni aus dem *Kast+Ehinger*-Druckfarbenkalender. (GER)

636 Feuille d'un calendrier mural de *Scholastic Magazines.* (USA)
637 Feuille de couverture d'un calendrier mural, dont le motif se réfère à «kabuki», un genre de représentation théâtrale qui reflète l'atmosphère et l'histoire du Japon au moyen de dialogues alternant avec des intermèdes de ballet. (JPN)
638 Calendrier de la série «art et technique» de *Rosenthal.* Plus de 1000 éléments en céramique de la gamme des produits techniques servent à symboliser les douze mois. (GER)
639 Feuillet d'un calendrier (à reliure spirale) intitulé «l'année typographique». (USA)
640–643 Feuille de couverture et motifs pour les mois de février, mai et juin du calendrier d'un fabricant d'encres. (GER)

AGENCY / AGENTUR / AGENCE – STUDIO:

636 Scholastic Magazines
637 Central Associates Inc.
638 Rosenthal AG/Abt. Verkaufsförderung
639 Container Corporation of America

638

641

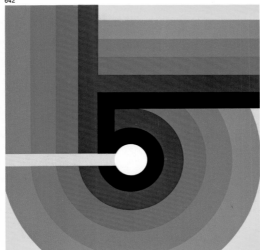

642

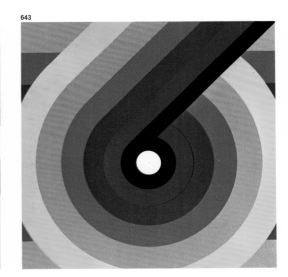

643

644

Calendars
Kalender
Calendriers

ARTIST / KÜNSTLER / ARTISTE:

644, 645 Dave Epstein
646 Josse Goffin
647–650 Roland Jenne

DESIGNER / GESTALTER / MAQUETTISTE:

644, 645 Dave Epstein
647–650 Roland Jenne

644, 645 Motif and complete sheet of a calendar published by Mercy College. The illustration, in an American primitive style, shows the college campus overlooking the River Hudson. (USA)
646 Motif from a wall calendar issued by the National Lottery of Belgium. Soft shades of brown, green, yellow, red and blue. (BEL)
647–650 Cover sheet and three motifs from a wall calendar published by the DVE printing and publishing house. All illustrations are black and white with one colour. Here a bluish-green fish, red peppers, a bluish-green fork and yellow "knitting" and yolk. (GER)

644, 645 Motiv und ganzes Kalenderblatt eines amerikanischen College. Gezeigt wird das College-Gelände am Ufer des Hudson Rivers. «Ein College für alle Jahreszeiten»; der Text gibt Aufschluss über die verschiedenen Lehrprogramme. (USA)
646 Motiv aus einem Wandkalender der belgischen Nationallotterie. Verhaltene Braun-, Grün-, Gelb-, Rot- und Blautöne. (BEL)
647–650 Deckblatt und drei Motive aus einem Wandkalender für DVE Druck und Verlag. Die Zeichnungen sind jeweils schwarzweiss mit einer Farbe. Hier ein blaugrüner Fisch, rote Paprikaschoten, eine blaugrüne Gabel und gelbe «Strickerei» mit Eigelb. (GER)

644, 645 Illustration et feuillet complet d'un calendrier publié par un lycée américain. Sous le titre «Un lycée pour toutes les saisons» on montre les différents sports pratiqués au lycée. Le texte donne des indications sur le programme pédagogique. (USA)
646 Illustration d'un calendrier mural publié par la Lotterie nationale de Belgique. Tons bruns, verts, jaunes, rouges et bleus atténués. (BEL)
647–650 Feuille de couverture et trois illustrations d'un calendrier mural de DVE, imprimerie et maison d'éditions. Les illustrations sont en noir et blanc avec une couleur sur fond noir: poisson en bleu-vert, poivrons rouges, fourchette bleu-vert, «tricotage» et jaune d'œuf en jaune. (GER)

645

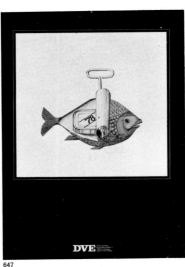

647

646

ART DIRECTOR / DIRECTEUR ARTISTIQUE:
644, 645 Dave Epstein/Andrew Nelson
646 Julian Key
647–650 Roland Jenne

AGENCY / AGENTUR / AGENCE – STUDIO:
644, 645 Dave Epstein, Inc.

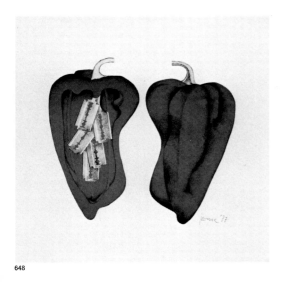

648

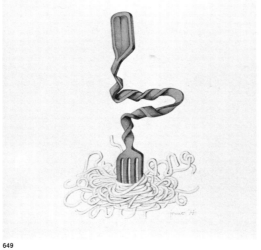

649

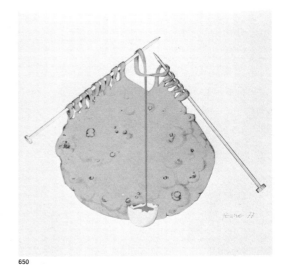

650

651

652

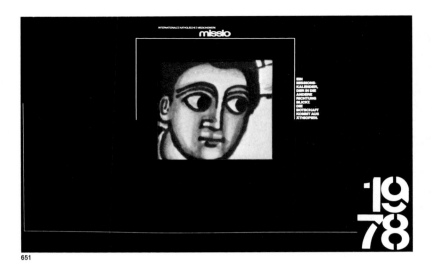

653

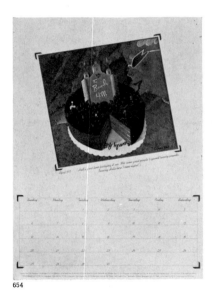

654

Catherine Loeb. 75.

655

Calendars/Kalender/Calendriers

651, 652 Cover and complete sheet from a wall calendar published by an international Catholic Mission using religious paintings from Ethiopia. Here a rendering of Cain and Abel. (GER)
653 Double spread from a spirally bound *Ansul* April-to-April calendar for tobacco growers. The woodcut shown is a tobacco label dating from 1700 from the British Museum. (USA)
654, 655 Complete sheet and detail of the artwork from a calendar issued by the Graphic Process Co. Brown cake, green foliage, pink building, blue glasses. (USA)
656 Full-colour motif from a desk diary published by the agency N.Y. Ayer International. (USA)
657, 658 Complete sheet and detail of the full-colour artwork from a wall calendar for Dalmine S. p. A. showing space-age fantasies. (ITA)

651, 652 Deckblatt und Seite aus einem Kalender des Internationalen Katholischen Missionswerks, mit religiöser Malerei aus Äthiopien. Thema der gezeigten Abbildung: Kain und Abel. (GER)
653 Doppelseite aus einem als Handbuch konzipierten Kalender (Spiralbindung) für Tabakpflanzer von *Ansul*. Der Kalender beginnt mit der Pflanzzeit April und enthält Ratschläge und Empfehlungen. Der abgebildete Holzschnitt ist ein Tabaketikett von 1700 (Britisches Museum). (USA)
654, 655 Ganzes Blatt und Detail der Abbildung aus einem Kalender der Graphic Process Co. Brauner Kuchen mit grüner Vegetation und rosa Gebäude, fleischfarbenes Gesicht mit blauer Brille. (USA)
656 Farbiges Blatt aus einem Pultkalender von *N. W. Ayer*. (USA)
657, 658 Ganzes Blatt und Detail aus einem Wandkalender. Jedes Blatt zeigt eine phantastische Szene aus dem Raumzeitalter. (ITA)

651, 652 Couverture et feuillet du calendrier de la société internationale des missions catholiques présentant des peintures religieuses de l'Ethiopie. Ici: Cain et Abel. (GER)
653 Page double d'un calendrier et manuel à reliure spirale destiné aux planteurs de tabac. Il commence au mois d'avril (saison de la plantation) et donne des instructions et conseils. Etiquette avec gravure sur bois du 18ᵉ siècle de la collection du British Museum. (USA)
654, 655 Feuillet et détail de l'illustration du calendrier de la Graphic Process Co. Gâteau brun avec paysage vert et hôtel rose, visage rose avec des lunettes bleues. (USA)
656 Feuillet d'un calendrier de bureau. En polychromie. (USA)
657, 658 Feuillet complet et détail de l'illustration d'un calendrier mural. Rue et maisons en jaune, vert, brun, rouge, ciel bleu. (ITA)

ARTIST / KÜNSTLER / ARTISTE:

651, 652 Selleke Uneto
654, 655 Catherine Loeb
656 Charles Santore
657, 658 Tiger Tateishi

DESIGNER / GESTALTER / MAQUETTISTE:

651, 652 Endrikat & Wenn
653 Jim Markich
654, 655 Keith Bright
656 Lee Estes
657, 658 Roberto Pieraccini

ART DIRECTOR / DIRECTEUR ARTISTIQUE:

654, 655 Keith Bright
656 Lee Estes
657, 658 Roberto Pieraccini

AGENCY / AGENTUR / AGENCE – STUDIO:

651, 652 Endrikat & Wenn
654, 655 Keith Bright & Associates
657, 658 Roberto Pieraccini

656

657

658

219

659

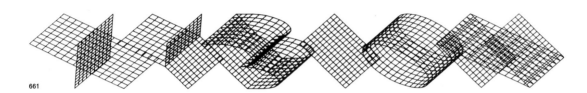

661

662

DESIGNER / GESTALTER / MAQUETTISTE:

659 George Jadowski
660 Herbert Wenn
661 Louis Danziger
662 Felix Beltran
663 Hans & Pat Schleger
664 Allan Miller
665 Roland Hirter
666, 667 Henry Steiner
668 Bruno K. Wiese
669 Ford, Byrne & Associates
670 So Man-Yee
671 Lewis van der Beken
672 Carlo Caligaris
673 Joseph M. Essex

659 Symbol for the US Energy Research and Development Administration. (USA)
660 Symbol for the German printing house *Emhart* of Aachen. (GER)
661 Computer-designed logotype for Xybion Corporation. (USA)
662 Symbol for a pottery designer by the name of Salles. (CUB)
663 Symbol for the Manchester Polytechnic. (GBR)
664 Trade mark for *Grupo Cinco*, a company specializing in five areas of design, planning and construction. (MEX)
665 Symbol for Bächthold + Brodmann AG, a rotary printing establishment. (SWI)
666 Symbol for the Hong Kong Hilton hotel. (HKG)
667 Symbol for Classic Jewellers. (HKG)
668 Symbol for a research institute for aeronautics and astronautics in Cologne. (GER)
669 Logotype for Geometric Data Corporation, makers of blood cell counters. (USA)
670 Trade mark for a fish marketing organization. (HKG)
671 Trade mark for Optima Corporation, Los Angeles. (USA)
672 Symbol for the typographers *Stimo*, Turin. (ITA)
673 Trade mark for *Ace* chainlink fences. (USA)

659 Symbol der US-Regierung für Energie-Forschung und -Entwicklung. (USA)
660 Symbol der Offsetdruckerei *Emhart*. (GER)
661 Mit dem Computer gezeichneter Schriftzug der Xybion Corporation. (USA)
662 Symbol eines Töpfers namens Salles. (CUB)
663 Symbol des Polytechnischen Instituts Manchester. (GBR)
664 Symbol der *Grupo Cinco*, einer Firma, die sich auf fünf Gebieten spezialisiert hat: Design, Konstruktion, Städteplanung, Architektur und Bauprodukte. (MEX)
665 Symbol der Rollenoffsetdruckerei Bächthold + Brodmann AG. (SWI)
666 Symbol für das Hilton Hotel in Hongkong. (HKG)
667 Signet für einen Juwelier (Classic Jewellers). (HKG)
668 Signet der Deutschen Forschungs- und Versuchsanstalt für Luft- und Raumfahrt. (GER)
669 Firmenzeichen für Geometric Data Corporation, die Blutzellenzähler herstellt. (USA)
670 Markenzeichen einer Marketing-Organisation für die Fischerei-Industrie. (HKG)
671 Schutzmarke der Optima Corporation. (USA)
672 Symbol der Typographenfirma *Stimo*, Turin. (ITA)
673 Symbol der Firma *Ace*, Hersteller von Metallzäunen. (USA)

659 Symbole du Centre américain de la recherche énergétique. (USA)
660 Symbole de l'imprimerie allemande *Emhart*. (GER)
661 Logo (conçu par ordinateur) pour la Xybion Corporation. (USA)
662 Emblème d'un potier qui s'appelle Salles. (CUB)
663 Symbole de l'institut polytechnique de Manchester. (GBR)
664 Symbole de *Groupo Cinco*, une société spécialisée dans les cinq domaines suivants: design, construction, urbanisme, architecture et matériaux de construction. (MEX)
665 Emblème de l'imprimerie Bächthold + Brodmann AG. (SWI)
666 Symbole de l'Hôtel Hilton de Hongkong. (HKG)
667 Emblème conçu pour un joaillier, Classic Jewellers. (USA)
668 Emblème du centre allemand de la recherche aéronautique et astronautique. (GER)
669 Logo de la Geometric Data Corporation. (USA)
670 Marque d'une organisation de vente de poissons. (HKG)
671 Marque de la compagnie Optima Corporation à Los Angeles. (USA)
672 Symbole de l'atelier Tipografia *Stimo* (ITA)
673 Symbole de la société *Ace*, fabricant de clôtures en fil métallique. (USA)

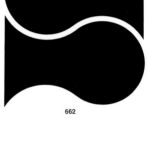

666

Trade Marks
Schutzmarken
Marques et emblèmes

670

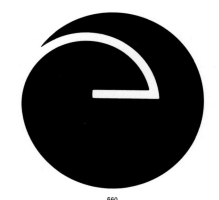

660

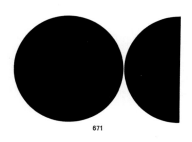

671

668

672

667

669

663

673

663

664

665

DESIGNER / GESTALTER / MAQUETTISTE:

674 Colin Knauf
675 Cato Hibberd Hawksby Design
676 Whaite & Emery
677, 681 John R. Rieben
678, 684 Clive Gay
679 René Bischof
680 Roland Hirter
682 Michael Vanderbyl
683 Eduardo A. Cánovas
685 Werner Weissbrodt
686 Heinz Grunwald
687 Ner Beck
688 Carlo Caligaris
689 Badian & Weinblatt
690 Lesniewicz/Navarre

ART DIRECTOR / DIRECTEUR ARTISTIQUE:

674 Colin Knauf
675 Cato Hibberd Hawksby Design
676 Whaite & Emery
677, 681 John R. Rieben
678, 684 Clive Gay
679 René Bischof
680 Roland Hirter
682 Michael Vanderbyl
683 Eduardo A. Cánovas
686 Heinz Grunwald
687 Ner Beck
690 Lesniewicz/Navarre

AGENCY / AGENTUR / AGENCE – STUDIO:

674 Pacific Rim Design & Direction
675 Cato Hibberd Hawksby Design Pty. Ltd.
676 Whaite & Emery
678, 684 Adam (Pty) Ltd
679 Werbeatelier Bischof
682 Michael Vanderbyl Graphic Design
683 Estudio Cánovas
686 Neish Tutt Grunwald Pty. Ltd.
687 Ner Beck Design
689 Badian & Weinblatt
690 Lesniewicz/Navarre

674

675

679

680

685

686

684

690

674 Logotype for *Grobermann,* distributors of rugs and floor coverings. (CAN)
675 Symbol for a firm of property consultants. (AUS)
676 Symbol for Baker Institute, a medical research centre. (AUS)
677 Trade mark for Vantage Home Builders, Denver. (USA)
678 Symbol for Security Life Assurance Company. (SAF)
679 Symbol for a company which sends prepacked ranges of basic foods to consumers. (SWI)
680 Symbol for the Swiss Radio. Winner of first prize in a competition. (SWI)
681 Symbol for *Chemelex,* a chemical company, Redwood City. (USA)
682 Symbol for *Met One,* manufacturers of wind speed indicators and other meteorological equipment, San Francisco. (USA)
683 Trade mark for *Thermopac* industrial boilers made by Industrias Técnicas Aire. (ARG)
684 Symbol for Videosound Studios, a sound recording company, Johannesburg. (SAF)
685 Symbol for the *Aquadrom,* a balneological centre in Hockenheim. (GER)
686 Trade mark for *Silverwood & Beck.* (AUS)
687 Logotype for The Educational Directory, suppliers of mailing lists and addresses in the educational field. (USA)
688 Symbol for the typesetting and lithographic establishment *Palestro,* Turin. (ITA)
689 Symbol for the *Chemometall* recycling company, Sollenau. (AUT)
690 Logotype for the Roofing Products Operating Division of Owens-Corning Fiberglas Corp. (USA)

676

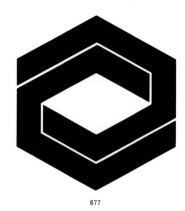

677

678

681

682

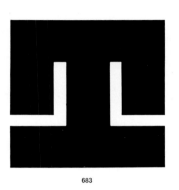

683

687

688

689

674 Symbol für *Grobermann*, Lieferanten von Teppichen und Auslegware. (CAN)
675 Symbol einer Firma für Immobilien-Beratungen. (AUS)
676 Symbol des Baker Instituts, eines medizinischen Forschungszentrums. (AUS)
677 Symbol eines Bauunternehmens, das auf Einzelhäuser spezialisiert ist. (USA)
678 Symbol einer Lebensversicherungsgesellschaft, Security Life Assurance Company. (SAF)
679 Symbol des OKD Konsumverbundes, Solothurn, Lieferanten von fertig abgepackten Grund-
nahrungsmittel-Sortimenten. (SWI)
680 Symbol für das Schweizer Radio. Es erhielt den 1. Preis bei einem Wettbewerb. (SWI)
681 Symbol der Firma *Chemelex*, ein Unternehmen der chemischen Industrie. (USA)
682 Symbol für *Met One*, Hersteller von Windgeschwindigkeits- und anderen meteorologischen
Messgeräten, San Francisco. (USA)
683 Markenzeichen für die *Thermopac*-Industrie-Kessel der Industrias Técnicas Aire. (ARG)
684 Symbol eines Tonaufnahmestudios, Videosound Studios. (SAF)
685 Symbol für das Bäderzentrum «Aquadrom» in Hockenheim. Originalfarbe blau. (GER)
686 Markenzeichen der Firma *Silverwood & Beck*. (AUS)
687 Logo für Education Directory, Lieferant von Adressen im Sektor Bildungswesen. (USA)
688 Symbol für *Palestro*, eine typographische und lithographische Anstalt in Turin. (ITA)
689 Symbol der *Chemometall*, Rückgewinnung von Chemikalien und Metallen. (AUT)
690 Logo der Roofing Products Operating Division (Dachdeckerei-Produkte) einer Firma. (USA)

674 Symbole de *Grobermann*, distributeur de moquettes et de revêtements de sol. (CAN)
675 Symbole d'une société de consultation en matière de propriété immobilière. (AUS)
676 Emblème d'un centre de recherche médical. (AUS)
677 Symbole d'une entreprise de construction. (USA)
678 Symbole d'une compagnie d'assurances sur la vie. (SAF)
679 Marque d'un distributeur d'aliments de base. (SWI)
680 Emblème de la Société Suisse de Radiodiffusion; celui-ci a remporté un premier prix. (SWI)
681 Symbole de la compagnie *Chemelex*. (USA)
682 Symbole de *Met One*, fabricant d'instruments météorologiques et d'anémomètres à San Francisco, Californie. (USA)
683 Marque pour *Thermopac*, chaudières industrielles par Industrias Técnicas Aire. (ARG)
684 Emblème d'un studio d'enregistrement. (SAF)
685 Symbole pour *Aquadrom*, un centre de bains à Hockenheim. (GER)
686 Marque déposée de la compagnie *Silverwood & Beck*. (AUS)
687 Logo de l'Educational Directory, une société qui distribue des listes d'adresses dans le
secteur de l'enseignement. (USA)
688 Symbole de *Palestro*, atelier de typographie et de photolithographie. (ITA)
689 Symbole de *Chemometall*, une compagnie pour le recyclage de métaux. (AUT)
690 Logo d'un fabricant de toitures. (USA)

Letterheads/Briefköpfe/En-têtes

691

P.O. Box 753   Trinidad, Colorado 81082   Telephone 505 445 3024

693

692

ARGOS VERLAG

ARGOS Gesellschaft für Verlags- und Druckproduktionen m.b.H.   Geschäftsführer: Robert Pütz
Oberbuschweg · Postfach 1940 · 5000 Köln 50 · Telefon 0223/876 4071 · Telex-Nr. 888 3508 · Bankkonto: (Blz 3705 0198) Stadtsparkasse Köln 5547 2968

Peter Fischer
8 München 81 · Sankt Emmeram 41 · Telefon 95 39 71

Bankhaus H. Aufhäuser · Bankleitzahl 70030600 · Konto Nr. 1809490

694

**This is Andrew Brogren speaking.
Do you hear me?**

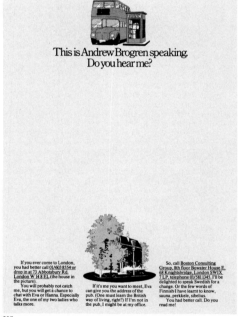

If you ever come to London, you had better call 01/603 8554 or drop in at 73 Abbotsbury Rd. London W 14 8 EL (the house in the picture).
You will probably not catch me, but you will get a chance to chat with Eva or Hanna. Especially Eva, the one of my two ladies who talks more.

If it's me you want to meet, Eva can give you the address of the pub. (One must learn the British way of living, right?) If I'm not in the pub, I might be at my office.

So, call Boston Consulting Group, 8th floor Bowater House E. 68 Knightsbridge, London SW1X 7 LF, telephone 01/581 1345. I'll be delighted to speak Swedish for a change. Or the few words of Finnish I have learnt to know, sauna, perkkele, sibelius.
You had better call. Do you read me!

695

696

Susana Rolando   Ravella 3, Ático 1, Barcelona 6 España Tel. 211 81 96

Susana Rolando   Ravella 3, Ático 1, Barcelona 6 España Tel. 211 81 96

ART FACTORY, INC.
FOUR EAST OHIO STREET
CHICAGO 60611
529-1370

THIS IS CLASSIC NATURAL WHITE, 24#

697

SUCCESS UNLIMITED MAGAZINE 6355 BROADWAY CHICAGO, ILLINOIS 60660 PHONE 312-973-7650

698

691, 692 Letterhead for the *Argos* publishing house with detail of vignette in blue/grey/black. (GER)
693 Letterhead for Lodge Wood, Trinidad, Colorado. Brown symbol, red logotype. (USA)
694 Letterhead for a restaurant in an old mill in Munich. Blue, red and ochre. (GER)
695 Letterhead for a Swedish consultant living in London. Red bus and phone booth. (GBR)
696 Stationery for a textile designer. (SPA)
697 Letterhead for Art Factory, Inc. (USA)
698 Letterhead for *Success Unlimited* magazine with blind embossed logo. (USA)
699 Letterhead for a Berlin photographer with round cut-out in the symbol. (GER)
700 Stationery for Carlyle & Warkulwiz, Inc. (USA)
701 Letterhead for *Greenhaus,* gardeners. (USA)
702 Stationery (squared) for an architect. (USA)
703 Letterhead for Report Production Associates. Letters in red, yellow and green. (USA)
704 Letterhead for a gold and silver smith. (GER)

691, 692 Briefbogen des *Argos*-Verlags mit Detail der Vignette (blau/grau/schwarz). (GER)
693 Briefbogen für Lodge Wood, Colorado. (USA)
694 Briefbogen für eine alte Mühle, heute ein Restaurant, in München. Blau/rot/ocker. (GER)
695 Briefbogen eines schwedischen Anlageberaters in London. Roter Bus und Telephonzelle. (GBR)
696 Briefpapier einer Textil-Entwerferin. (SPA)
697 Briefkopf einer «Kunstfabrik». (USA)
698 Briefbogen des Magazins *Success Unlimited* mit Logo in Blindprägung. (USA)
699 Briefbogen eines Berliner Photographen mit rundem Ausschnitt im Symbol. (GER)
700 Briefpapier einer Gruppe von Kreativen. (USA)
701 Briefbogen der Gärtnerei *Greenhaus.* (USA)
702 Briefbogen auf Millimeterpapier für einen Architekten. Rotbraune Schrift. (USA)
703 Briefbogen für Report Production Associates. Buchstaben in Rot, Gelb und Grün. (USA)
704 Briefbogen einer Gold-Silberschmiedin. (GER)

691, 692 En-tête de la maison d'éditions *Argos* et détail de la vignette. (GER)
693 Papier à lettres de Lodge Wood. Typographie rouge, symbole brun. (USA)
694 Papier à lettres d'un restaurant munichois se trouvant dans un vieux moulin. Bleu, rouge et ocre. (GER)
695 En-tête d'une société de consultation. (GBR)
696 Papier à lettres d'une dessinatrice. (SPA)
697 En-tête de l'Art Factory Inc. (USA)
698 En-tête du magazine *Success Unlimited* avec logo gaufré à sec. (USA)
699 En-tête d'un photographe avec cercle découpé à l'emporte-pièce. (GER)
700 Papier à lettres d'un groupe d'artistes. (USA)
701 En-tête d'un horticulteur. (USA)
702 Papier à lettres d'un architecte à réseau carré. Typographie brune. (USA)
703 En-tête de la Report Production Assoc. (USA)
704 Papier à lettres d'un orfèvre. (GER)

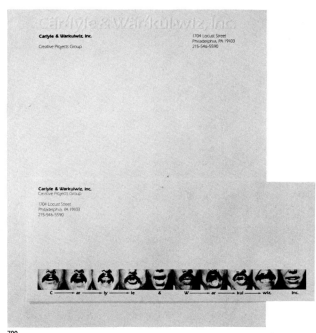

699

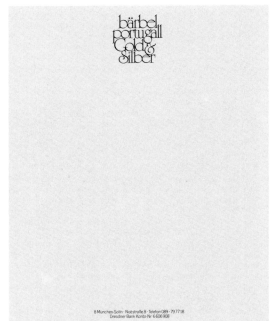

700

701

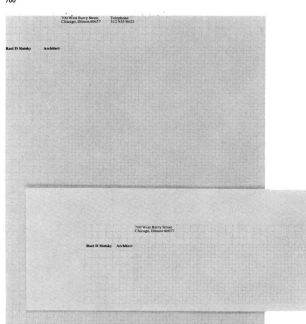

702

703

704

705

ARTIST / KÜNSTLER / ARTISTE:
708 Karin Welponer
712 Shigeru Akizuki

DESIGNER / GESTALTER / MAQUETTISTE:
705 Bill Bundzak
706 Oswaldo Miranda
707 E. Meichtry
708 Günther Link
709 Nobuyoshi Ito
710, 711 Alex Steinweiss
712 Shigeru Akizuki

ART DIRECTOR / DIRECTEUR ARTISTIQUE:
705 Bill Bundzak
706 Oswaldo Miranda
708 Günther Link
709 Nobuyoshi Ito
710, 711 Kenneth J. Neuman
712 Shigeru Akizuki

708

709

706

707

AGENCY / AGENTUR / AGENCE – STUDIO:

705 Young Goldman Young Inc.
706 P.A.Z. Criação e Comunicação
707 AWG AG für Werbeplanung und Gestaltung
708 Herrwerth & Partner
710, 711 Steinweiss, Inc.

712

710
711

Packaging/Packungen/Emballages

227

713, 714 Labels and bottle styling for a special beer made by the Blitz-Weinhard Brewing Company of Portland, Oregon. The label is printed in blue and gold on white. (USA)
715 From a series of matchboxes for *Eddylites*. The designs are formed by matches with heads in blue and pink. (CAN)
716 Tin box for shortbread made by the Fujiya Confection Co. Stripes in shades of pink and gold on dark red. (JPN)
717 Packages for *Rabat* coffee. Labels in gold and blue, white lettering on red package. (NLD)
718, 719 Gift cartons for champagne. Fig. 718 white with black lettering, Fig. 719 black and white with contrasting lettering. (USA)
720 Pack for *Chanceller 100* cigarettes. In shades of blue, fading from dark to light, with dark blue lettering. (BRA)
721 From a series of matchbooks for *Eddylites*. Orange, blue, light brown and white on black. (CAN)
722 Can and bottle styling for *Hi-C* fruit drinks from *Coca Cola*. The labels are in the colour of the fruit referred to. (USA)
723 Packages of sweets made by Curtiss Candy Co., with logotype in red, pink and yellow. (USA)

713, 714 Etikett- und Flaschengestaltung für ein Spezialbier, Henry Weinhard's Private Reserve Beer, das, so ist auf dem Etikett zu lesen, nach den im 19. Jahrhundert angewandten Braumethoden hergestellt wird. Emblem in Gold und Blau, Beschriftung in Gold und Weiss. (USA)
715 Zündholzschachteln für *Eddylites*. Die Muster werden durch Zündhölzer mit Köpfen in Blau und kräftigem Rosa gebildet. (CAN)
716 Blechdose für Mürbeteig-Gebäck von einem japanischen Hersteller. Streifen in verschiedenen Rosatönen und Gold auf Weinrot. (JPN)
717 Packungen für *Rabat*-Kaffee aus Holland. Leuchtend rotes Papier mit goldenem und blauem Etikett, weisse Schrift. (NLD)
718, 719 Geschenkverpackung für Champagner. Der Karton in Abb. 718 ist weiss mit schwarzer Schrift, der andere ist schwarz und weiss mit kontrastierender Schrift. (USA)
720 Packung für eine neue Zigarette, *Chanceller 100*. Abstufungen von Hell- bis Dunkelblau, mit dunkelblauer Beschriftung. (BRA)
721 Zündholzbriefchen für *Eddylites*. Orange/blau/hellbraun/weiss. (CAN)
722 Dosen- und Flaschengestaltung für *Hi-C*-Fruchtgetränke von *Coca-Cola*. In den Etiketten überwiegt die Farbe der betroffenen Frucht. (USA)
723 Verpackungen für *Curtiss*-Süssigkeiten mit buntem Schriftzug. (USA)

713, 714 Etiquette et bouteille pour une bière spéciale, brassée selon les méthodes traditionnelles pratiquées au 19e siècle par Henry Weinhard. Emblème en bleu et or, typographie en or et blanc. (USA)
715 D'une série de boîtes d'allumettes pour *Eddylites*. Design crée par des allumettes dont les têtes sont bleues et roses. (CAN)
716 Boîte métallique pour du sablé. Rayures en différentes teintes roses et or sur fond rouge foncé. (JPN)
717 Emballages pour le *Rabat-Koffie*, une marque de café néerlandaise. Etiquettes en or et bleu sur papier rouge. (NLD)
718, 719 Emballage-cadeau pour du champagne. Fig. 718: carton blanc avec typographie noire, fig. 719: carton en noir et blanc avec typographie contrastante. (USA)
720 Paquet pour les cigarettes *Chanceller 100*. Typographie en bleu foncé sur fond passant de bleu pâle à bleu foncé. (BRA)
721 Pochettes d'allumettes d'une série pour *Eddylites*. Orange, bleu, brun pâle et blanc sur fond noir. (CAN)
722 Boîte et bouteille pour une boisson à goût fruité. Les étiquettes sont imprimées dans la couleur du fruit en question. (USA)
723 Emballage pour des sucreries. Typographie en couleurs vives. (USA)

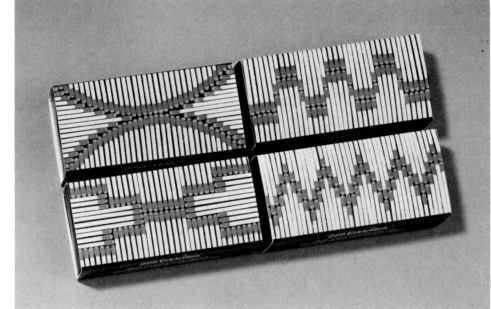

715

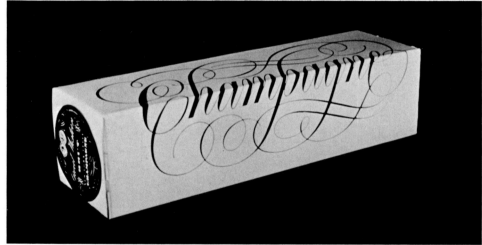

718

713

714

719

ARTIST / KÜNSTLER / ARTISTE:

713, 714 Mark Jones/Primo Angeli
715 Dawn Cooper Tennant
716 Shigeru Akizuki
717 Ten Cate Bergmans Design b. v.
718, 719 Bill Reid
721 Dawn Cooper Tennant/Glynn Bell
722 Person Long

DESIGNER / GESTALTER / MAQUETTISTE:

713, 714 Primo Angeli/Tandy Belew
715 Dawn Cooper Tennant/Robert Burns
716 Shigeru Akizuki
717 Ten Cate Bergmans Design b. v.
718, 719 Philip Gips
720 Dimas Soares
721 Dawn Cooper Tennant
722 Morton Goldsholl/Sheldon Rysner
723 James Lienhart

716

717

720

721

722

723

724

728

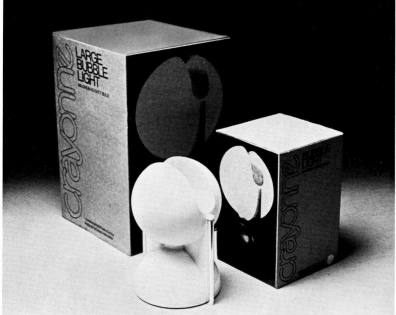

729

724 Tubes from a range of *Winsor & Newton* artists' colours with copies of works by famous artists showing the use of the colours. The range won a British award. (GBR)
725 Packages for *Ilford* black-and-white films. (JPN)
726 Hinged carton for the books of a reading course published by Encyclopaedia Britannica Educational Corp. (USA)
727 Folding box for a disposable eating set marketed by J.G. Holmes Pty. Ltd. (AUS)
728 Packaging for *Shorty,* a short thick pen from *Parker.* (GER)
729 Packages for *Crayonne* "bubble lights". (GBR)
730 Dispenser pack for paper tissues made by Wellcome (Pty.) Ltd. (SAF)
731 Bags for *Tipiti* foods, lettering in various colours. (BRA)

724 Tuben für Künstlerfarben aus einer Reihe für *Winsor & Newton,* mit Abbildungen von Gemälden berühmter Künstler als Anwendungsbeispiel. (GBR)
725 Verpackung für Schwarzweiss-Rollfilm von *Ilford.* (JPN)
726 Faltkarton für die Bücher eines von der Encyclopaedia Britannica Educational Corp. verlegten Lesekurses. (USA)
727 Faltschachtel für ein Wegwerf-Tischgedeck. (AUS)
728 Verpackung für *Shorty,* einen kurzen, dicken Bleistift von *Parker.* (GER)
729 Verpackungen für Lampen der Marke *Crayonne.* (GBR)
730 Schachtel für Papiertaschentücher von *Wellcome.* (SAF)
731 Packungen für *Tipiti*-Nahrungsmittel, mit farbiger Beschriftung. (BRA)

ARTIST / KÜNSTLER / ARTISTE:

726 Richard Laurent
728 Manfred Schipper

DESIGNER / GESTALTER / MAQUETTISTE:

724 Bev Whitehead
725 Helmut Schmid
726 Richard Laurent
727 Cato Hibberd Hawksby Design
728 Manfred Schipper
730 Derek Spaull
731 Oswaldo Miranda

ART DIRECTOR / DIRECTEUR ARTISTIQUE:

724 Michael Peters
725 Helmut Schmid
726 Paul McNear
727 Cato Hibberd Hawksby Design
730 Derek Spaull
731 Oswaldo Miranda

AGENCY / AGENTUR / AGENCE – STUDIO:

724 Michael Peters & Partners Ltd.
725 Nippon International Agency
726 Lipson-Jacob & Assoc.
727 Cato Hibberd Hawksby Design Pty. Ltd.
728 Parker Pen GmbH, Marketing Services
729 Conran Associates
730 Derek Spaull Graphics
731 S. J. de Mello Propaganda

725

726

727

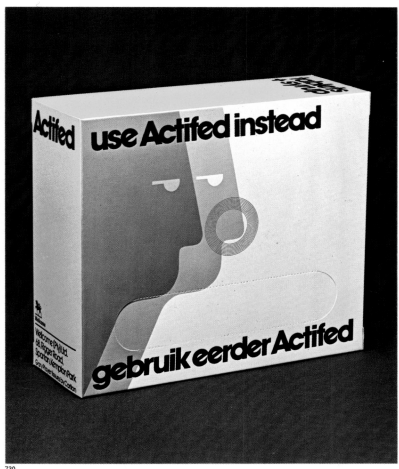

730

731

724 Tubes pour une gamme de couleurs pour artistes avec des reproductions d'œuvres d'art de peintres renommés. (GBR)
725 Emballages pour les pellicules *Ilford*. (JPN)
726 Carton pliant contenant un cours de lecture publié par les éditions Encyclopaedia Britannica Educational Corp. (USA)
727 Boîte pliante pour un couvert à jeter après usage. (AUS)
728 Emballage pour *Shorty*, un crayon court et gros de *Parker*. (GER)
729 Emballages et lampe conçues par *Crayonne*. (GBR)
730 Boîte pour les mouchoirs à papier *Wellcome*. (SAF)
731 Emballages pour les produits *Tipiti* avec typographie en couleurs. (BRA)

732

732 Bottle styling for *Opium*, a perfume by *Yves Saint Laurent*, reproduced in actual size from a brochure. (FRA)
733 Boxes for a wrapping paper made by Zonart & Co. Ltd. Red on white. (JPN)
734 Service bags sold in the *Zonart* paper boutique. (JPN)
735 Carton containing a collection of seashells as a mailer for the Insurance Company of North America. (USA)
736 Carton envelope, black with brown lettering, containing a promotional gift to the fur trade. (SAF)
737 Packages for *Bonds* hipster briefs (ladies' underwear), offering a view of the fabric design and colour. (AUS)
738, 739 Packaging of a calendar from the Container Corporation of America, with detail. The calendar is of heavy board with a satin surface, folded in the middle. Each month is in a different colour combination. (USA)

732 Flacons für das Parfum *Opium* von *Yves Saint Laurent*, in Originalgrösse aus einer Broschüre reproduziert. (FRA)
733 Verpackung für Einwickelpapier. Das Bild zeigt eine aufeinander abgestimmte Kombination aus drei Kartons. (JPN)
734 Tragtasche und Tüten aus der *Zonart*-Papier-Boutique. (JPN)
735 Werbesendung einer Schiffahrtsversicherung in Form einer Kartonschachtel mit echten Muscheln. (USA)
736 Karton-Umschlag, schwarz mit brauner Schrift, für ein Werbegeschenk an den Pelzhandel und Kürschner. (SAF)
737 Verpackung für *Bonds*-Damen-Slips. Durch die durchsichtige Folie sind Muster und Farbe sichtbar. (AUS)
738, 739 Verpackung und Detail eines Kalenders der Container Corporation of America. Die Seiten sind durch aufeinandergeklebte, dicke Pappstücke und eine glatte, in der Mitte geknickte Kartonoberfläche miteinander verbunden. Jeder Monat hat eine andere Farbkombination. Der Kalender steckt in einem durchsichtigen Halter aus Plastik. (USA)

732 Flacons pour le parfum *Opium* de *Yves Saint-Laurent*, reproduits en grandeur nature d'une brochure. (FRA)
733 Boîtes contenant des papiers d'emballages de cadeaux de Zonart & Co. Ltd. Rouge sur blanc. (JPN)
734 Sacs en papier en vente dans la boutique du papier de *Zonart*. (JPN)
735 Carton publicitaire distribué par une compagnie d'assurances. Il contient une collection de coquilles. (USA)
736 Enveloppe en carton (noire avec typo brune) distribuée aux pelletiers en tant qu'élément de publicité. (SAF)
737 Emballages pour des slips pour dames. Couleurs et dessins sont visibles à travers la feuille transparente. (AUS)
738, 739 Emballage d'un calendrier de la Container Corporation of America et détail. Les pages du calendrier en carton fort avec surface satinée sont pliées au milieu. Chaque mois se présente par une combinaison de couleurs. Le calendrier est inséré dans un support en matière plastique transparente. (USA)

737

DESIGNER / GESTALTER:

732 Dinand
733, 734 Katsu Kimura
735 Ford, Byrne & Associates
736 Lutz Reinhardt
737 Ed Kysar
738, 739 Bill Bonnell

ART DIRECTOR:

733, 734 Katsu Kimura
735 Gerry Reimel
736 Lutz Reinhardt
737 Jerome Gould
738, 739 Bill Bonnell

AGENCY / AGENTUR:

732 Mafia
733, 734 Packaging Direction
Co., Ltd.
735 Ford, Byrne & Associates
736 Swakara-Team/
J. W. Thompson
737 Gould & Associates
738, 739 Container Corporation of America

733

734

735

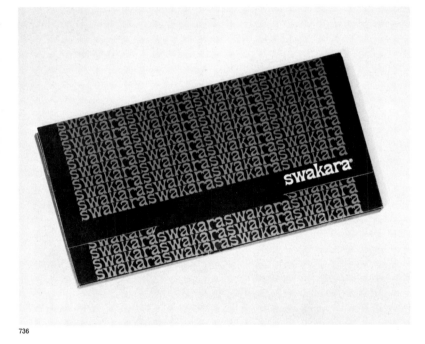

736

738

739

740

742

743

740 Specimens of a series of folding boxes containing paper puzzles. (JPN)
741 Family of packs for a range of tableware and household utensils designed by Roberto Sambonet. Purple lettering on brown board. (ITA)
742 Packaging for sets of records issued by the American Book Company, New York. (USA)
743 Notebook block and folding box for Carton y Papel de Mexico SA, Mexican associates of the Container Corporation of America. (MEX)
744 Boxes containing books and cassettes for an English course by International Communications Inc. Green box, white lid, lettering in green and blue. (JPN)
745 Paper carrier bag (shown from two sides) for Japan Electronic Products Import Association. Blue and white. (JPN)

740 Beispiele einer Reihe von Faltschachteln, die mehrere Papier-Puzzles enthalten. (JPN)
741 Verpackungsreihe für *RStset*-Haushaltsgegenstände, wie Töpfe, Pfannen, Bestecke, Geschirr. Brauner Karton mit violetter Aufschrift. (ITA)
742 Verpackung für Schallplattensets der American Book Company. (USA)
743 Notizblock mit dazugehöriger Schachtel von der mexikanischen Tochterfirma der Container Corporation of America. (MEX)
744 Schachtel mit vier Büchern und neun Tonbandkassetten für einen Englischkurs. Der untere Schachtelteil grün, der obere weiss mit grüner und blauer Schrift. (JPN)
745 Tragtasche von zwei Seiten gesehen, blau mit Weiss und weiss mit Blau, von einem japanischen Importverband für elektronische Produkte. (JPN)

ARTIST / KÜNSTLER / ARTISTE:
743 Herbert Bayer

DESIGNER / GESTALTER / MAQUETTISTE:
740 Katsu Kimura
741 Roberto Sambonet/Bruno Monguzzi/Maria Zacchetti
742 James G. Hansen
743 Arie J. Geurts
744 Sadao Sugaya
745 Helmut Schmid

Packaging/Packungen/Emballages

741

744

740 D'une gamme de boîtes pliantes contenant des puzzles. (JPN)
741 Exemples d'une gamme d'emballages pour des ustensiles de ménage, p. ex. des pots, des poêles, des services et de la vaisselle. Carton brun avec typographie violette. (ITA)
742 Emballage pour une série de disques de l'American Book Company. (USA)
743 Bloc-notes avec boîte distribué par la compagnie mexicaine d'une société américaine de conditionnement. (MEX)
744 Boîte contenant quatre livres et neuf cassettes pour un cours d'anglais. La partie inférieure est verte, la partie supérieure blanche avec typo verte et bleue. (JPN)
745 Sac en papier vue de deux côtés (bleu et blanc ou blanc et bleu) d'une association japonaise d'importation (équipement électronique). (JPN)

ART DIRECTOR / DIRECTEUR ARTISTIQUE:

740 Katsu Kimura
741 Roberto Sambonet
742 Mary Mars
743 Arie J. Geurts
744 Sadao Sugaya
745 Helmut Schmid

AGENCY / AGENTUR / AGENCE – STUDIO:

740 Packaging Direction Co., Ltd.
742 Source/Inc.
743 Carton y Papel de Mexico SA,
    Laboratorio de Diseño y Mercadotecnica
744 Sugaya Design Office
745 Nippon International Agency

745

746

747

750

751

746 Examples from a range of *Leslie Blanchard* hair care products. Logo and lettering in gold with closure in a code colour. (USA)
747 Bottles for a dandruff and cream shampoo made by Tamanohada Sekken Ltd., Tokyo. (JPN)
748 Package for *Dentrol*, a new liquid denture adhesive. (USA)
749 Container for a children's foam bath designed as a toy with turnable sections. (USA)
750 Labels for foam baths, blue for seaweed (left) and green for dwarf fir (right). (GER)
751 Package for injection vials of a preparation made by Taino Pharmaceuticals, Tokyo. (JPN)
752 Dispenser in gold and black, with non-slip base, for packs of *Betadine*, an antiseptic for external application. (AUS)
753 Range of containers and folding box for *Emlin* cosmetics. Light brown with white lettering and gold caps. (USA)

746 Beispiele einer Reihe von Haarpflegeprodukten der Firma *Leslie Blanchard*. Beschriftung und Logo in Gold mit Schachtelverschluss jeweils in einer Code-Farbe. (USA)
747 Flaschen für verschiedene Shampoo-Sorten eines japanischen Herstellers. (JPN)
748 Verpackung für *Dentrol*, ein flüssiges Fixierungsmittel für künstliche Zähne. (USA)
749 Behälter für ein Kinderschaumbad, der gleichzeitig ein Spielzeug ist. (USA)
750 Etikett für ein von Mann & Schröder hergestelltes Duftschaumbad. Hier blau für Meeresalgen und grün für Fichtennadel. (GER)
751 Packung für *Mecron-M*-Injektionen in Hell- und Dunkelbraun. (JPN)
752 Behälter in Gold und Schwarz mit rutschfestem Boden für die Entnahme kleiner Packungen mit einem antiseptischen Mittel. (AUS)
753 Verpackungsreihe für *Emlin*-Kosmetik, hellbraun mit goldfarbenen Deckeln. (USA)

746 Exemples d'une gamme de produits pour les soins des cheveux. Typographie et logo imprimés en or. Couvercles dans une couleur codée. (USA)
747 Flacons pour deux shampooings d'un fabricant japonais. (JPN)
748 Emballage pour *Dentrol*, une colle liquide pour les dents artificielles. (USA)
749 Récipient-jouet pour un bain de mousse pour enfants. L'extérieur en couleurs vives est constituée de trois parties, dont deux sont mobiles. (USA)
750 Flacons pour des bains de mousse aux essences de plantes: algues marines (flacon bleu), pin (flacon vert). (GER)
751 Boîte en brun foncé et brun pâle contenant cinq ampoules pour des injections. (JPN)
752 Distributeur-présentoir (imprimé en or et noir) pour un produit antiseptique. (AUS)
753 Gamme d'emballages pour les produits cosmétiques *Emlin*. Brun pâle et or. (USA)

Packaging/Packungen/Emballages

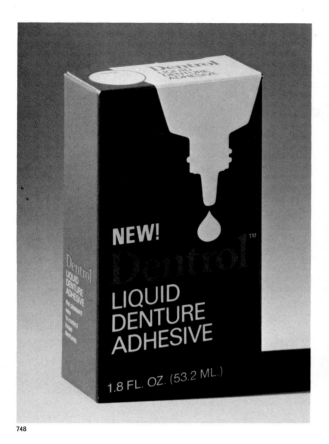

748

749

ARTIST / KÜNSTLER / ARTISTE:

749 Milda Vizbar
750 Dieter Zembsch
753 Horst Mickler

DESIGNER / GESTALTER / MAQUETTISTE:

746 Wallack & Harris, Inc.
747 Shigeru Akizuki
748 James M. Keeler
749 Milda Vizbar
750 Dieter Zembsch
751 Helmut Schmid
752 John Nowland
753 Madge McKinley

ART DIRECTOR / DIRECTEUR ARTISTIQUE:

746 Bob Wallack
748 Edward C. Kozlowski
749 Ned Harris
750 Dieter Zembsch
751 Helmut Schmid
752 John Nowland
753 John Dolby

AGENCY / AGENTUR / AGENCE – STUDIO:

746, 749 Wallack & Harris, Inc.
748 Ed. C. Kozlowski Design, Inc.
750 Zembsch'Werkstatt GmbH
751 Nippon International Agency
752 John Nowland Graphic Design
753 BBDM Inc.

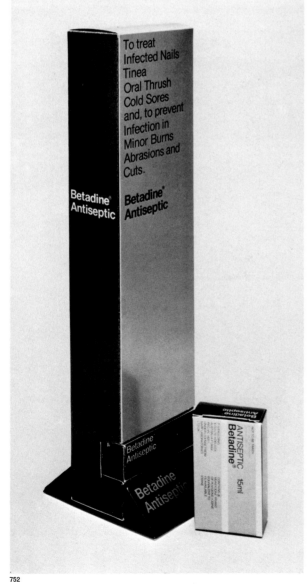

752

753

754 Cover for a recording of rock music by Tom Scott and his group. Dark colours. (USA)
755 Cover for a recording by the rock group Blue Oyster Cult. Illustration chiefly in dark blue and grey with an allusion to the title, "Agents of Fortune". (USA)
756 Cover for a collection of favourites by the English rock band Yardbirds. (USA)
757 Cover for a recording of music created on the electric music box. The illustration, with flowers in yellow, blue and pink shades, is an interpretation of the title. (USA)
758, 759 Complete cover and detail of the artwork for a recording of soul music by Eric Gale and his group. (USA)

754 Hülle für eine Rock-Platte von Tom Scott und seiner Gruppe. Dunkle Farbtöne. (USA)
755 Hülle für eine Platte der Rock-Gruppe Blue Oyster Cult. Die vorwiegend in dunklen Lila- und Grautönen gehaltene Illustration spielt auf den Titel (Die Glücksbringer) an. (USA)
756 Schallplattenhülle für eine Zusammenstellung der bekanntesten Stücke einer englischen Rock-Band. Mehrfarbige Illustration. (USA)
757 Schallplattenhülle für eine Aufnahme reiner Synthesizer-Musik. (USA)
758, 759 Detail der Illustration und vollständige Plattenhülle für eine Aufnahme von Soul-Musik von Eric Gale und seiner Gruppe. (USA)

754 Pochette d'un disque de musique rock de Tom Scott et son groupe. Tons foncés. (USA)
755 Pochette pour un enregistrement du groupe rock Blue Oyster Cult. L'illustration en lilas et gris foncé devrait évoquer le titre du disque (Agents de la fortune). (USA)
756 Pochette contenant une collection des pièces les mieux connues d'un groupe anglais de musique rock. Illustration en polychromie. (USA)
757 Pochette d'un disque de musique composée sur un synthétiseur. Illustration en couleurs. (USA)
758, 759 Détail de l'illustration et pochette complète pour un enregistrement de musique soul d'Eric Gale et son groupe. (USA)

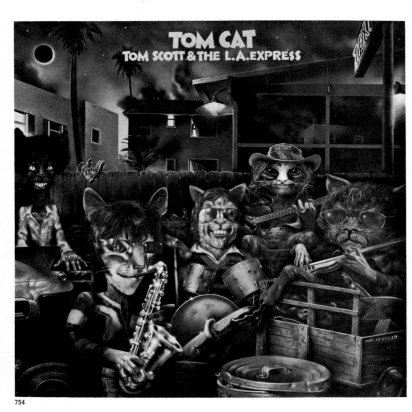

754

755

756

757

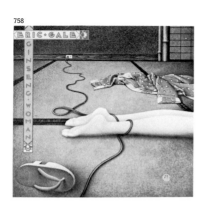

ARTIST / KÜNSTLER / ARTISTE:

754 David B. McMacken
755 Lynn Carlee
756, 758, 759 David Wilcox
757 Clifford Condak

DESIGNER / GESTALTER / MAQUETTISTE:

754 David B. McMacken
755 Andy Engel
756 Paula Scher
757 Henrietta Condak
758, 759 Paula Scher/Andy Engel

ART DIRECTOR / DIRECTEUR ARTISTIQUE:

754 Chuck Beeson
755 John Berg
757 John Berg/Paula Scher
758, 759 Paula Scher

AGENCY / AGENTUR / AGENCE – STUDIO:

756 Push Pin Studios

PUBLISHER / VERLEGER / EDITEUR:

754 A & M Records, Inc.
755, 757–759 CBS Records
756 Epic Records/CBS Records

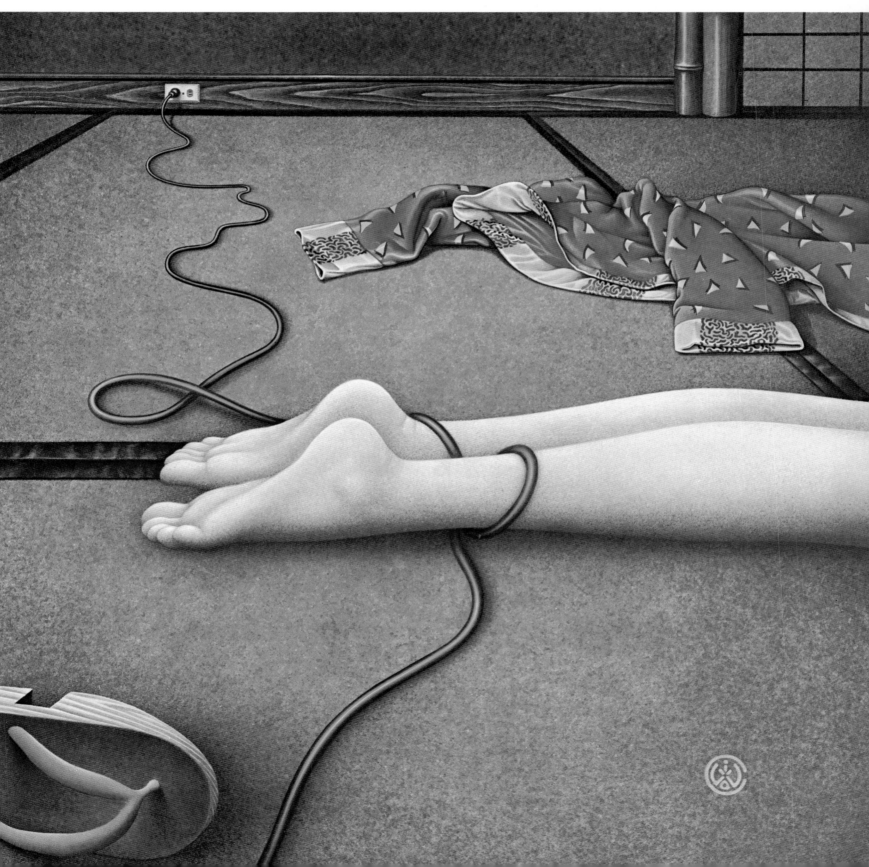

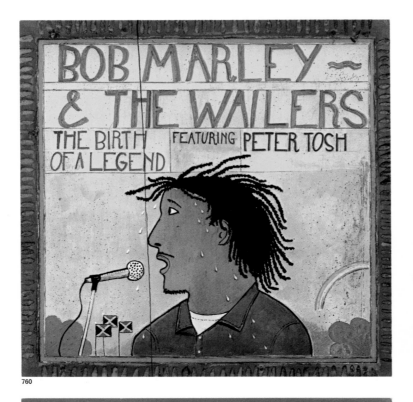
760

761

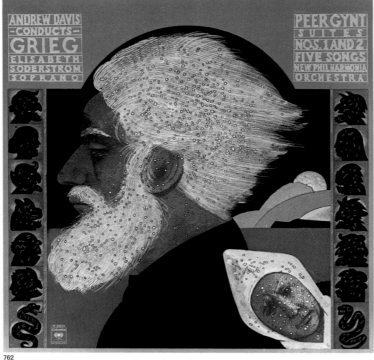
762

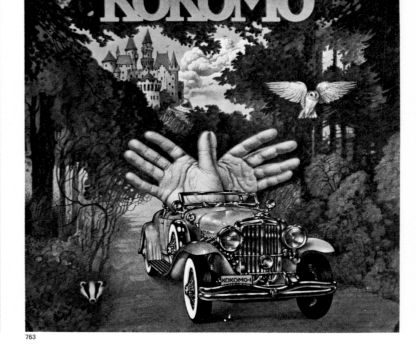
763

760 Cover for a recording of Reggae by Bob Marley. (USA)
761 Cover, predominantly in yellow shades, for recordings by Heat Wave. (USA)
762 Cover for a recording of Peer Gynt and other pieces by Grieg. (USA)
763 Cover in dark colours for the recordings of a folk-rock band. (USA)
764 Cover of a Ramsey Lewis record. "Tequila Mockingbird" is one of the songs. (USA)
765, 766 Cover (black and blue) and inside spread (blue ground, beige clouds, dark blue wings) of an Ian Hunter record. (GBR)
767 Polychrome cover of a CBS record. (USA)
768 Black-and-white cover for music written for pianos and percussion. (SWI)
769 Cover of a record issued instead of a catalogue for an exhibition of Topor's work at the Stedelijk Museum, Amsterdam. (NLD)

760 Hülle für eine Reggae-Platte von Bob Marley. (USA)
761 In Gelbtönen gehaltene Plattenhülle für die Disco-Gruppe Heat Wave. (USA)
762 Hülle für eine Aufnahme von Peer Gynt und anderen Stücken von Grieg. (USA)
763 Plattenhülle in dunklen Farben für Aufnahmen einer Folk-Rock-Band. (USA)
764 Hülle für eine Ramsey-Lewis-Platte. «Tequila Mockingbird» ist eines der Stücke. (USA)
765, 766 Vorderseite (schwarz/blau) und Innenseiten (blauer Hintergrund, beige Wolken, dunkelblaue Flügel) einer Hülle für «Overnight Angels» von Ian Hunter. (GBR)
767 Mehrfarbige Hülle für eine CBS-Platte. (USA)
768 Schwarzweisse Hülle für eine Platte mit Klavierstücken von Strawinsky und Bartok. (SWI)
769 Hülle einer Platte, die anstelle eines Kataloges zu Topors Ausstellung im Stedelijk Museum, Amsterdam, herausgegeben wurde. (NLD)

760 Pochette pour un disque de Reggae de Bob Marley. (USA)
761 Pochette d'un disque de musique du groupe Heat Wave destinée aux discos. (USA)
762 Pochette pour un enregistrement de Peer Gynt et d'autres pièces de Grieg. (USA)
763 Pochette d'un disque enregistré par un groupe de musique folk-rock. Prédominance de tons sombres. (USA)
764 Pochette de disque avec une illustration qui fait allusion au titre. (USA)
765, 766 Recto et intérieur d'une pochette de disque de Ian Hunter intitulé «Overnight Angels». Recto en noir et blanc, intérieur en jaune et bleu prédominant. (USA)
767 Pochette du disque «Pierce Arrow». (USA)
768 Pochette pour un enregistrement de musique de Stravinski et de Bartok. Noir-blanc. (SWI)
769 Pochette du disque tenant lieu de catalogue pour l'exposition de l'œuvre de Roland Topor au Musée Stedelijk à Amsterdam. (NLD)

Record Covers
Schallplattenhüllen
Pochettes de disques

764

765

766

767

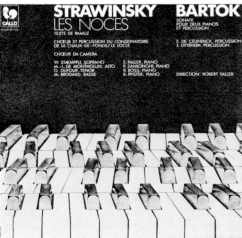

768

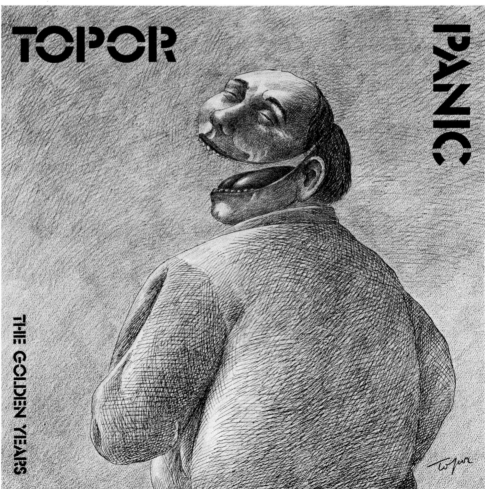

769

770

771

772

773

770 Cover of a jazz recording as a tribute to Louis Armstrong, whose portrait appears in pale pastel shades of beige and pink. (USA)
771 Cover of a recording marking the 25th anniversary of the Munich Radio Orchestra. Vignettes in full colour. (GER)
772 Cover of a work by Berlioz. Pastel shades of brown, pink, beige, green, lilac. (USA)
773 Cover for a guitar selection by David Bromberg. Muted colours. (USA)
774, 775 Detail of the artwork and complete cover for a recording of rock music by the group American Tears. The illustration relates to the title, "Powerhouse". (USA)

770 Schallplattenhülle für Aufnahmen des Thad Jones-Mel Lewis Jazz Orchestra, ein Tribut an Louis Armstrong, dessen Portrait in blassen Pastelltönen zu sehen ist. (USA)
771 Hülle für eine Platte zum 25jährigen Bestehen des Münchner Rundfunkorchesters. (GER)
772 Plattenhülle für ein symphonisches Werk von Berlioz. Pastelltöne in Braun, Rosa, Beige, Grün und Violett. (USA)
773 Hülle für eine Platte mit den erfolgreichsten Aufnahmen von David Bromberg. (USA)
774, 775 Detail der Illustration und vollständige Hülle für Aufnahmen einer amerikanischen Rock-Gruppe. Die Illustration bezieht sich auf das Titelstück («Kraftwerk»). (USA)

770 Pochette d'un disque enregistré par le Thad Jones/Mel Lewis Jazz Orchestra, avec le titre «Suite for Pops» (Pops était le nom donné à Louis Armstrong par ses amis). (USA)
771 D'un disque publié lors du 25e anniversaire de l'orchestre de la radio munichoise. (GER)
772 Pochette pour un enregistrement de Harold in Italy de Hector Berlioz avec l'Orchestre de Paris et Pinchas Zukerman, violon. Prédominance de tons bruns atténués. (USA)
773 Pochette pour un enregistrement de mélodies populaires de David Bromberg. (USA)
774, 775 Pochette (recto et verso) et détail de l'illustration pour le disque d'un groupe américain de musique rock. L'illustration se réfère au titre. (USA)

Record Covers

Schallplattenhüllen

Pochettes de disques

774

ARTIST / KÜNSTLER / ARTISTE:

770 David B. McMacken
771 Walter Tafelmaier
772, 773 Seymour Chwast
774, 775 Robert Giusti

DESIGNER / GESTALTER / MAQUETTISTE:

770 Phil Shima
772 Seymour Chwast
773 Robert Biro
774, 775 Paula Scher

ART DIRECTOR / DIRECTEUR ARTISTIQUE:

770 Roland Young
772, 774, 775 Paula Scher
773 John Berg

AGENCY / AGENTUR / AGENCE – STUDIO:

772 Push Pin Studios

PUBLISHER / VERLEGER / EDITEUR:

770 A & M Records, Inc.
771 Bayerischer Rundfunk
772–775 CBS Records

775

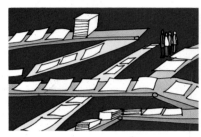

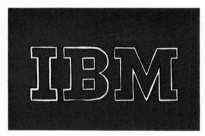

788

789

776–787 Sequence for a commercial promoting IBM data processing equipment. (USA)
788–790 Three frames from a titling sequence for *Come Back Little Sheba* presented by Laurence Olivier on *Granada* television. (GBR)
791–798 Titling sequence used by Radio Canada for special programmes on the occasion of the 25th anniversary of its French transmitting station. (CAN)
799–801 From a film for *Matarazzo Textil* presented at an international fashion show. (BRA)
802–807 Sequence from a film dealing with medicines in the framework of the relations prevailing between physician, nurse or other administrant, and patient. (FRA)

776–787 Sequenz aus einem Werbefilm über Datenverarbeitungs-Geräte der IBM. (USA)
788–790 Bilder aus der Titelsequenz für den Farbfilm *Come back little Sheba* (Komm zurück, kleiner Sheba), präsentiert von Laurence Olivier für die Fernsehanstalt *Granada*. (GBR)
791–798 Titelsequenz als Einleitung zu Spezialsendungen der Société Radio Canada anlässlich des 25jährigen Bestehens des Senders für das französische Sprachgebiet. (CAN)
799–801 Bilder aus dem Film einer Textilfirma für eine internationale Modenschau. (BRA)
802–807 Bilder aus einem Film über das Verhältnis Arzt/Patient/Pflegepersonal und die symbolische Bedeutung des Medikaments, dessen Annahme oder Ablehnung. (FRA)

776–787 Séquence d'un film publicitaire de l'IBM. (USA)
788–790 Extraits du générique d'un film couleur de Laurence Olivier, intitulé «Come back little Sheba» (Reviens, petit Sheba). Il a été réalisé par la TV *Granada*. (GBR)
791–798 Stills extraits du générique que la Société Radio Canada utilisa pour annoncer les émissions spéciales en langue française diffusées à l'occasion de son 25e anniversaire. (CAN)
799–801 Images du générique d'une émission sur une présentation internationale de modes. (BRA)
802–807 Du générique du film *Le médicament relationnel*, réalisé par le laboratoire *Delalande*. Il discute la valeur symbolique du médicament conçu comme un médiateur dans la relation qui s'établit entre le médecin, le malade le médicament et la personne qui l'administre. (FRA)

790

CBFT 2

ARTIST / KÜNSTLER / ARTISTE:
776–787 Otto David Sherman
788–790 Anna Farrar
791–798 André Théroux
799–801 Zélio Alves Pinto
802–807 Martine Robin/Annie Garnier

DESIGNER / GESTALTER / MAQUETTISTE:
776–787 Otto David Sherman
791–798 André Théroux
799–801 Zélio Alves Pinto
802–807 Jean Caillon

ART DIRECTOR / DIRECTEUR / ARTISTIQUE:
776–787 Sal Hardi
788–790 Anna Farrar

AGENCY / AGENTUR / AGENCE – STUDIO:
776–787 Otto David Sherman
788–790 Granada Television
791–798 Société Radio Canada/
         Service de la Publicité
802–807 Films 33

PRODUCER / PRODUZENT / PRODUCTION:
776–787 IBM
788–790 Granada Television Ltd.
791–798 Société Radio Canada
799–801 Thomas Sheier Studios
802–807 Films 33

Film/Television

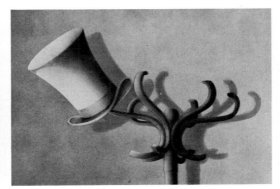
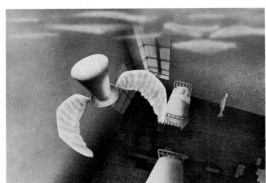

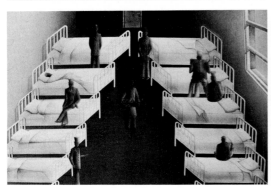
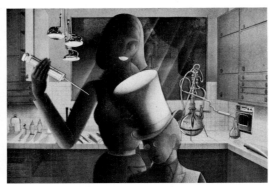

808

809

810

811

812

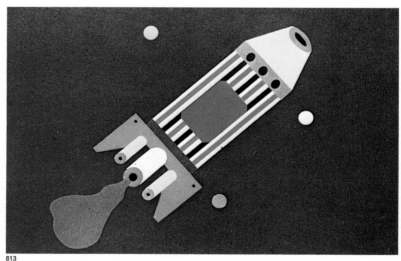

813

808–815 Frames from audio-visual films for children produced by the OMAVA organization. Figs. 808 and 809 are from *Ovid the Mouse,* the story of a mouse who makes friends with children and uses their shoes as a means of transport. Figs. 810 and 811 are scenes from *My Friendly Ant,* the adventures of a hard-working ant who even drives a tractor to earn some pesos. Figs. 812–815 are from *Green Parrot, Parrot Green,* the tale of a parrot who flies to the moon. (ARG)
816 Frame from *Hickory House,* a *Granada* television film about a fat man. (GBR)
817 Title slide for a film broadcast by a Maryland transmitting station. (USA)
818–823 From a film for young people about the views of Marshall McLuhan, on Austrian TV. (AUT)

808–815 Beispiele aus einem audiovisuellen Erziehungsprogramm für Vor- und Primarschulen in Argentinien. Abb. 808, 809 zeigen Szenen aus *Ovid, das Mäuschen.* Ovid hat Freundschaft mit den Kindern geschlossen und wohnt in der Schule. Unterwegs in der Stadt benutzt Ovid Schuhe als Transportmittel. Abb. 810, 811 sind Szenen aus *Die Ameisenfreundin,* der Geschichte einer hart arbeitenden Ameise, die sogar einen Traktor fährt, um ein paar Pesos zu verdienen. Abb. 812–815 gehören zu einem Film über einen Papagei-Astronauten. (ARG)
816 Szene aus einem Zeichentrickfilm über einen dicken Mann (Fernsehsender *Granada*). (GBR)
817 Titelbild eines Films für die Fernsehstation von Maryland: «Warum ich?». (USA)
818–823 Sequenz aus einem Jugendprogramm des ORF über Marshall McLuhan. (AUT)

808–815 Stills extraits d'un programme pédagogique audiovisuel destiné aux écoles primaires en Argentine. Fig. 808, 809: scènes du film *Ovid, la souris.* Ovid s'est installé dans l'école où il s'est fait l'ami des enfants. Lorsqu'il va en ville, un soulier lui sert de moyen de transport. Fig. 810, 811: scènes du film *L'amie-fourmi.* Ce film raconte l'histoire d'une fourmi qui travaille dur. Fig. 812–815: extraits d'un film qui traite d'un perroquet-astronaute et de ses aventures. (ARG)
816 Image d'un film d'animation sur un homme gros, diffusé par la TV *Granada.* (GBR)
817 Still d'un film émis par la TV du Maryland: «Pourquoi moi?». (USA)
818–823 Du générique d'un programme pour la jeunesse, diffusé par la TV autrichienne. (AUT)

ARTIST / KÜNSTLER / ARTISTE:

808–815 Ayax Barnes
816 Anna Farrar
817 Thomas Gecan
818–823 Rudi Böhm

DESIGNER / GESTALTER / MAQUETTISTE:
808–815 Ayax Barnes

Film/Television

814

815

816

817

ART DIRECTOR / DIRECTEUR ARTISTIQUE:

808–815 Eduardo & Eva Becker
816 Anna Farrar
817 Thomas Gecan
818–823 Erich Sokol

AGENCY / AGENTUR / AGENCE – STUDIO:

816 Granada Television
817 Maryland Center for Public Broadcasting

PRODUCER / PRODUZENT / PRODUCTION:

808–815 Organización de Medios Audiovisuals Aplicados
816 Granada Television Ltd.
817 Maryland Center for Public Broadcasting
818–823 ORF

818–823 ⟶

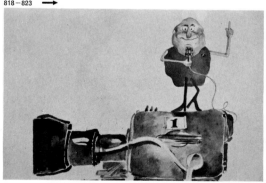

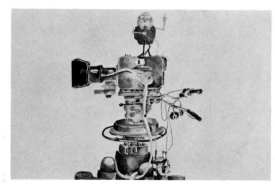

Paper/Papier: Papierfabrik Biberist – Biber GS SK3, blade coated, pure white 120 gm2 and Biber Offset SK3, pure white, machine-finished, 140 gm2 / Biber GS SK3, hochweiss, satiniert, 120 gm2 und Biber-Offset SK3, hochweiss, maschinenglatt, 140 gm2

Printed by / gedruckt von: J. E. Wolfensberger AG, Zürich (Colour pages/ Farbseiten), Merkur AG, Langenthal (black and white/ schwarzweiss)

over / Einband: Buchbinderei Schumacher AG, Bern / Schmitten ossy lamination / Glanzfoliierung: Durolit AG, Pfäffikon SZ